Phone Man

A Memoir

By

Allan Rankin

© 2017 Allan Rankin

All rights reserved. No part of this publication may be reproduced in whole or in part, stored, or transmitted in any form or by any means without prior written permission obtained from the author.

ISBN-13: 978-1981805372

ISBN-10: 1981805370

First edition.

Also by Allan Rankin

Prostate Cancer: From the Bottom Up
E-book, published 2012
Available from Amazon.com books

Dedication

To my wonderful children, Leslie and Daniel, who were never far away from any of what follows, and especially Leonard, who couldn't always be there but was always in my thoughts. And to my amazing grandchildren, Melanie, Mathew, Alexandra, and Gordon, in order of appearance, along with Zoe and Nora and all those who follow. This book is for them.

Contents

Foreword 8

Part I

Chapter 1: Infancy and early development
   1934-46 Brights Grove, Ontario 11
Chapter 2: School age and adolescence
   1946-53 Sarnia, Ontario 26
Chapter 3: Adolescence to young adulthood
   1953-55 Vancouver, British Columbia 40
Chapter 4: A sort of adult
   1955-63 North Vancouver, British Columbia 56
Chapter 5: The first start-up
   1963-65 Palo Alto, California 75

Part II

Chapter 6: A man in full
   1965-72 Montreal, Quebec 92
Chapter 7: A man in free fall
   1973-75 Magog, Quebec 111
Chapter 8: Back to adolescence
   1976 Dorval, Quebec 127
Chapter 9: Gone boy
   1977 Nowhere and Everywhere 143

Part III

Chapter 10: A whole new ball game
 1977-79 Palo Alto, California **152**
Chapter 11: Into the light
 1979-82 San Francisco, California **161**
Chapter 12: LD riding the wave
 1983-86 Atlanta, Georgia **181**
Chapter 13: Back to the loop
 1986-92 Pleasanton, California **200**
Chapter 14: ISDN (It Still Does Nothing)
 1992-97 Bellingham, Washington **212**
Chapter 1:5 The fall of giants
 1998-2001 Dana Point, California **229**

Part IV

Chapter 16: Hopi holiday
 2001-03 Dana Point, California **243**
Chapter 17: Way down south in Dixie
 2003-04 Savannah, Georgia **251**
Chapter 18: Enough with the clubs
 2004-13 Mission Viejo, California **275**
Epilogue...**286**

Foreword

Phone Man is the story of my life. It starts on a golf course near a beach, and ends on a golf course near a beach. In between, it bears no similarity. No life can be mapped out ahead of time. Mine wasn't, but not for lack of trying. It was constantly changed by events, circumstances, and people around me. Always, my eye was on something or somewhere else.

It's a story of change humorously woven into the telecom revolution that shaped the world we live in. Old industries and technologies fell by the wayside, along with many of us who worked within it. The revolution changed the way we consumers think, act, and how we spend our money. It changed the way we raise our children, how we learn, what serves as entertainment, and even the way we communicate.

It will take you all over North America, from rural towns in Canada to Silicon Valley—from magneto phones to the latest technologies. For me it was a long learning curve with each change presenting new challenges. But the biggest challenge happened when we discovered our youngest child had cerebral palsy.

Part I starts with my parents on a golf course in Brights Grove, Ontario, Canada. When I was thirteen we moved to the closest town, Sarnia, across the river from Port Huron, Michigan. For the next sixteen years I went to high school, started my career with Bell Canada, and then worked for British Columbia Telephone Company, in Vancouver, British Columbia. I got married and had three kids before everything really changed.

Part II explains why we moved to California and then back to Canada. We returned only to find the extent of the challenge we faced and how it would set the stage for years to come. What was salvaged was finally destroyed by an ill-advised campground venture that ended in financial ruin. It's only the beginning.

Part III will take you into the greatest technological leaps in history. It's a ride that takes you to the peak of the dotcom bubble, and the crash that took down the entire industry that got us there. This is a story of survival in the midst of competing monolithic entities.

Part IV changes the pace with two completely different cultures: the Hopis in Arizona, and the Deep South. We move to Savannah, Georgia, for a year, but after a lifetime of travel the story doesn't end there. If it had to be somewhere it had to be California. We returned and remained there for an unbelievable ten years. Does this mean that it was the last move? Don't count on it. My life in telecommunications was over, but I still had the freedom to travel.

I didn't choose telecommunications as my life's work, it chose me. *Phone Man* is only one man's story within that vast industry. If you were lucky enough to have made the same choice, you should enjoy reading about another's experience and conclusions. If you chose something else, this is your opportunity to learn what went on behind the dial tone. In fact, even if you never worked a day in your life but at least at some point used a telephone, you should read this book. If you do, you will know what happened. If you don't read this book, then read another. If you don't read anything, those who own the technologies of this century will own your mind. It's called the Information Age; information that has little to do with books and much to do with the Internet.

Part I

1934 – 1965

*Lakeview Golf Course – Brights Grove, Ontario.
Bill Rankin standing at left, Annie Rankin sitting next to
Hank Forbes with hat (brother-in-law).*

Chapter 1

1934-46

Brights Grove, Ontario

Infancy and early development

No matter how much you plan, you never know what's coming next. To use a worn-out metaphor, life is like a deck of cards. It arrives neatly stacked from top to bottom with every card falling in place. But crack the deck and shuffle it, then see what happens. Chaos! There are many games you can play, but you must have rules. Even then, you can never be sure how it will pan out. Luck is a factor. You can forget that. If you intend to win, you'll need more than luck.

    We constantly make decisions that affect our lives. As in cards, others are in the game. There are many ways to play, and some don't play by the rules. Even a simple game of stud poker can provide an equal measure of joy and disappointment. Maybe you will up-the-ante and win the pot. Or lose the farm. Competition is fierce, but you can always decide to drop out; sometimes that's the best move. You can play a different hand or find another game. If you plan on winning, you'll need to do more than just learn the rules. You have to read the other players as well as you can read the cards, and where they are at any given point in the game. Otherwise you will end up a loser.

    That's what I was, when I found myself trying to cross the border into the United States. I had little more in my pocket than I had the first time—when I was eighteen and on my way to British Columbia. That time I sailed through barely noticed. Since then, I'd been back and forth many times. I'd had many ups and downs but nothing like this. This time I was recovering from a world-class midlife crisis. I had quit my job and had another on hold in California. Just when I thought my problems were behind me, an immigration officer took away my papers and sent me back to Canada. He held a better hand or maybe a stacked deck. In a matter of minutes, the future looked worse than what was behind me.

Without a green card I could see endless rejection slips while job hunting in places unknown. Montreal was out; I wasn't going back there. Toronto was where I should have been, but it was too late now. I had too many good memories in Vancouver to go there in this predicament. That would be far too embarrassing. Maybe Calgary, nobody would know me there. But wait, I'm getting ahead of myself. There's more to this story than that. Let's start at the beginning.

I was born in Brights Grove, Ontario, in 1934. Well, actually I was born in the Sarnia General Hospital. I was supposed to be born at home like my two siblings were, but complications developed at the last minute. It necessitated a rush to the hospital where I tried to enter the world by elevator. My mother, Annie Rankin, was five feet three, and I weighed ten pounds five ounces. I almost killed her and may have suffered a few side effects myself. It was normal at that time for children to be born at home. Doctors sometimes rushed through sleet and snow by horse and buggy to get there; it was more likely in a Ford Model A by my time. Eight years earlier my parents' first-born had died at birth. The next two, Bill and Ross, arrived intact, and then I came along quite by accident. I have this on good authority too. My father reminded me more than once.

Even my middle name, *McDarmid*, was a mistake. Someone apparently misspelled it, thereby distancing me from the many McDiarmids before me. My brother Bill was named after many generations of Williams. He was called Billy for longer than you would expect but always carried the distinction of being known as Bill Jr. My other brother, Ross, was named after Ross Somerville who won the US Amateur Golf Championship on the day he was born. It must be nice to be named after a champion. In 1950, Somerville was picked as Canada's top golfer in the first half of the twentieth century. I, too, had to carry a high handicap, but it never came from golfing. As the fourth and last of a string of boys, I was merely redundant.

There was another mistake in Brights Grove that year. John Labatt of brewing fame had rented the Grove's only "manor house" for the summer. It later became well-known as Wildwood on the Lake and had numerous summer cabins scattered around the property. Anyway, big mistake! One day, shortly after leaving for a meeting in London, he was kidnapped. Three individuals secreted him in a cabin on Lake Muskoka, chained to a bed. The ransom note demanded $150,000 and was signed by *three-fingered Abe*. It served to remind "Grovers" that these were dangerous times of gangland violence during the Great Depression. Mobsters were in their midst! This stuff was expected in Detroit and Chicago, but not Brights Grove; not even in Canada. Labatt survived the ordeal, but it reportedly sent him into near seclusion for the rest of his life. On the other hand, my life was just beginning.

The Rankin family came from Scotland via Nova Scotia. My branch didn't leave many tracks until reaching Vantleek Hill, east of Ottawa. My great-grandfather Daniel was born on a farm there. His father had married Margaret McDiarmid, and the farm became the Rankin farm as they continued to multiply. Dad was born just before the changing times of the twentieth century. He moved to Forest, Ontario, where he and his father owned a livery business on King Street. Soon horses were out and automobiles were in. An old news caption from the Forest paper read: *Bill Rankin, eighteen, has just returned from Ford Motor Company in Detroit.* They were converting their livery stable into a Ford dealership.

My ancestors were Baptists, but Dad gave that up too. He cut his baptism short after the minister decided he needed an extra period of immersion. He came up swinging, claiming "the SOB tried to drown me." As a child he wasn't allowed to play with the French-Canadian children who arrived at thrashing time. When he told me this, I called it weird and bigoted. He defended the practice by saying, "Hell, we weren't allowed to play with the Presbyterians either." I assume they wanted to protect the children from confusion and, heaven forbid, intermarriage. Good luck with that one!

The Baptist Church is still there with its formidable rock walls, looking as if it were intended to last for centuries. The cemetery behind it is just as impressive. The Rankin and McDiarmid names are carved into a good many of the granite tombstones. They, too, will remain for centuries. Descendants, however, have widely scattered.

Airplanes arrived just in time for World War I. The RFC (Royal Flying Corps) assigned Dad to the Deseronto training center in Ontario, where he ran a powerboat on the Bay of Quinte to rescue downed pilots. In the early days of flight, enemy fire was never needed to take out even the best of pilots. When the Americans entered the war in 1917, the RFC sent him to an air base in Fort Worth, Texas. As a mechanic, his job was to keep bi-planes in the air while the US military strived to rapidly train hundreds of young pilots. Many crashed during training, but in combat a fighter pilot's life expectancy was only a few weeks. Had my father been a pilot instead of a mechanic, you very likely wouldn't be reading this.

My mother was a Wells. In the book *The Wells of Wantage* by Merla Wells Patton, her genealogy can be traced back to 1580. It started in Wantage, England, but judging by the size of the book it will never end. The original Wells family made weatherproof clothing (from hides) for the Royal Navy for generations. After immigrating to America, William Wells moved from New York State to Upper Canada. As a United Empire Loyalist, he was appointed a major in the British army. Along with four of his sons he fought in the War of 1812, all surviving. My great-grandfather Peter Wells bought and cleared land close to Forest, Ontario, where he died from being kicked in the stomach by a horse. His son, Burton Wells, married Florence Spearman. She was from a family of blacksmiths who had emigrated from Ireland around 1900. Burt and Florence had four children, one of whom was my mother, Annie Matilda Wells. She grew up on their fruit farm a few miles from Forest.

After getting married my parents bought land in Brights Grove, intending to grow vegetables for market. In the affluence of the Roaring Twenties they saw a growing interest in tourism and decided a golf course had better prospects. Many came from Detroit to enjoy the beautiful, wide sandy beaches that ran for miles up the east coast of Lake Huron. Unfortunately, when the stock market crashed in 1929, many golfers hung up their clubs until after World War II. Adding to the hardship, my parents' house burned down one night when they were visiting a neighbor. Baby Billy was with them, but their beloved pet dog perished in the fire. Coal-fired furnaces with large coal bins in the basement were common until well into the fifties. Like all self-sufficient people of the time, they rebuilt the house with the help of neighbors.

Lakeview Golf Course remained open until appropriated by the army for training new recruits at the start of World War II. Dad watched despairingly as they marched across uncut greens and fairways turning to weed. Having lost his main source of income, he took a job in Windsor at Ford Motor Company where they were building army vehicles. Ross and I delighted in marching behind drill formations, with little thought of becoming more cannon fodder should the war continue.

Religion was Mother's domain. She strove to maintain the same Christian values she'd grown up with. She also belonged to the Order of the Eastern Star, the female arm of the Masonic Lodge of which Dad was a member. They didn't talk about it, but I suspect many in the community also belonged. They didn't talk about it either. In Brights Grove, St. John in the Wilderness Anglican Church was as close as it got—it was the only church available and was presided over by Reverend G.G. Stone. It was due to our mother that we were obliged to attend regular services and Bible studies. Unable to carry a tune, Ross and I mouthed all the right moves as we watched others enthusiastically singing hymns. If we could sit through one of his sermons, the good Reverend would have to put up with us faking it. In winter Ross was assigned the duty of lighting the fire in the pot-bellied stove on Sunday mornings. Being first to arrive, he'd be sure to sample Reverend Stone's sacramental wine.

At four I resented sitting out the school year when Ross entered grade one, just prior to his sixth birthday. We were close enough in size for me to assume we were twins. One night we were waiting for Dad to come home to kiss us goodnight. Mom was impatiently waiting to turn out the light and tuck us in. He finally arrived. I wanted to get the first kiss, so I scrambled out of bed to meet him just inside the doorway. It caught him by such surprise to have a pajama-clad kid clamp onto his leg that he fell ass over teakettle to the floor. I wasn't that big, but after a couple of hours of drinking he wasn't all that steady. He picked me up in a rage and held my head under the bathtub's cold-water tap, yelling, "I'll drown the little bastard! He's nothing but a damn accident anyway." It burned into my brain, never to be forgotten.

Fortunately, Mother was there to back him off. I could hear her screaming over my own wailing: "Bill, for God's sake have you lost your mind?" Given his condition, I guess he had. I think I lost a piece of mine too. It's amazing what gets planted inside the brain, to remain dormant until switched on by some unexpected trigger, whether external or internal. Mom dried me with a towel and carried me to bed where I continued crying until asleep. Later, Dad woke me with prickly whiskers and a cheek-burning kiss to say he was sorry. I wasn't having any of it. I just wanted to run away and vowed I would.

Children carry the burden of every traumatic experience in the same way veterans do with PTSD. With children, it's more likely harmful in terms of confidence, enthusiasm, and the capacity to trust and express love. Unconsciously, it can affect such things as participating in school plays and public speaking—anything that might bring criticism, ridicule, or embarrassment. It can be permanent, lying dormant only to be triggered at unexpected times regardless of age. There are two things that most cats, dogs, and kids never forget: physical or emotional abuse on one hand, and noteworthy acts of kindness on the other. Either way they burn in, and even if seldom thought about, can affect behavior and personality. Based on how my dad reacted, I was convinced I'd done something incredibly stupid. I wasn't about to stick my neck out again. I became less confident. Everyone in our family was very good at understatement and sucking up the bad with the good. In my case, emotional concealment became entrenched, at least to the best of my ability.

Fortunately, there were also many memories of much kindness, so I wasn't totally screwed up or introverted. I just felt less significant than my brothers, who in my mind were wanted and smart. If I asked my dad to help me fix my bicycle chain, he'd say, "Get Ross to help you. He knows how to do that." And I'd think, yeah, but you had the time to show him, didn't you? It was only natural for my parents to be more hands-on with the first child and practically AWOL by the last. Bill was the eldest, and I still remember all the fuss over his schooling, clothing, ponies, golf game, first rifle, girlfriend, dance, job, and you name it. Ross, being four years younger than Bill, got far less attention and wouldn't have wanted it anyway. When Mom bought guitar lessons for the two of us, he refused to go. I didn't go either, even though I wanted to. If she bought clothes that didn't suit him, he wouldn't wear them, so neither would I. He wouldn't even allow her to kiss him, and that meant I'd fight that too. In spite of everything, she made me feel as if I was her favorite. One of my favorite things was to join her on a car ride to someplace new. I'd be leaning into the windshield like a hound dog drooling in the wind with its head out the window. Out of the gene pool I think Bill inherited the English ones, Ross the Scottish, leaving me the Irish. I should have been a girl; Mom would have liked that.

At five there was no way I was going to sit out another year while Ross went to school. I'm sure it was an easy decision for my mother. After looking after the cabin business all summer, she'd be glad to see the back of us as we plodded off with new lunch boxes and pencils. On my first day of school I had to sneeze and wasn't sure if it was allowed. With the teacher busy at the blackboard, I crawled up the row between desks to where Ross sat. It took him by surprise to have me poking his side.

"What are you *doing*?" he whispered.

"I have to sneeze," I whispered back, while twitching my nose to suppress it.

"Well go back to your desk and sneeze," he replied, indicating it was okay as long as not around him. I did, and nobody paid much attention. Days later, the teacher gave the class a short lesson on the importance of covering one's mouth during a sneeze. I was shocked to learn that millions of germs could be spread beyond twenty feet in an ever-widening cone. I could have taken out the entire school!

Another fabric at the center of the community was Nicholson's Store. This was the place where men gathered around the stove during long winters to swap stories while smoking pipes and chewing tobacco. None of us would ever get within ten feet of them while wearing a new pair of shoes. New shoes were important, and you didn't get them until the other pair wore out. It was difficult to resist showing them off, but these guys had a warped sense of appreciation and could spit tobacco juice with the accuracy of a Kentucky squirrel shooter. Copenhagen Snuff was Dad's favorite. He'd slip a wad of it in his cheek or under his lip, and when required could spit an odious projectile of black juice halfway across the store. The Nicholson brothers also had a bathhouse across the road, where people could change into swim trunks in the summer. Some of the kids would sneak into the attic to peak down into the lady's changing stalls. I wanted to; I just didn't want to get caught.

Embarrassment was never a problem for one of my friends. In sixth grade he taught me the art of playing "knockout." He tried it on me and it felt weird enough for the two of us to practice on some other boys. It was merely a matter of putting your arms around the victim's midsection and squeezing. It was much like the Heimlich maneuver, only maintaining pressure until they fainted. Do not try this at home—it takes a professional! Of course, one of the girls ran inside and tattled, which put an end to it. Our teacher had a daughter of her own in class. I suspect that's where the leak came from, but more likely there wasn't a girl in the entire school who could have resisted.

The teacher took out the dreaded rubber strap with which she threatened us periodically. She marched us down the stairs to the boys' smelly toilet in a dungeon-like cellar below the classroom. There was a drain at one end of a high-backed copper trough urinal that enabled peeing up against the wall with a good healthy backsplash. My friend was first to be strapped. He dutifully held out his hand for a series of good whacks. On his second hand she became a little overzealous and hit him on the wrist. It must have really hurt because he started crying and screamed, *"You French bitch! You hit my wrist."* She wasn't French, but her husband had been. At that time, many in Ontario thought they all should be in Quebec.

I thought, now we're really in trouble, but actually it worked for me. I was up next, and she was more careful. Anyway, I'm sure she knew who the real instigator was: My friend was the son of the local bootlegger, who was a single parent and always in some kind of trouble. Having survived the ordeal without a whimper, I thought I was a hero. I re-entered the classroom grinning with pride after my partner-in-crime's disgraceful teary-eyed appearance, only to be met with disdain. Everyone knew she'd gone easier on me.

Nicholson's grocery store had a restaurant and soda fountain, along with gas pumps. Right beside the store they had an open-air dance floor with a covered bandstand. At a very young age many of us worked as ticket-takers, letting couples onto the dance floor. Blackie, our pet crow, would follow us from tree to tree when we went to work. Having a pet crow was another one of Ross's ideas. He'd spotted the nest high up in a pine tree and sent me up to flush the young ones out. Circling crows complained loudly as I climbed closer to the nest. Suddenly, there was a burst of young ones fluttering to the ground on their first flight. We managed to capture one and called him Blackie. By clipping his wing, we kept him grounded until he became a close companion. The old timers advised us to slit his tongue to enable him to talk, but we never did. With his raucous voice, from high up in the trees above the dance floor, he would drive the bandleader berserk by singing along with them. Eventually, Blackie tired of domestic life and submitted to the call of the wild, presumably to raise his own family. He returned for occasional visits but eventually found life more interesting elsewhere. I like to think he was my first role model.

Prior to being shipped overseas, many servicemen visited the Grove with plenty of young ladies in attendance. One night I innocently ventured to the beach to watch some Navy guys swimming. Just as I arrived, one of the girls saw me. She squealed, "Oh my God! They've stolen our clothes!" I took off running when I saw a nude sailor rushing out of the water at me. The safest place was in a crowd of people, or so I thought. Spinning through the turnstile I looked back to see him leap clean over it. I ran past the next ticket-taker into the middle of the dance floor. I was sure I'd lose him there. To the amusement of everyone he charged through the dancers, grabbed me by the scruff of the neck, and proceeded to haul me back to the beach. I figured I was done for. He expected me to tell him where the clothes were, and I didn't have a clue. Just as we arrived his girlfriend called out, "Never mind. It's okay, I found them." He gave me a stern warning not to spy on them again and turned me loose with a shove. Never again did I doubt the outcome of the war. It takes a lot of guts to run buck naked into the middle of a crowded dance floor.

After the war, a Sarnia bandleader named Jack Kennedy purchased the property between the golf course and the lake. He developed a modern dance pavilion called *Kenwick-on-the-Lake*. His wife's maiden name was Warwick, hence the name Kenwick. The land was previously known as Corrinians Grove. He was a former mayor and wheeler-dealer from one of the satellite cities around Detroit. Suddenly, the Grove became a hotbed of activity with people visiting from far and wide. Crowds grew into the hundreds when big-name bands came to entertain: Glen Miller, Les Brown, Duke Ellington, Tommy Dorsey, Guy Lombardo, Lionel Hampton, they all came. The golf course was back in business too.

The Grove was always a summer playground for everyone, and it provided plenty of opportunity for local kids to make money. Ross and I had a lock on the golf course with caddying, cutting grass, retrieving golf balls, and more. We even speared frogs and cut off their legs for Dad to sell to cabin customers. Fried frog legs taste like chicken, but Mom hated cooking them because of their creepy tendency to jump around in the pan while frying. That was the main reason we brought them home; she was freaked by our insistence they were still alive.

Child labor was perfectly acceptable in those days. We worked at Kenwick's concession stand whenever the bands were playing. Actually, I got fired for dropping a crock of orange concentrate used for mixing the orange juice. I was lifting the bottom while another kid guided the spout into another container on the floor. His container flipped over and I lost control. The crock broke on the cement floor, littering the entire work area with gooey orange syrup. I could never figure out why they fired me and not both of us. He was on the receiving end, but then he was first to blame me. Never mind, there were plenty of other jobs. Whatever I did I was happy as long as I didn't have to put up with a boss, and vice versa.

Golfers would usually toss us a nickel or a dime when we retrieved golf balls from the creek. You couldn't see the creek bottom, but by wading chest deep in muddy water full of slugs, catfish, and snapping turtles, you could see where the ball dropped in. We'd find it with our feet before diving down to retrieve it. Aside from the golf course, my favorite place was the pony ring. This was volunteer work with no shortage of volunteers. The rides were worth it. Those ponies would take us flat-out around the ring before ending with an abrupt right turn to an immediate halt in their stall, as was their habit. Normally, we'd lead them around by hand while giving kids a ride. The best ride was at the end of the day when the ponies couldn't wait to get back to the farm. Once there, you could see their joy at rolling on their backs before hitting the water trough.

Tips were rare, but I refused one once. It was a couple from Detroit. He wanted to take a picture of her sitting on a pony. The girl was white. He was not. He may have been the first black person I'd ever seen and was certainly the first I ever talked to. They were happy and laughing together. He asked me to hold the pony outside the ring while he took a picture. Then he looked surprised when I wouldn't take the quarter he insisted on giving me. It was likely the first time a guy from Detroit had trouble giving someone a tip. But I couldn't take his money. It felt good just holding the pony and watching them interact in such a loving manner. It was the kind of relationship I imagined for myself when I grew up. I'd never seen my parents act that way.

Of course, it wasn't all work. There were plenty of kids to play with. The beach was the best attraction. Dad used to say, "Damn kids could swim before they could walk." In fall, the park became a football field, and then later it was flooded for free skating and hockey in winter, followed by baseball in spring. No matter what sport, there was never any organization, teams, or coaching of any sort. It was more of a free-for-all for people aged anywhere from seven to twenty. Inevitably, come summer it would revert back to picnics, ball games, and races when the large crowds returned. This was the best time; the unbelievable freedom of being out of school for two months superseded the rest of the year. We'd run barefoot all summer until the soles of our feet were like leather.

After Labor Day it was back to the one-room, red brick schoolhouse overlooking Lake Huron with its miles of sandy beaches to taunt us. One teacher taught all eight grades with close to thirty kids. How we learned anything is a testament to the quality of the teachers dispatched across Canada to take on such a daunting task.

It was a small community, but we were not just a bunch of hicks. The local Conservative Member of Parliament sent all four of his children to the same school we went to. His twin girls were the same age we were. We always attended each other's birthdays, along with others, although I'm sure invitees were carefully selected by parents. We always wanted our close friends—boys—to come to our parties, but Mom had an equal measure of girls on the list in a futile attempt to civilize us.

Dad's best friends were three local brothers who all had their own fishing business. During the long winters, with much time on their hands, they'd sit around a table shooting the bull while drinking whiskey. The unwritten rule was nobody could refill their shot-glass until all were empty. In that manner they progressed, or regressed, at an equal pace. Dad liked holding back with his glass half full when the others were dry. All eyes would be on him, waiting for him to stop talking and catch up. He'd repeatedly bring it to his lips and then set it down to continue talking while the others eyed him like predatory vultures. It was only a matter of time before one of them would crack. Then they all would be shouting as one, "Drink the damn thing for Christ's sake!"

The brothers were commercial fishermen on Lake Huron when they weren't rum-running to Michigan. The eldest brother's property was at the mouth of the creek where it ran into the lake not far from the golf course. He had rowboats for rent and always gave us the use of one. The second brother was a tough-looking, solidly built guy you'd never want to meet in a dark alley. His place was closest to us, and Ross and I spent hours around his boathouse where we'd interact with the Chippewa First Nation fishermen from Kettle and Stony Point reservations. They taught us how to use a netting needle to repair nets. One was a large man known to all on the lake as "Big Bish," since his last name was Bishop. He was the only one who could single-handedly carry a piling the size of a telephone pole over his shoulder from the boathouse down to the beach to be loaded on a boat. The poles were used for off-shore nets by pile-driving them into the bottom of the lake. When the nets filled, the Chippewas hauled them up and emptied them into the boats. We pleaded with them to take us out, but they discouraged us by claiming every new man had to be thrown from the boat into the lake without his pants on, to make sure he could swim. Ross persisted until they finally took him out. Sure enough, they pulled off his pants and threw him overboard.

The youngest brother was a good-looking man who when drunk turned into an unrecognizable Neanderthal throwback. More impressive was his daughter, who I thought was the prettiest girl in school. Earlier, after Walt Disney's *Snow White and the Seven Dwarfs* movie came out, I had to have a Dopey Doll. She made so much fun of me that I was forced to smash his head in to prove I was normal. When she went home, I quickly repaired him with adhesive tape and spent the rest of his short tenure apologizing to him. She continued to tease me until I had to choose between her and the doll. Dopey won! Later, as a teenager, I would rethink that one.

The Nicholson brothers lived across the street from each other, one block from their store and other enterprises. Today, the store is the location of Skeeter Barlow's Grill and Bar. When I visit Brights Grove, I go there to reminisce about the days when it was a gas station, store, soda fountain, and dance hall—a place where everyone gathered regardless of age. We'd watch and interact with adults all year long, and play with kids indifferent to any standing or status. Even the dogs ran free. They followed us everywhere, sometimes as many as twenty—unleashed and unaltered—and sometimes with surprising results.

Wives and mothers collaborated through the good and the bad of it. They were the backbone of the community and leaders of all social activity. The knitting and quilting club was called the "chit and chatter club." Dad called it the "shit and splatter club" and disappeared when they met at our house. They'd plan social events and other things, like ways to raise money or deliver food to the poor. Dad's activities of duck, deer, and rabbit hunting received far more attention from all three of us boys. Mom would be left high and dry if we could join him on a local hunting trip.

Half of the kids in our school were from farms one or two miles in either direction. Eventually, their lakeshore properties were sold for subdivisions now populated with beautiful homes along Old Lakeshore Road. Some of our friends were vacationers whose parents had cottages in the Grove. Today, many permanent residents live in those same cottages, now winterized and updated. The golf course, too, had a cottage and several cabins for summer vacationers. A couple from Windsor came every summer. He was a teacup reader, and once when we were visiting them in Windsor he read my mother's teacup. He told her that when we returned home she'd find her cat had gone missing. He also told her that one of her three boys would always live a long way away from home. Both predictions turned out to be true. Sure enough, when we returned home the cat was gone, never to be seen again. I suspect they thought Ross would be the next one, but the leaves had already picked me.

After the war, the golf course fairways, tees, greens, and sand traps were all totally unrecognizable. Before long it was returned to its former pristine beauty. Many returning veterans were pilots, and some continued flying as a means of making a living. One pilot landed a floatplane on the lake right in front of the golf course. He taxied to the beach and started taking three or four people for rides at fifteen dollars a head. I ran home and gathered up all my savings which only amounted to five dollars. It wasn't enough to convince him, but I stood around all day watching him come and go. At the end of the day there were only two other customers. He said, "Okay kid, gimme your five bucks and let's go." We flew over the lake where I could look down on the one-room red brick schoolhouse and all the farms where many of my schoolmates lived. We circled back over the golf course and made a neat landing close to shore. That was it; I was going to be a pilot.

I could never think of a better place to grow up, but after twenty years of running a business through times of economic depression and war, Dad must have thought a regular forty-hour job with benefits looked pretty attractive. He sold Lakeview Golf Course and for the next three decades it was called Bright's Grove Golf Club. That, too, will soon come to an end. Plans for another residential development are already in place.

No matter what becomes of it, if you look at Google Maps you'll see the winding creek that occupied so much of our time. That's where we'd take our first skinny-dip of the season after the ice melted. In spring, if the outlet wasn't opened to the lake, the lower part of the golf course would flood just as it had for centuries. It was great fun to dig a trench through the sand and watch the widening ditch spill trapped water into the lake. We'd build rafts, play pirates, or cut a tree down for a bridge across the creek. In summer we'd dive for balls, and in winter we'd watch Dad cut ice for the summer cabins. Ross didn't need me for any of this, but I stuck to him as if joined at the hip. And then we moved to Sarnia.

*Brights Grove School 1945 (I'm 2nd from left in front).
Ross is back row 4th from right.*

Chapter 2

1946-53

Sarnia, Ontario

School age and adolescence

Sarnia is located where Lake Huron flows into the St. Claire River on its way to Lake Erie. It's a beautiful setting and home to one of Canada's largest grain elevators; a setting not likely to be thought of as an oil town. But nearby, Oil Springs was the first place in North America to be commercially drilled for oil. With a natural harbor and excellent midpoint location on the Great Lakes, it was inevitable that a refinery would be built in Sarnia. The demand for oil far exceeded anything coming out of the ground in Southern Ontario. Soon, pipelines brought in crude oil from across the country to fill tankers on the Great Lakes. By 1959, with the completion of the US/Canadian St. Lawrence Seaway system, Sarnia was connected to the Atlantic Ocean and global markets. It was oil that made it into a multi-industrial community with all the spin-off petroleum products. During World War II, Polymer Corporation produced five thousand tons of artificial rubber to help defeat the Nazis.

Sarnia was sitting on one of the world's busiest waterways, with lake and ocean-going vessels traveling in both directions. Detroit is fifty miles downstream from what was soon be called Chemical Valley. Immigrants were moving in from all the war-torn countries of Europe. Many farms were purchased by people of Polish, Dutch, and other nationalities capable of making them profitable with their large families. All Big Oil needed to be profitable was war.

When the golf course sold, Dad purchased a rather sad-looking house with a peeling exterior and even grubbier interior. It had potential. The surrounding houses had been well maintained in a nice neighborhood. He was working at Polymer as a guard, and later was in charge of the laundry. I was assigned his helper for the house renovations and had no idea what I was doing. Nonetheless, I threw myself into it with as much enthusiasm as any twelve-year-old could muster.

Old wallpaper had to be removed with pressurized boiling water and a lot of scraping. I got off to a bad start when a hose flew loose. It sprayed hot water over my lower left leg, causing enough pain and howling to confirm he'd taken the wrong son. Too bad! I was the only one available. After my dad patched me up we were back in business. Old carpets were removed from the dining, living, and bedrooms. He rented a floor sander to restore the original softwood floors before applying several coats of highly toxic varnish of some sort. They came out beautifully. The bathroom and kitchen received new linoleum, and soon the walls were painted in Mom's tastefully selected colors. We moved in and continued scraping and burning off decades of old, peeling exterior paint with a blowtorch. Overall I did little of this, but the experience served me well for the rest of my life.

Johnson Memorial Elementary School seemed immense after the one on Lakeshore Road. I wondered if I could possibly pass grade eight after seven years in a one-room schoolhouse. This school had two floors containing many classrooms plus a basement for woodworking and other activities. They had a football team that competed with all the other public schools in Sarnia. The weight limit was 110 pounds and I assured the coach I could easily lose a couple of pounds to qualify. He needed some weight in the line and never asked again. I was given a uniform and put into the line at inside left, next to center. My job was to make a hole for the quarterback or backfield when on offensive, and stop anyone from coming through when on defensive. It sounds easy. I received a few bruises and one split eyebrow followed by a shiner lasting two weeks. At the end of the season we made it to the finals, but were beaten at Athletic Field—Sarnia's equivalent to the Coliseum. After the game, while still in a uniform now torn and covered in grass stains and mud, I rode home alone on the city bus. The only reason I remember the occasion is because I noticed one of Mom's lady friends eyeing me with a wee smile of sympathy. I looked pathetic but appreciated her support. Nobody else I knew even watched the game.

Football is very different from hockey. In football you have a position to play and may never touch the ball. In hockey everyone on the ice is all over the puck. There was no school hockey league, so I played on ragtag teams on outdoor rinks all around Sarnia. Without any coaching it was rather hectic and I soon lost interest. When spring rolled around, I tried out for the school baseball team. I would like to have played first base since I already had a bucket-size first baseman's mitt. The only option for a greenhorn from the sticks was the outfield. That's when I discovered baseball wasn't my game either. I had trouble catching a fly ball. I'd have it lined up, only to have it suddenly shift position seconds before arriving. It wasn't until I was in high school that I learned my depth perception was flawed due to one eye being short-sighted and the other long. The optometrist advised me to be very careful when passing a car in traffic since I could possibly misjudge how close an oncoming vehicle was. It was even more disappointing when he mentioned I shouldn't fly airplanes either. Landing would be problematic when I suddenly discovered I was closer to the ground than I thought. My two brilliant careers, sports and flying, had suddenly vanished. My future was over before I was out of grade ten.

Sarnia Institute and Technical School offered a general, a technical, and a commercial curriculum. If you expected to go to university you went with general. My brother Bill had already graduated by the time I got there. After honing his drafting skills at Sarnia Bridge Company, he went to work for Coles & Jeffery Construction Company. If university was not on the table for him and with Ross already in Tech, my chance of going to university was bleak. I opted for general, just in case. At thirteen I envied those who knew what they were going to do in life. Bill was never around much but he was always on the go with lots of friends and obviously heading for a secure future. As a natural calligrapher he was an outstanding draftsman and would have made a good architect. Instead, he later started his own construction company. Ross became his partner. I had no idea where I was going.

Grade nine went well academically but with minimal success at understanding what girls were all about. Social and conventional activities were not my long suit; work in one of the downtown stores after school was far more rewarding. Finding a job was never a problem. Sometimes when I told them my name, they'd ask, "Are you Bill Rankin's son from the golf course?" Many Sarnia cops remembered too. On a couple of occasions, I got off easy for some minor driving violation. They said, "Your old man used to let me play golf during the Depression." During that time, he let many local cops and business men play all day for fifty cents or a buck. Usually he made up the difference in beer sales from the icehouse. I was still profiting from it.

Army Cadets – 1947.

An unexpected gap had sprung up between Ross and me at this time. Suddenly he'd grown much older. It would take me a couple of years to catch up, but I was a very observant understudy. Other than school, everything important in life came from Ross. He was eighteen months older, stubborn, and a determined leader. I trusted his instincts and wanted to hang out with him. We were always about the same size until age created a more distinct difference around the time of puberty. Before that, he was my brain. If he liked something, I did. If he didn't, I didn't. I'm afraid he did most of my thinking for me until my early teens. I realized this was a conditioned reflex by the time I was sixteen and taller than he was. On the other hand, I experienced far more with him than I ever would have on my own.

Ross hung out with his mates from Tech. Many were from immigrant families in the South Ward. This was not only across the railway tracks, but next to the shack town, Blue Water, jammed between the Indian Reservation and the Imperial Oil refinery. With the construction boom, workers came from all over Canada and Europe. Unfamiliar Eastern European families were mixed in with French Canadians migrating from Quebec. It looked more interesting than anything I was doing. As the maturity gap between us narrowed, I started to hang out with him again, and the South Ward became my second home.

I was introduced to formerly unknown rarities such as kielbasa sausage, stuffed grape leaves, homemade wine, and other delicacies, including girls. Many doors were opened that shouldn't have been until I was older. Ross's friends were always older than mine, so I'd drop mine to follow his. I followed him up the food chain every time he moved on to the next crowd always older than he was. Life was more exciting, full of freedom and lack of discipline. I enjoyed more cars, smoking, and drinking than I ever would have experienced on my own. I soon found out this lifestyle had a price.

There was never a question about what to do. Every night we'd migrate across the tunnel-cut (tracks leading to the tunnel under the river to Port Huron) to the South Ward. The gas station was a hangout for all the kids in the neighborhood where something was sure to develop. Often we played cards games like euchre and cribbage, but poker was more popular. It was usually dealer's choice. Whoever was dealing could apply their own rules to five or seven-card stud with variations of deuces wild, eights-or-better, lowball, two-in-the-hole, or five-card draw. Sometimes it got pretty creative. The confectionery store at the gas station was the gathering spot, supplemented by shabby trailers and pickups with campers in the back. There were a couple of questionable characters who spent more time in jail for drinking and fighting than holding a job, but most of us were still in high school. We were more interested in partying. That was my downfall.

It started with vino (homemade wine) in a perfectly normal European family's kitchen. Soon it moved on to beer or cheap wine, and then Lemon Hart rum became a favorite. It liberated me from my inhibition and lack of confidence. Under the influence I could be the life of the party, or so it seemed. Jaw-dropping imitations of Frankie Laine—"That Lucky Old Sun," Vaugh Monroe—"Ghost Riders in the Sky," and Johnny Rae—"The Little White Cloud That Cried" were complete sell-outs, as I recall, while getting lit up before going to a dance. There was no more standing in the wings too shy to talk to a girl. Under the influence I could talk, dance, and end up taking her home. Her house, not mine! Clothes were important too. Tailor-made double-breasted suits with wide lapels and high-waist, baggy-knee pants with a tight cuff were de rigueur. No wonder we drank! I thought we were following New York zoot suiters or Hollywood movie characters. I had no idea it was largely inspired by Hispanic gangs and ragtag bands which caused many riots across the United States during the forties. The downside of being cool was devastating on school performance. It not only ate into my homework, but I needed a job in order to afford it. There was never enough time left for homework. Any observant person could see I was on a slippery slope to failure.

As Bill's position at Coles Jeffery advanced, the summer of '49 found all of us working there. Ross, recently graduated, was driving a dump truck as far away as Toronto. When I was fifteen, my summer employment was with their land surveyor, Reiner Anderson. We were a two and sometimes three-man crew. He quickly gave me a lesson in work ethic on our first outing. "When I say do something, move your ass," he shouted. "Don't walk, *run*!"

I reminded him fifty years later when he stopped in to see me in Bellingham after visiting his daughter in Vancouver. I asked him, "What's the big attraction in Vancouver?" Many kids from Sarnia ended up in Vancouver.

He replied, "You should know. You started it." I guess I did. You'll read more about that in the next chapter.

In 1949, Reiner was a football jock who played for the Sarnia Imperials in a tough industrial league. At work I was his "chain man." Under his direction from the transit, I would measure off a long straight line with a hundred-foot thin steel tape, sticking "pins" in the ground every hundred feet until reaching the end. Then I'd drive a permanent iron post into the ground to indicate a corner of the property. He would move the transit to that stake, set up to make the turn at the proper angle, and we'd measure off the next property line. When we traveled to any job site, time was money. We really had to move in order to complete the project as quickly as possible, sometimes working until after dark. Often, we were parceling up land or laying out a new subdivision straight through thick brush where many trees had to be cut down in order to achieve a line-of-sight. At the end of the summer, he asked if I had any suggestions for my replacement. Without hesitation I recommended a friend who had graduated the previous spring. I owed him one for all the times I'd listened to him play his clarinet while we enjoyed his parents' homemade wine and kielbasa. He hadn't found a job since graduating, but he got this job. Recognizing a good fit for a job was a hidden talent I never realized I had. Years later he became a major residential builder in Kingston, Ontario.

No matter what summer job I had, I always quit in time to allow a two-week vacation in Brights Grove before school started. This was where I met Harry Lockwood and we became lifelong friends. The following summer we found work with the Canadian Army at nearby Camp Ipperwash. We were civilian personnel, doing maintenance work while the camp held cadet training. There was a lot of grass to cut, but mostly we whitewashed curbs and delivered goods from the commissary. When we found out that the corporal who drove the truck had a scam selling cigarettes and canned goods to his fellow soldiers, we went along with him once to see how it went down. Our life of crime ended after we distanced ourselves from him. One day found us carrying a rack of pies into the officers' mess hall. Going up the back steps the tray tipped enough to make all the pies slide off all over the steps. There was nothing to do but sit down and sample them by the handful. The sergeant major came along and made a lot of noise when he found us filling our faces and laughing our heads off. We never took him too seriously. He had an obsessive interest in "were we getting any" in Grand Bend, a nearby summer beach town. It was more difficult than he thought, but we went along with him by promising to hook him up if he'd cut us some slack. At the "Bend," whenever we saw him looking for us in a crowd, we'd disappear until he swaggered past. His fortyish appearance, with hairy arms, a thick waist, and an army crew-cut, was far too old for any girls we met.

Harry was my first cut-out from Ross. He lived in the tiny village of Delaware and went to high school in London, Ontario. His father had died from poison gas many years after World War I, leaving Harry as the man of the house. This may have contributed to his confidence and take-charge attitude which led to a successful career in business. Ross was a my-way-or-the-highway type of guy. At least that's how he was with me. But I could see that he, too, was influenced by others. If I wanted in the game, I'd shut up and follow him. With Harry, I was on a more equal footing. He was confident enough to be self-deprecating; often the butt of his own joke, he drew people to him with laughter. But he also wanted to know your story, hear your ideas. He had plenty of his own but always welcomed a new gig. I'm not sure who set the agenda, but if I came up with something, Harry was sure to be all in.

Harry Lockwood and me at Camp Ipperwash – 1950.

Harry's mother owned a summer cottage in Brights Grove, and Ross had taken up with Harry's older sister. She lived at our place for a while after she moved to Sarnia for work. Living there was Mom's idea. She had visions of Ross settling down with a steady girlfriend until he got married. Ross didn't see it that way. Unfortunately, Harry was a lot more fun and always persuaded his sister's friends to carouse with him instead of getting serious about her. His penchant for adventure made it difficult for her to keep any boyfriend. I always suspected it was Harry's way of protecting her. His curly blond hair and innocent looks did little to disguise a wicked sense of mischief, but did little to discourage Marco Oreskovitch who married her.

Marco, Harry, and me – 1952.

In spite of the sixty miles between Sarnia and London, Ontario, Ross and I fell into a regular pattern of hanging out in one city or the other. We had access to Mom's '40 Ford, and Harry had the use of his mother's '49 Ford after he wiped out her previous car. Dad added to the carpool with his ancient '34 Ford sedan, but soon we all had our own cars anyway. My first car was a robin's egg blue '37 Ford customized coupe with smoke pouring out the exhaust. I pestered Dad until he helped me do a ring and valve job on it. After an electrical fire burnt up all the wiring, I tried to recruit him again.

He told me, "Go ask Ross. He knows how to do that." Ross had the advantage of having studied auto mechanics in school. He was busy but took the time to tell me what to do. Soon, if anyone had a car problem the first thing I'd do was pop the hood and look for a loose distributor cap, spark plug wire, or some other connection. My reputation spread when one of my friends needed a broken valve spring replaced on his '37 Ford. I borrowed a valve lifter from a local garage with the promise of having it back in the morning. It took until midnight. Then we woke up the entire neighborhood by starting the car without wasting time hooking up the manifold. A Ford V-8 without a muffler was the most beautiful sound in the world—unless you were trying to sleep.

Cars were easier to work on back then. No matter how much work I did on mine, I could never get it much over sixty-five. Anything over that and it would start fluttering as if starved of fuel. Under sixty-five, it performed like a rocket. I never tried too hard to solve the problem. It served me well as a governor. And just as well! The well-worn mechanical brakes were totally incapable of stopping anything faster. Automobiles had been around for fifty years. After the war, teenagers were the first generation with the opportunity to own their own. For many, it was a recipe for disaster—but I didn't need a car for that.

It started with smoking, then drinking, and of course girls. Later generations would add drugs to the mix to further complicate their lives. At sixteen I had little interest in school and was failing halfway through grade twelve. The option of knuckling down to months of serious study had little appeal compared to keeping the party going. I didn't have the sense to seek out guidance or some level of mentoring. In three-and-a-half years of high school I never once talked to a teacher or counselor about what I was studying or where I was going. Not even at home did I receive much encouragement. If the others had sought jobs after high school and started paying board, why wouldn't I?

Sarnia was not a college town back then. High school was more of a blue-collar machine turning out workers for Chemical Valley. If you wanted a higher education, you had to get out of town. The option of working for wages was far more appealing than another four years of abject poverty while struggling through university. After I quit school, I had no idea what I was going to do. The explanation to my mother went something like this: "I'll take a commercial art course by correspondence. Yeah! Really! I saw an ad in Dad's *True Detective* magazine." That was it!

Suddenly there was a great deal of interest in how I intended to make a living. Suggestions such as Polymer and Imperial Oil, with the long-term prospect of punching a clock or pulling shift work, had little appeal. Mueller Canada, which manufactured plumbing products, had possibilities. High school taught me how to run a lathe. Maybe I'd be a tool and die maker? I went with Mueller.

Then the unexpected happened. The wire chief from Bell Canada called to ask me if I was interested in coming in for an interview. Apparently, he'd called the high school looking for candidates and my drafting teacher offered me up. I had no idea he saw potential in me. Hence, it was Bell Canada that decided I was destined to be a telephone man. Or more likely, since that sounds far too presumptuous, it was divine intervention. Whatever it was, after a couple of brief weeks with Mueller, I picked up my Christmas turkey and left.

Bell Canada started me at twenty-five dollars a week. The job promised incremental raises over a seven-year apprenticeship toward being a journeyman. I could see myself after multiple training courses knowing everything there was to know about telephony. After two years I was still a line and station installer-repairman, having learned everything I needed to know in the first six months. The training consisted of working with two or three journeymen for short periods of time until most field situations had been encountered. The only courses I had were defensive driving and tool sharpening. Others had been there for years and never questioned it. I had the impression that the apprenticeship program was merely a way of prolonging low wages, but I wasn't complaining. They gave me a truck full of tools and equipment and turned me loose. I loved the job.

Many of the guys I worked with were World War II vets. On paydays we'd occasionally go for a few beers after work. I was relentless in pumping them for combat stories and what part they played in the war. It was difficult to get them onto any subject other than women and booze. The majority of the fighting stories were brawls in bars and often within their own regiment. They were not interested in talking about their mates getting blown away, or even killing the enemy. One unforgettable story was told by a fellow who met and then married an English girl before returning home. Before the wedding, her older sister spirited him off for a picnic and gave him an unexpected very good time as a wedding present. Considering my immature concept of the sanctity of marriage and the propriety of the English, I was having more trouble getting my head around that than all the blood and guts of war.

There was lots of variety in being a telephone man. Aside from toll line maintenance and restoring service after major sleet storms, phones were needed everywhere—homes, offices, factories, oil refineries, and businesses of all kinds. Dial tone was fed from central offices all over the county by copper cable, open wire, and drop-lines until it ran out of juice. The town of Oil Springs needed to be converted from magneto to common battery. Petrolia needed to be converted from common battery to automatic dialing in order to eliminate the operator. I had the privilege of working at industrial, commercial, and residential sites.

My job was to establish the best method of installation to suit Bell's standards and customer requirements. Inside wiring often involved squirming through insect and rat-infested crawl spaces, basements, and attics, to get a phone installed with little or no sign of wiring. You quickly learned a lot about house construction. On one occasion I was drilling a hole up from the basement to fish a wire from the space between the walls. It seemed as if there was no space. After drilling to the extent of the eighteen-inch bit, I went upstairs to see if there was any sign of it. Sure enough, the end of the bit had finally emerged about halfway up the leg of a grand piano. Safety was always a concern. Believe it or not, there is a safe way to single-handedly string a drop wire across a busy highway without stopping traffic or getting yanked off a pole by some fast-moving vehicle.

Occasionally, I could be found doing toll line inspection along some lonely right-of-way climbing poles to replace glass insulators shot out for target practice. There was no way I would attempt to reach a broken insulator at one end of a six-foot cross-arm while clinging precariously to a rock-hard, sixty-foot pole by a pair of climbing spurs. The possibility of falling and being found crumpled at the bottom of a pole was above my pay grade. I preferred installations where I met people, lots of people. That's how I met Doris Bisson.

Doris was a French-Canadian girl from Timmins. After her father died she moved in with her sister, Anne, and her husband, Oscar. He was a pipe-fitter superintendent who had worked in Venezuela on oil refinery projects. The death of his first wife necessitated his return in order to look after their three children. By this time, his eldest was a preteen juvenile delinquent with a younger brother in the wings. The youngest, at three, was still in a high chair and not yet walking. Oscar urgently needed a wife. Somehow he managed to convince Anne that this was a good idea. When Anne got a load of the kids, she convinced Doris to come and live with them and go to Business College. Oscar was never short of ideas about how to make money. His mind was whirling with madcap schemes, always daring and original but never fully thought out. In fact, they were mostly disasters. The neighbors around Tecumseh Park on Parkinson Street were horrified to see him moving a dilapidated structure down Ontario Street to be placed on the corner. "Just wait," he told them through his infectious grin gripping on a cigar, "this will be the best-looking building on the street."

The house came from Blue Water, possibly off the reservation, to become a variety store. A baseball park across the street had convinced Oscar that a store would make his fortune. When finished, it had a plate glass corner store-front with a large sign and respectable living quarters upstairs. The outside needed help, and Oscar had a solution for that too. Permastone was a stone-like product that he could install himself. He bought the franchise and used his place as a showroom. Being an eternal optimist, he assumed others would want a similar enhancement to their home or office. Massive profits would pay for his installation and launch a whole new business. Indeed, the store looked good. Even the neighbors settled down to enjoy the nearby shopping convenience.

Under Anne's tutelage the kids were better off than ever, but not without some cost to her own state of mind. The eldest was contained, but never controllable. The middle one could have done better if Oscar hadn't given him quarters for beating up on kids hanging around in front of the store. Then there was the youngest. He was a sweet child who progressed further than any of them but still lagged far behind his own age level. Oscar knew if Doris came to live with them, Anne would have more time to work in the store. Eventually, I too would be caught up in Oscar's sphere of influence time and time again, and never-ending for the next twenty-some years.

A phone extension was needed. That's where I came in. I normally wouldn't have spent much time on a simple installation, but I'd never seen a family like them. Anne and Doris were attractive with slightly dark complexions. I found them exotic, if not erotic. Adding to the novelty of the situation, Oscar had brought a monkey back from Venezuela. Seeing a monkey jumping around a living room was a first for me. It was normally caged, but often let out for exercise and entertainment. Oscar went to great lengths to make me feel welcome, and a friendship developed between Doris and me. It never ceased to amuse everyone to have me pretend to hit Doris in order to excite the monkey. It would drive him crazy until he'd jump on my back trying to bite me around the neck and ears. The monkey grew to hate the sight of me. The feeling was mutual. One of us had to go.

It wasn't long before they all had to go. Oscar's job was coming to an end at the refinery and his Permastone business was going nowhere. His next job was at a mining site in Kimberley, British Columbia. With no other options available at the time, British Columbia seemed a good idea. He leased out the store and started packing. His TV was one of the few in Sarnia, and Ross and I bought it. We installed the twenty-foot antenna on our roof, foreshadowing the technical revolution soon to follow.

Doris could easily have stayed in Sarnia. She had a good job in the office of a local photographer. But for reasons unfathomable to me she was unable to give up the family. It was not long before I started receiving letters describing the incredible beauty of the mountains. As promised, Doris had a job in the office at the construction site. Kimberley even had a ski jump. Not long after their arrival, Oscar's eldest boy, in keeping with his perpetual tormenting of Anne and Doris, broke his leg on his first jump. With Christmas coming, I sent her an art kit with easel, brushes, and paints. Painting was something she always wanted to do. With all the fun they were having, they couldn't understand why I wasn't joining them. When she wrote a letter telling me that Oscar had a job lined up for me, I couldn't resist. Forget Bell Canada! I was off to British Columbia to make my own fortune.

Chapter 3

1953-55

Vancouver, British Columbia

Adolescence to young adulthood

Nobody I knew in Sarnia knew where Kimberley was. I'd never heard of it, and when I cast around for someone to travel with, nobody was interested in finding out. Jim Haggerty was a friend from the South Ward, a couple of years older than I was. When I was younger I thought he was pretty cool. I envied his thick, wavy black hair which he spent much of his time combing. My hair was thin and beyond management unless kept unwashed. I also had pimples. Between the two, I never thought much of myself, unlike Jim who appeared quite pleased. When I first met him, he had a steady girlfriend, and I thought he had it all together. After she dropped him I can't ever recall him hooking up so well again. It was not a surprise when he was the only one who wanted to join me. By that time, he was depending on me.

    My car at the time was a '46 Chevy with a minor flaw of leaking oil. Without time or money to look into it, I solved the problem by carrying a glass jug filled with used oil readily available from any gas station. We left a trail of oil across the Northern States and up into Alberta before turning left to Kimberley. I knew approximately how many miles per gallon of oil we'd get and when to stop for a top-up. One stop was between Shelby, Montana, and Lethbridge, Alberta. Between the two there weren't many better places to stop around midnight. The wind was blowing snow sideways, but the sky was full of stars with no competition from any city lights. Jim sat tight, as was his habit, while I grabbed the gallon jug from the back seat and rounded the front of the Chevy. On the way I slipped on the ice and fell, hitting the car and making a loud thump. I lay in front of the car, unhurt and totally silent. It took only a few seconds before Jim stirred.

    "Al!" he shouted. "Al?" he called again after several seconds of silence. Then, "Al, are you alright?" All was quiet except for the howling wind. Suddenly he jumped out of the car and rushed around to find me spread-eagled, still holding the glass jug of oil. He was panic-stricken. Being alone two thousand miles from home in the middle of a frozen prairie can do that to you, especially if you're looking at a dead man.

"Are you alright?" he shouted, "Al, Al, talk to me. Can you hear me?" he continued, grabbing my coat and shaking me.

"Yeah, I can hear you," I said. "But since you're here, why don't you take the oil and top up the Chevy?" For as long as he lived, which wasn't all that long, I don't think I ever saw him looking so happy. We laughed, but still, he was pissed.

The next day we reached our destination. Kimberley is located in southeast British Columbia between the Purcell and Rocky Mountain ranges at an elevation of about 3,800 feet. Oscar had rented a house, and Jim and I piled in on top of them. Sure enough, the job Oscar promised was waiting and I started right away. That left Jim to wander the streets of a strange town looking for work but without many prospects. In Sarnia, he filled oil drums for Imperial Oil. Nothing had prepared either of us for a mining town like Kimberley. The only construction job in town was the one I was working on, and construction work was typically controlled by unions. In British Columbia, unions controlled everything. I don't know what strings Oscar thought he was pulling when he got me the job of delivering material around the construction site in a pickup truck, but he certainly never consulted any union. Strings or not, it didn't take long for them to notice. It started with suspicious looks and whisperings, and then progressed to outright antagonism. One day I blew the lid off and made it easy for them. I figured I could drive a pickup through any narrow gap, but that was forward, not reverse with a trailer behind.

"Take this welding rig over to the admin building," an officious-looking hard-hat shouted at me.

It was mounted on a single-axle two-wheeled trailer. I hooked it up and took off. No problem! When I arrived, the welders were waiting, along with numerous other trades people and a few office girls keeping tabs on the riggers. Various engineering types were going in and out of a prefab office building carrying blueprints rolled up under their arms.

"Back it up in here," shouted a cigar-smoking welder, indicating a narrow passage between stacks of pipes, steel beams, lumber, and various clutter.

I'd never backed up anything with a trailer attached before. Every time I thought I had it lined up, it went the wrong way. I'd pull forward and try again, only to have it go in the other direction.

The welder was standing there scratching his head. Others were throwing their hands in the air while various spectators stopped to watch in amusement. Finally, I got the knack of turning the wheel in the opposite direction I wanted the trailer to go. After unhooking the beastly contraption, I made a quick retreat. The next day I was called to the office, where administration wanted to know how I'd gotten the job. And was I a union member?

"No," I said, "but give me the paper and I'll sign up right now."

"You can't do that," he answered. "The union office is in Vancouver and they assign all the jobs. That's the only place you can join."

"But Vancouver is five hundred miles away," I complained. "All the roads are closed through the pass for winter. How am I supposed to do that?"

"That's your problem," he said. "You can't work here anyway. The union jobs are all filled." He was not only getting rid of me, but making damn sure I never came back.

Oscar was nowhere around. That evening I asked him, "What the hell were you thinking?"

The only way to Vancouver was through Spokane and Seattle. We were old hands at cross-country migration by this time. In fact we were looking forward to it; especially Jim, who was starting to doubt the wisdom of the move. We drove through New Westminster and stayed on Kingsway until we ended up in skid row at Main and Hastings. *So this is Vancouver*, I thought, *maybe that shack-town Blue Water wasn't so bad after all.* We soon discovered there was much more to Vancouver. But even Gastown which is adjacent to skid row was beyond our reach. At least skid row had lots of cheap hotels. All the union offices were located there as well. They all had the same answer whether it was construction, lumber, or fishing unions: "Nope, nothing going on until spring. Come back then and maybe we'll find you something."

Jim had sold his car to finance his trip, and funds were running low for both of us. If things turned grim, I had a two-year leave of absence from Bell which I didn't intend to exercise. Meanwhile, I needed money and wanted adventure. But there was no way either of us could afford to wait until spring. I needed to check out the telephone company.

BCTel was founded by William Farrell in 1904. It was still about twenty years behind most Bell companies in terms of standards and service offerings. Phones were like Henry Ford's early cars: You could have them any color you wanted as long as it was black. Antiquated switchboards were all older-style Automatic Electric products from their factory in Bellevue, Ontario. Bell Systems may have been the enemy BCTel envied, but they were in the process of catching up. I called and talked to the plant manager.

He was interested in my Bell experience. I laid it on thick about Bell standards, colored phones, and coil cord offerings—dumb things I knew something about. When he asked about 1A Key equipment, I had to stretch it a bit. I knew it was a system of multi-line phones with lights and hold features, but I'd heard more about it than I'd ever seen. I couldn't say much about private branch exchanges either. There was not much call for PBXs in Sarnia. Only one guy worked on them. Maybe if I'd stayed another ten years I would have gotten lucky.

The plant manager said changes were coming. "Maybe we'll have some openings in the PBX department soon." Meanwhile, he wanted me to start as a regular installer until I became familiar with the inner city. He recommended I join the union right away although it wasn't necessary. It was more of an association than a union, but more serious than Bell's token effort. Since the pay was better than Bell, I didn't hesitate to join like everyone else.

My first day was a cultural shock. I showed up at the garage to find a hodgepodge of old panel trucks and cars, with only a few converted pickup trucks that looked similar to Bell's dark green beauties. The panels were driven by old geezers in suit, shirt and tie, looking like dress rehearsals for a Depression-era movie. It was discouraging to learn I would be paired up with one of these guys. He turned out to be a cantankerous, old, chain-smoking Icelander who rolled his own and stuck them in a chewed-up cigarette holder. Ash fell constantly on his clothes while driving, leaving minor burn marks all over his suit. He felt my job was to be his gofer, and his was to do all the customer interface and planning of the job. For my part, I feared I was expected to keep him alive for another year until he retired.

The next shock was my first union meeting. When employees retired they got a thousand dollars along with a few words of recognition from the union. They looked so old and decrepit I didn't expect any of them would live long enough to reach the bank. Was that me in forty-seven years? As my relationship with the Icelander soured, I doubted I'd outlive him. I played along just to learn the inner city with its back alleys, hotels, and high-rise buildings, and then I started bitching. My mantra to the plant manager was, "Where's that move I was promised to PBX installation?"

"Soon, soon," he would reply. "Be patient."

After one particularly frustrating day of quarrelling with my partner, I couldn't wait to get back to the garage and threaten to quit. I went at my foreman with such fury that I surprised myself with what could only be described as an out-of-body experience. From an advantage point of about two feet above my head, I could hear myself shouting so clearly that it shocked me back into my body to grab the controls and shut up. He pacified me by moving me to another old geezer. This was supposed to hold me over until the plant manager's supposed secret plan came to fruition. He always assured me that changes were on the way.

My second partner declined to wear false teeth, if he had any, and was just as grisly as the first. But I liked him. He didn't care a whit about driving or talking to customers. All he wanted to do was the pole work. At first I insisted it was better for him to stay in the truck while I did everything. Old as he was, he was more at home up a pole than I was. We developed a good relationship. Still I wasn't satisfied. If I had to work with someone, I needed to be learning something. As much as I liked working alone, I would work with anyone to get into the PBX department. That was where I could learn something. Otherwise, I was sunk.

After I started working we needed a place to live. While living downtown we got to know some of the waiters in skid row beer parlors. One had the perfect solution. He and his wife, who was a good cook, had an empty bedroom in their Kitsilano apartment. He talked to her and they offered us room and board on a weekly basis. I would pick up the tab until Jim found a job, which he eventually did. This time it was filling oil drums for Shell Oil near East Hastings Street on Burrard Inlet.

Jim had problems adjusting to life in the big city so far from home. Having expressed this to his mother, she immediately cooked a chicken and sent it to him by mail. The potent package of rotting chicken arrived a few weeks later. The landlady met him at the door saying, "I don't know what it is, but you'd better get rid of it or leave." He continued filling drums until he retired thirty years later, whereupon he shortly died. The single highpoint in his life was a brief marriage, only to have his wife leave him not long after the honeymoon.

I had issues with the landlady, too. The first day there she asked, "What kind of eggs do you want for breakfast?"

I said, "Oh, I don't know, scrambled is good." Three weeks later we were still eating scrambled eggs.

I asked her, "Can we have something besides scrambled eggs?"

She was offended and whined, "You said you wanted scrambled. I don't know what you want. Why didn't you tell me you didn't like them? I can't read your mind......"

She went on until I backed off, saying, "I like them. I love them. They're wonderful, just not every day. Can you poach or fry sometime?" For the rest of my life, *scrambled eggs* would be a code word for unwanted redundancy.

Other than my mother, this was my first experience of living with a woman. I learned they can get testy over things that men would never think of. I wrote Doris about some of the landlady's idiosyncrasies. After she had responded, I noticed another anomaly. The landlady was reading my mail. I wondered what her reaction to Doris' comment was, when she wrote, "When I come to Vancouver I'll beat her up for you." I'm sure the landlady had no concerns about that, but she must have wondered what I was saying.

I'd promised to visit Doris at Easter and took a Greyhound through Washington State back to Kimberley. One thing led to another, and the next thing I knew, we were engaged. Anne asked me, "When's the wedding?" It took me by surprise, having never thought about it.

"Well, at least not until July," I answered without thinking and feeling a little overwhelmed. I knew engagements meant a promise of marriage, but didn't they go on forever? July wasn't that far away, but when I left town there'd be safety in distance.

Oscar had a plan for that too. When he lost his job at the end of May, he moved to Vancouver and rented a house in Burnaby. I asked him when he was going back to Ontario. He said not until after the wedding. It was a foregone conclusion that I was now part of the family. Doris found a job downtown at Pacific Lumber Inspection Bureau. Since Kitsilano was much closer, we moved into a tiny apartment. She was in, and Jim was out. It was hard to argue with that.

I think I was mostly attracted by her innocence. She'd led a sheltered life, surrounded by a large and very close family. Her siblings, being several years older than she was, no doubt treated her as the baby of the family. Catholicism was a mystery too. I had no idea how much the nuns had influenced her. I'm not sure what her attraction to me was. It could have been the times. Women still feared becoming old maids if not married by their early twenties. Doris would never have left the family on her own accord. I, too, felt alone in the big city. Perhaps we both saw each other as security where we could meet our comfort zones, even if her zone was different than mine.

I'd left the Chevy at a used car lot on East Hastings that said they would fix the leak and get me $500 for it. It was a step backward when I started riding the bus; something I hadn't done since turning sixteen. I was no longer someone from a semi-privileged background with an easy life. Now I was an immigrant. At least I started to think and act as one. I worked hard and played less. With no fallback plan or support system, I didn't want to screw up. I'd turned nineteen and suddenly realized my youth was gone. I was an adult and had done everything a youth could aspire for. I was ready to settle down. We talked about buying a house and starting a family. I was looking forward to it—a starting point from which we could grow. I knew nothing about married life, parenting, the world at large, or even life itself. With no real knowledge, I was complacently allowing events to move along. Doris had no idea how naive I was.

There was one advantage in having Oscar in my camp. Weeks went by without my car ever being seen again and I was being put off by the car lot manager. One night when Oscar and I were taking the girls out to dinner, I told him that I thought I was being ripped off, and asked what he thought I should do about it. Without hesitation he swung the car around and headed for the used car lot. He pulled into the only entrance and stopped the car where nothing could get in or out. We headed straight to the office, leaving the girls locked inside the car. Oscar told them to not let anybody in.

"Yeah, that's the guy," I said as we entered the office.

Oscar said, "My friend here tells me you stole his car."

"I didn't steal anything," he replied. "It's just that we sometimes can't trust people from Ontario. We have to check on things. It takes time."

I said, "Well we don't trust people from BC. If you haven't got the money, give me the damn car back."

"There is no money. We had a hard time selling it and the repairs cost a lot more than expected."

"Bullshit," I said. "You likely sold it to the first sucker who showed up." I was pretty cocky with Oscar backing me up.

One of the salesmen came in and complained about Oscar's car blocking all his customers. The manager told the salesman to go move it. As he was leaving, I started to protest, but Oscar said, "Don't worry, he won't get inside."

The owner reached for the phone and said, "Move it or I'm calling the cops."

"Good!" Oscar said, "Go ahead and call them. We're not going anywhere."

We waited until a uniformed officer arrived. After looking at the car's disrupting position, he came into the office where the air was rife with tension. He was big enough to be intimidating, but years of service allowed him to remain calm and laid-back; the kind of cop everyone likes to see walking their neighborhood.

"What's going on?" he asked the manager.

"These guys are blocking my entrance and refuse to leave," he complained.

"What's your problem?" the cop asked me.

"He took my car on consignment three weeks ago and owes me five hundred bucks," I wailed. "He's sold it and hasn't paid me a cent."

"Have you sold the car?" he asked the owner.

"Er, I'm not sure. We had a lot of expensive repairs and, ah, had to farm it off to another lot. I'll have to check. Anyway, the car had more problems than he told me and there ain't no five hundred dollars."

"How much do you think you owe him?" the cop asked with infinite patience.

"Well, it might be as much as three hundred. But no more," he quickly added.

The cop turned back to me and asked, "Does that satisfy you?"

"It does if he gives me the three hundred bucks right now," I said.

The cop slowly pivoted back to the manager and asked, "How about it?"

"I can't do that. A check has to be made out by Accounting and that will take a few days."

"Bullshit!" I said again for lack of better vocabulary. "Either you have it here tomorrow at this time, or I'm calling the cops and taking you to court."

The cop took one final look at the guy and said, "I've got better things to do. I'd suggest you have it ready." He looked at Oscar and said, "Now get your car off the lot."

Oscar said, "No problem! But we'll be parked here again tomorrow and every night of the week until my friend here gets his money."

The check was there and just as well. My Dad had co-signed at his bank for my loan, and the three hundred dollars just covered the balance. I'd never needed to ask him for money and wasn't about to start now. I was broke again, but money wasn't all that important since I'd never had much. I kept my expectations geared to my income which was pretty low. Anyway, I was feeling a whole lot better with no debt. I'd been able to support myself since I was sixteen, and always got by on the innocence of youth and blissful ignorance. Credit was not an option. That was about to change. Once married, we would want to buy a house.

On July 1 we were married in a Roman Catholic Church. The plan was almost scuttled when the priest insisted I convert or forever be condemned to Purgatory. He assured me that there would be no entrance into heaven unless I was a member of the "one true faith." I thought it was nonsense—my mother had already told me God was everywhere. That was even more confusing. The priest doubled down by assuring me she wouldn't get in either. He had this on good authority, too, as it had been ordained from one priest to another all the way back to Jesus. I'd never given much thought to that subject either, but I wondered how he could know that? To the best of my knowledge, Jesus was a blond-haired, blue-eyed Jew who was killed by the Romans at the request of his own religious leaders. Then the Romans continued to persecute both Jews and Christians for another three hundred years before accepting Jesus as the son of God, if not God Himself for good measure. No wonder I was confused.

It was still too much for me. All I wanted to do was to keep Doris happy by getting on with it. Eventually, I consented to allow our future children to be baptized in the faith. She would be the greater influence where religion was concerned while I remained beyond redemption. I was okay with Jesus; I just didn't approve of all the trappings. Jim was my best man at the wedding. Mom and some ladies drove all the way across the country to see the event. My clearest memory of the ceremony, as we walked back down the aisle after exchanging vows, was wondering, what the hell have I done now?

The reception was at Oscar and Anne's house. I borrowed Mother's car for a quick honeymoon in Kelowna, where one of my grandfather's brothers, Will Rankin, lived. He had gone to the Yukon during the turn-of-the-century gold rush and actually came back with enough gold to buy land in Kelowna where he planted apple trees. When I first met my ninety-something-year-old great uncle, he was digging up septic tank leach lines at his lakefront house. By this time, his son Percy was running the fruit ranch with his wife. They had two sons: One was a rancher with a string of horses, and the other a flight instructor in the RCAF.

A year later I visited again, and Percy offered me a ten-acre piece of the orchard for ten thousand dollars. With that in mind I visited Okanogan Telephone Company and thought seriously about moving. It was a subsidiary of BCTel and I could easily have transferred, but I wasn't sure. Had I gone there first, instead of Vancouver, I would never have hesitated. But now I was hooked on the city where there was more opportunity for advancement. In Kelowna, I could see the future. Somehow, it didn't look big enough.

Not long after the wedding, Oscar and Anne moved back to Ontario to chase another construction job. Doris was free of her family and winging it on her own with me. Jim was content to be our Sunday dinner guest for several years. To her, that was little substitute for a robust family such as hers, but she still had a cousin in town, Cecile, and husband René. He was the sous chef at Hotel Vancouver, which was the top CN hotel in Canada and one of the great ones in the British Empire. When Queen Elizabeth visited in 1959, it fell upon René to cook Prince Philip's steak. When the waiter was called to pick up the dishes, he asked, "How was the steak?" Prince Philip responded, "Piping hot!" I suppose he meant it as a compliment to the waiter. My interpretation at the time was, "Tough as nails old boy—tasted like crap, but piping hot," done with a poor imitation of a royal accent. The chef was René's best friend. We all became friends and enjoyed many house parties with gourmet food. It was a place for Doris to keep her French up, otherwise she would never have survived with only me to live with.

302 E 20th North Vancouver.

There wasn't much housework in our small apartment. Often I was home before Doris and would have something related to dinner prepared. You can only do so much with canned goods. With my specialty, creamed peas on toast, I was a better cook than she was.

We bought our first house in North Vancouver. Doris quit her job and started a new one as housewife. That suited us both since we were anxious to start a family. I needed to teach her how to drive and bought an old Chevy coupe from BCTel's aging fleet. I was not going to be a chauffeur for grocery shopping and all the other things required of a stay-at-home mom.

The house was much older than the Chevy. The ground-level basement had a wood floor apartment subject to periodic flooding, dry rot, and rat infestation. There was also an attached garage that had seen better days. Essentially, it was a one-room apartment occupied by Joe Gatto, an emaciated alcoholic fellow who had some health problems, judging from his persistent coughing between cigarettes. It was rumored his family was connected to the mob, but I felt sorry for him and wanted him to stay. I also wanted his rent of twenty-five dollars a month.

As soon as BCTel's expansion got underway I transferred to the PBX department. This was a big deal! There were no more thoughts of moving to Kelowna. In 1955 the US-based General Telephone and Electronics acquired 50.2% ownership of BCTel.

Automatic Electric Strowger step-by-step switch selector bay for a PABX (Private Automatic Branch Exchange).

Suddenly they were buying the latest products from any number of manufacturers. There was a lot of training required to master all the different switches being introduced. With so many being installed there was plenty of overtime due to cutovers from one system to another. Also, there were a number of new employees coming in from different cities across Canada and England. All had previous telephone experience and were in demand.

My first apprentice was from Vancouver Island where he grew up on a dairy farm. In the 1920s, his parents had emigrated from Germany with centuries of family dairy experience. Their three boys grew up working as hard as their parents on the farm, but their dairy days were numbered. Like most kids of immigrant families, they were as wild as any other car-crazy kids in Canada. All three, in turn, left for Vancouver just as soon as they were old enough.

Derek Oliver's lifetime phone - Automatic Electric Model 80 from 1954.

Among other locations, we installed telephone equipment at various sites for the 1954 British Empire and Commonwealth Games. I was at the stadium when Roger Bannister and John Landy both beat the four-minute mile with Bannister taking the lead at the finish line. Poor Landy! Nobody ever hears of him today but everyone in the world knows about Bannister. And all because Landy looked over his shoulder before the finish line and lost the race by microseconds. There's a lesson in there somewhere. Another interesting event was in '59. I was assigned to make sure the leased direct line for security stayed up when Queen Elizabeth and Prince Philip opened the Queen Elizabeth Theatre. I was looking the right way when against all protocol I locked eyeballs with the Queen for a brief two seconds as they made their grand entrance through the lobby. She may have been smiling for everyone, but I knew better. Although, she never once looked my way as they watched the Flamenco dancers, which I totally didn't get.

At first it was a challenge to be selected for courses. I can recall my foreman saying, "Maybe you shouldn't apply. You've been out of school for a long time now and may not be able to cut it against all these younger guys." Coming from him it really ticked me off. It was more of a self-reflection, I thought. But considering my performance in high school, it weighed on my mind as well. Besides, many of them were not younger but older than I was, including my apprentice who'd quit UBC in his first year. He couldn't wait to get off the ranch, quit school, and get a job. Failure was no longer an option for me. I knew if I went on a course I'd give it all I had. I never liked being stuck in the same job. No matter what course I was on, I spent many a night poring over blueprints on the dining room table until I knew every switch inside out.

The investment in training was paying off for BCTel as well as for those of us who believed an apprenticeship should cover all aspects of the craft. Not everyone was interested in taxing themselves to that extent. It was a complex industry, and the company only needed so many in each discipline. My objective was one day to break out of the craft into engineering or management. I knew nothing about either, but it would be a challenging career move with a path to further advancement. I needed additional experience with some specific knowledge to compensate for my lack of education.

Doris missed her sisters and maintained correspondence. Eventually, Oscar decided to try Vancouver again. He also convinced another sister and her husband, Laurette and Art Gibbons, that there was plenty of work in Vancouver. Art and Laurette had two children, Conrad, and Dennis who was wheelchair bound. Art was trained as a paratrooper but broke his back on his last jump before going overseas. That same day, Dennis was born with a lump at the base of the spine. Tragically, an army doctor operated to remove it. Art walked again, but Dennis was left a paraplegic for life. If that's called Sins of the Father—"visiting the iniquity of the fathers on the children to the third and fourth generation"—it seems damnably unfair.

We had not been in the house more than six months before all nine of them moved in. Art and Laurette took the second bedroom, and poor old Joe Gatto had to vacate the garage in order to make a bedroom for Conrad and Dennis. I rigged up a buzzer system between the garage and their parents' room in case either of the boys had a problem. Oscar and Anne took the ground floor apartment with their three. Neither Art nor Oscar had jobs, nor were they successful in finding one. Doris loved having her sisters there, and it was possibly the happiest period in her married life. I, too, enjoyed the sudden influx of male companionship. The age gap was too large for any romantic entanglement with the sisters, but we did become lifelong friends. Only Harry Lockwood could see the humor in it. He sent letters addressed to me *c/o Doris' family* to her extreme annoyance.

Art was an avid hunter; Oscar and I, not so much. We'd often take off for a Saturday of hunting in the nearby mountains north of Abbotsford. It wasn't long until Art dubbed me "Thunderfoot" for occasionally sending a pile of rocks rolling down the mountain while stealthily stalking deer. After several months Art moved back to Ontario and was hired on the construction of the new Welland Canal. When that was finished, he became Construction Manager for the City of St. Catharines until his retirement. Laurette became a very successful realtor in the area. She would live well into her nineties and long outlive all the rest of her family including her children.

Without Art around, Oscar and I no longer felt obliged to show any pretense of being hunters. For Oscar, it was about not being outdone. For me, it was a hike in the woods. Yet there's something appealing about the excitement of the hunt while packing a high-powered rifle. It was power, a license to kill. It's the same feeling you can see in the eyes of those worked up in a mob when the adrenalin is pumping. Let's face it; we're animals. We're hardwired for survival. Mankind has a right to be proud of having fought nature and all comers for thousands upon thousands of years. That doesn't make us irredeemable; we also have our better angles. Maybe hunting is just the same primitive part of the brain that relishes sitting around a campfire. In any civilized country, hunting is not bloodlust, it's just a sport—a necessary sport—in the proper management of wildlife, culture, and traditions. It's just not for everyone.

My problem was I always saw both sides of things, rendering me somewhat flaky. The last thing I wanted to do was shoot a deer and then have to bleed, gut, clean, and maybe quarter it before hauling it out a couple of miles to the camp or car. Even worse would be wounding one and then having to track it for miles before finishing the job. Some stalwarts just want the head for a trophy over their fireplace to impress friends. I'd have to be pretty hungry for food or attention before doing either.

Eventually, Oscar was hired as a pipe-fitter superintendent on a job in Kitimat, up the remote coast in northwestern British Columbia. This left Anne and the kids in the apartment, where the eldest, Vince, drove her to distraction. To provide some perspective, one incident was a fight in a dockside café, where he broke a bottle over some guy's head. It was during this time that the youngest, Terry, had problems in grade one. It had also happened in Ontario, and this was the second year they couldn't teach him anything. The teacher advised Anne he needed special education. When Oscar returned, he wouldn't accept that his son could not master the first year of school. He started teaching him how to add one and one, two and two, etc., until the boy would have it, only to blissfully forget everything an hour later. Soon, Oscar gave up as well. They all returned to Sarnia to start another variety store. Years later, when Oscar was throwing out a broken washing machine, the challenged youngster spent some time fooling with it in the garage. He went to Oscar with a broken part and said, "Dad, if you could buy me one of these things I think I can fix the washing machine for you." And he did, proving too late that Oscar didn't need a new machine after all. More importantly, it gave a whole new meaning to special education. Even today there is too little of it.

Our house was no sooner vacated than Harry Lockwood and family moved to Vancouver. He was working for a finance company where he quickly learned "the art of repossessing television sets from little old ladies living on pensions." I don't think he enjoyed doing it, but he was good at it. I persuaded him to stay in the basement apartment as long as they wanted, which wasn't all that long. The girls didn't get along with each other, while Harry and I happily went off to work. The next tenant from Sarnia was Bill Grabove with his wife and daughter. Sometimes it felt as if I'd started a wagon train west.

Chapter 4

1955-63

North Vancouver, British Columbia

A sort of adult

Time moves slowly when we are young. My brief youth felt like a lifetime. The short time in Vancouver already seemed like a second life. I was so disconnected from everything prior, that it felt as if I was a different person. That other person was young and impressionable, with no plan of his own. He was easily led; life was fun, a playground. The Vancouver person could see he needed to grow up and take responsibility for his life. Now, he too was gone. The new me was married with children and the pace was quickening.

Leslie was born in October, and Doris' mother, Rosa, was there for the occasion. She had a lot of experience with babies and knew exactly what had to be done. She'd spent most of her married life cooking in her husband's two bush camps with up to twenty men in each. Often she cooked for both camps. The meat generally came from a deer or moose carcass hung in a shed where she'd do all her own butchering. She did this while raising eight kids. Doris was the baby of the family and several years younger than her siblings. By her time, "ma mère" didn't have a lot of time for children as she worked around the kitchen and dining hall. The older ones were also too busy with their own shenanigans to give Doris much time, but they gave her anything else she wanted. Being married to me meant she'd have to become independent. It's amazing how quickly women learn how to shop, cook, raise kids, and take care of a household once they're married. She was already proving to be a good homemaker, and then instantly adapted to the additional responsibility of being a parent. These are skills well beyond me even now. I might add that it also seems well beyond the inclinations of many from both gender today, where being married and raising children is no longer a priority.

By the following summer it was time to show off our baby girl. We took a trip by car across the States to return to Ontario for a grand reunion. It was a '52 Chevy Sedan and I installed a cut-down sheet of plywood across the back seat to make a playpen for Leslie. She quickly learned to stand up, wanting to join us in the front. Nobody gave any thought to seatbelts or child restraints in those days. I didn't even pay much attention to the tires until I had a blowout in Montana and changed out all four. This was our first trip on a vacation back home.

Doris and I with Leslie in my parent's back yard – 1956.

Doris had told me about her father. He was deceased by the time I met her. It was almost a forgotten folklore that he had a brother. She would have heard the details from her mother or possibly an older sister. The story was that her father was one of two sons from a Wilson family of Scottish origin. Both boys were adopted after some tragic accident on the St. Lawrence River while immigrating. Her father was adopted by the Bisson family and named Ovide. The other boy was adopted by an American family and named Larry (alias). He was still alive and living in Washington State at the time of our trip. We couldn't resist looking him up. As expected, he received us warmly. Doris thought the resemblance to her father was apparent although he could not have been more different otherwise.

Ovide had been a north-woods French Canadian bush-camp operator who had no need to speak English. He was a devout Catholic, but his Scottish genes delighted in spirited debates with the family priest. I never met him, but I did meet Larry, in Spokane. He said that he and Ovide had only met once, as adults, but their cultural and language differences meant they had little in common.

Larry's life had no similarity to Ovide's religion, language or bush-camps. His idea of roughing it was a summer cottage on a lake outside Spokane. He took us waterskiing, but I failed to rise to the occasion. That was a luxury I wouldn't experience for another decade. After his death, many years later, we were told that his widow retired to a mobile home park in Anaheim, California. Another version of his story differs greatly from my rather benign account. The other story, being more interesting by virtue of ships, pirates, captivity and escape, will no doubt prevail as the family genealogy over the centuries. Whatever their history, from my perspective both were honorable and hard-working men. Ovide's life was harder and decidedly more challenging. In my opinion, Larry hit the jackpot.

We entered Ontario at Sault Ste. Marie. Our first stop was to spend a few days with yet another sister, Jeanne, and her husband, Lyle. He was a hard-drinking foreman in the steel mill, and a World War II war hero. As a sergeant he was decorated twice: Once for diving into a frozen river to hook a chain onto an army truck that had broken through the ice, and the second for single-handedly taking out a German machine-gun position with a flame thrower while driving a jeep.

He was the real McCoy and had the scars to prove it. I noticed them while we were shaving one morning and asked, "How did you get that?"

Being Lyle, he said, "Oh, that. It's what's known as a furlough."

"What does that mean?" I asked, even more curious as I doubted the truth of his explanation.

He grinned at me, and said, "You know! You stick your shoulder around the corner until someone gets a shot at you." Veterans are like that. They'll talk for hours about the fun they had, but you can't learn much about what they really went through. I received more information from Jeanne, who had saved the newspaper clippings.

Lyle in Sault Ste. Marie – 1956.

Next stop was Timmins to greet some more of the Bisson clan: Alcide, Irene, Conrad, and Aurèle, siblings all. Alcide, having spent much of his life following in his father's footsteps, was now an independent landscape contractor working on government highway projects. Conrad had a successful TV store and was the spark plug of the family. When the war started, he was too young and not heavy enough to be accepted. He ate bananas by the dozen until he gained enough weight to join anyway. Once overseas, it didn't take long before Lyle found him and got him assigned to his squadron. They both claimed to have had the time of their lives, fighting the war together. For a while, Conrad was a dispatch rider taking messages from the front lines back to headquarters. When he got tired of German pilots shooting at him, he rigged up a machine gun to his handle bars so he could shoot back.

Conrad Bisson in Timmons.

Conrad's younger brother, Aurèle, also sold and serviced TVs. Being a younger brother myself, I thought he would have been better served had he shaken off Timmins and moved to Toronto at a younger age. It was too late for either of them by the time I met them. They were already mature men with their own families and destined to remain in the north they clearly loved. They'd come a long way from where they started, working in bush camps and gold mines. Many of their peers would not do as well.

Their cousin, Henri Beauchamp, was visiting as well. His parents had moved to Montreal where he grew up. He became a typesetter for *La Presse*, the leading newspaper in Montreal. Later, in the sixties, as a shop steward in the union, he fought tooth and nail to prevent the conversion to phototypesetting. But technology was on the march. All the unions in the world couldn't stop further job cutting when computers entered the fray in the seventies. Henri's aunt (Doris' mother) was a Beauchamp. She was the only girl in a family of seven boys and far more responsible than all the boys put together. As men they all worked in the bush, and when in Timmins spent most of their money on booze and women. Henri's cousin, Norman, also moved to Montreal and ended up a multi-millionaire in the radio broadcasting business.

The Beauchamp ancestors landed in Quebec directly from France, possibly before the Battle of Quebec in 1759. There was no connection to another group of Beauchamps—the ones who landed in England with the Normans in 1066, who ended up centuries later pronouncing it *"Beecham."* Timing—hundreds of years—made a world of difference between the hard-drinking Canadian fiddle players in Timmins and the powerfully connected kingmakers of England. But still, Aurèle's son, Gilles Bisson, was elected as the New Democrat Party's Member of Provincial Parliament, for the northern riding of Timmins to James Bay, in 1990. He's been reelected in every election since. Maybe there *is* a connection! After all, genetics trump genealogy every time. You can fiddle with both, but one is randomly inherited through genes, and the other depends on records, history, memory, error, and maybe a little wishful thinking.

Eventually we arrived in Sarnia. Bill and Ross were both married by this time. They had formed a partnership in RANKIN Construction Company. Bill was the administrator who did the estimating, sales, and public relations—the wheeler-dealer who never said no. Ross was left to make things happen. Saying *no* was never a problem for him when it came to running a job site. Mom and Dad were happy to finally meet Leslie, our one-year-old. It was not until the following year that Daniel was born. He wouldn't get to see Ontario until he was three. On that occasion he gained more attention by having extreme pain in his side. It was an appendix attack requiring an operation. Fortunately, Ross' wife, Chris, was a nurse and able to diagnose Daniel's problem early enough. With Daniel in the hospital, I waited anxiously for word. It came by a local telephone call with someone reading the contents of a Western Union telegram, saying, "The operation was successful and Daniel is doing fine." That also said a lot about the cost of toll calls back in the days when telephone companies held a monopoly. On the other hand, I never received a hospital or doctor's bill.

Daniel at new house in North Vancouver.

While they went ahead for a few weeks extended vacation, I remained in Vancouver until my vacation came up and then joined the family for two weeks before we all returned home. When Doris saw me getting off the plane in London, Ontario, she remarked to Ross, "Gosh, he's lost so much weight." I never thought about it until I weighed myself and realized I'd lost about twenty-five pounds. As a bachelor for a month, aside from not cooking I played tennis in

Stanley Park on many evenings. Once back in Vancouver with Doris in the kitchen, I had to put my foot down: "No more pies!"

That fall, the house was void of guests. I was able to tear down the garage and gut the apartment to put in a concrete foundation before rebuilding the apartment and renting it out. I'd organized a Saturday working bee with Harry Lockwood and a bunch of friends from BCTel to mix and pour the foundation. Their incentive to get it done was a laundry tub full of beer sitting on ice. It wasn't long until someone got thirsty. By the second quenching it was obvious the job was not going to get done to any reasonable degree of workmanship. With a solemn promise from all to return on Sunday, I shut down the bee and continued partying for the rest of the day. On Sunday, the only one to show up was Harry. It took all day, but we finished the job by ourselves—sans beer.

The house was sitting at the back end of one side of a double lot. I split the lot and had a second house built. Doris and I moved in and rented the two units in the older house. It wasn't long before we bought another fixer-upper in Lynn Valley. We moved in there and added two bedrooms in the attic. I still don't know how Doris put up with it. You could say I was restless but that would be far too generous. With two kids and one on the way, I was motivated to succeed. I was too young to regret quitting high school, but not too young to know I had to do something to make up for it. A few more years in school would have made a world of difference. Now, I wonder why I couldn't see it earlier. The truth is I couldn't wait. Nothing has changed. There's always another hill to look over.

My former apprentice and I went hunting occasionally. Someone had told him there was a good location for hunting near where he lived out in the Frazer Valley. On the way, he said, "I invited a friend of mine from the island to join us. I hope you don't mind? We can pick him up on the way through downtown." His friend was sound asleep. We eventually roused him by banging on the door; actually, his mother's door. She was happy to send him out at 6:00 a.m. since he'd just come home drunk around four. No doubt she preferred to teach him a lesson rather than listen to him fart and snore on the couch all day. He came out to the car carrying a half-full bottle of Slivovitz, a potent Serbian brandy. "Wanna swig?" he said, by way of introduction. We declined. "Y'shur? Helps snap the old eyeballs open!"

Upon arriving at the recommended location, we loaded up and headed down a dirt road into the woods. Before long we came across a large clearing with an old dilapidated shack in the middle of it. Our hung-over friend said, "Look, there's a cat in that old abandoned building."

"Where," I asked. "I don't see anything."

"Right there, on the screened porch. Never mind I'll show you." Without hesitation he lifted his 30-06 rifle and fired a round right at it. The cat let out an ear-piercing scream and leapt out of sight. Silence prevailed. We looked at him with open mouths. It was only a matter of seconds before a loud voice was heard from the shack.

"What the hell do you think you're doing?" It was exactly what I was about to say.

"Oh shit," he said, "somebody lives there."

While backtracking, my workmate replied, "We better get out of here."

"Walk, don't run," I whispered as I joined him. "Best that fellow stays inside for a while." It lasted for less than a minute. Once out of sight, we broke into a run and made a beeline for the car.

"Unload and lock them up." I shouted. "This hunting trip is over."

I was sure it would take the guy in the cabin a while to get over the shock. No doubt he'd soon hike out to a phone. We'd be back in Vancouver having dumped the "friend" and finished lunch before he could call the game warden.

The acquaintance who lived in that area knew we were going to be hunting there that day. He kept asking exactly where we were, and did we see anything unusual. Apparently, a bunch of hunters shot up some old guy's house and almost killed his cat. The only answer was, "Nope, hunted way over in the other direction; didn't see a thing all day." At the very least we would have had our guns confiscated, and maybe that would not have been a bad idea. At worst, we could have been charged with attempted murder. Other hunting trips to the Caribou and Okanogan Valley were less dim-witted. But we did return to the Frazer Valley.

I'd read a story about a mysterious gold mine in the mountains just north of Pitt Lake near Coquitlam. Around the turn of the century, there was this "Indian Joe" fellow who would disappear up the Fraser River. After a month or so he'd return with a pile of gold dust and nuggets and cash them in for thousands of dollars. The papers of the day claimed he often took a "squaw" with him who was never seen again. The speculation was that he'd drown them on the way out before returning to New Westminster in order to keep his secret. Unidentified bodies found floating down the Frazer River gave plenty of weight to the claim. The papers even credited him with putting a curse on the location. It promised death and destruction to anyone following him or venturing anywhere near the north end of the lake towards his secret gold mine. No doubt reporters blew the facts out of proportion over the years. But time and time again in the early 1900s, there were numerous prospectors trying in vain to find it. Some did and often ended in disaster. Others lived long enough to deposit enough gold to verify there was a mother lode there somewhere, just waiting to be picked up by someone. We figured it might as well be us.

I had a clinker-built boat with a ten-horse Mercury outboard motor that was perfect for the job. I couldn't really afford such extravagance; it was an impulse decision made on credit early in the spring, with the intention of selling it before the end of summer. It wouldn't cost me anything. I just wanted to know what all those rich guys did with their boats. On a Friday night we drove as far as we could before pitching a tent in darkness on the edge of the Pitt River. At dawn we launched the boat and proceeded north on what appeared to be a beautiful day. An hour later we closed in on our destination. We could see it was an ominously primitive beachhead scattered with brush around ancient tree stumps and driftwood. It looked as if it hadn't been visited in fifty years, and for good reason. It was a time capsule with a questionable background. The hair stood up on the back of my neck, almost electrified, as we looked for the best spot to pull in the boat. Normally, I was drawn like a magnet to places like this. What the hell was going on?

Beyond the beach, the mountains rose straight up to look down upon us. It was beautiful, but I could feel nothing but scorn with no respect. There was a single canyon where the river flowed down into the lake. Looking up that canyon was hypnotic and frightening at the same time. It dared you to try and enter, but left much doubt over the outcome. Before we could land, the wind started to blow. We could see the sky filling up with clouds as it became increasingly darker. There was a sudden chill in the air as waves angrily slapped at the boat. I looked at my friend and said, "What do you think, is that a storm coming up?"

"Yeah, no kidding, how good is this boat in rough water?"

I thought about it. I wanted to reassure him. "I've taken it all over Burrard Inlet," I told him. Another friend from work and I had taken a trip up Indian Arm. "We went as far as Wigwam Inn and never had any trouble." But he already knew that. He and I were in Burrard Inlet when the Second Narrows Bridge fell down. I swear we had nothing to do with it.

"What about English Bay?" he asked, looking for a better case.

I said, "No problem! Except near the first narrows, where the changing tide will lift you up and drop you more than twenty feet with each swell." The bravado was suddenly lacking in my voice. I became more fearful as the black shroud coming out of the canyon crept ever closer. It spilled over the beach toward us. "I almost got swamped once trying to round Point Atkinson," I quickly added.

I could tell that whatever was bothering me was affecting him as well. He said, "These damn lakes get pretty choppy, too, you know." Still, neither of us was willing to be first to throw in the towel.

I threw out a teaser instead. "Well, we came up here to do some exploring." It sounded too persuasive. I tried again. "I'm not sure I'd be interested in getting any closer, you know, with the weather and all. How about you? Do you feel like following that river up the canyon?"

"I'd hate to get stuck in here," he replied. "I've definitely got to get home tonight."

"Me too," I said, already turning the boat south into the increasingly white-capped water. This place was scaring the crap out of me. It took us hours to fight the beating waves all the way back to the safety of Pitt River. I don't know what old Indian Joe did to all those maidens but he wasn't going to get me. He could keep his damn gold as far as I was concerned. And fifty years later it seemed a lot of folks agreed. Even now, over a hundred years since he started cashing in, the mine still hasn't been found.

Back-east relatives and visitors still remained a constant. Oscar's son Vince showed up needing a place to stay for a few days. The thought of it terrified Doris. He was no longer just a teenager with a bad attitude. Now he looked pure outlaw with a Texas drawl so imbedded it could have come from the bottom of the Rio Grande. It was not that he wasn't handsome. I would never have recognized him except for the same disarming, sly grin that Oscar always charmed people with. Vince stood in our doorway wearing cowboy boots and a western shirt tucked into tight jeans. A belt with a massive buckle emphasized his already narrow waist. Everything above that was well filled out with muscle.

Doris wasn't buying any of it, especially the grin. She'd had too many fights with him while helping Anne raise the three of them. Besides, he wasn't blood. Everything in her family was related to family. The only blood between them would have been spilt at Oscar's hand. He had a flip side with a cruel streak that would have whipped Vince plenty while growing up. But if Vince disliked Doris as much as she disliked him, she thought he could be dangerous. It was unwarranted, of course. He always affected women that way and usually to his benefit. Actually, he was reasonably fond of his Aunt Doris. He found her a little excitable, but harmless. Against her wishes I said we could put him up for a few weeks until he found a job. After two weeks she still had the willies just looking at him. I told him his time was up, but not before finding him a job.

Vince had been living illegally in Texas for a number of years while driving long-haul eighteen-wheelers from state to state. Of course he always packed a gun—this was Texas, after all. Along the way he was trying to establish a wife in each state in which he laid over. One lady in Oregon took him seriously until she found out about the others. She turned him in to the immigration authorities and they kicked him out of the country. That's the short version of how he landed on our doorstep. Whenever I received visitors with no job and no other place to go, I became very creative in conjuring up employment. We had a neighbor living behind us who was a supervisor on the docks. I told him about Vince and suggested he'd be a natural.

"Is there any way of getting him a job as a longshoreman?" I asked.

"It's not easy," he said, "but there is a way if he has the patience."

"I know he'd love the job," I promised optimistically. "In fact I think he'd kill for it!" He thought I was kidding.

"Tell him to show up Monday morning and submit his name. There'll be a hundred guys hanging around waiting to get called, and that's just the union members. As long as there are union members available, he'll never be called. Tell him not to get discouraged, just keep showing up. Sometimes it takes weeks until one day there'll be a shortage of members. That's when they start calling from the non-member list. I'll be watching for his name."

It didn't sound promising, but it only took a couple of weeks. By that time everyone on the docks knew who Vince was. It wasn't long before he was a card-carrying longshoreman. Without further contact we lost track of him.

We'd no sooner gotten rid of one nephew when than another showed up. Lyle and Jeanne Young's son, Reggie, had written to us while in the Navy. He said he'd like to talk to us about getting his "land legs while adapting to Civvy Street." He was on shore leave and coming to Vancouver. I had an installation job in Kamloops, south-central British Columbia. I wanted to take the family along to combine work with a camping trip. Since we were leaving town before his arrival, I left a note on the front door explaining where we were.

In spite of the prosperity and peace of the fifties, it was also a time of great anxiety over the arms race and nuclear bombs. Canada and the U.S. built lines of defense—the Distant Early Warning (DEW) line and the Mid-Canada Line (MCL)—to give the United States time to get its intercept planes off the ground in case the Russians came over the North Pole to bomb us all back to the Stone Age. But not to worry, the kids in school were being drilled to hide under their desks while adults considered building bomb shelters in their backyards.

There was another radar line near Kamloops where BCTel was installing the communications for an early warning radar site. I believe it was appropriately called the Pinetree Line. Nearby was a lake where we could camp much closer to the site, rather than commute from Kamloops. It was a perfect opportunity for all of us, Doris, Leslie, Daniel, and me along with the boat, to pre-empt the Russians in going back to the Stone Age. The rest of the crew stayed in town at a motel. When Reggie showed up at the motel, we were forty some miles north in the mountains.

Doris at campsite with Reggie on right.

By coincidence, a co-worker on the same job was walking by the desk as he was asking for my room number.

"They checked out a couple of days ago," the desk clerk said. Reggie was with a navy buddy and they were hitchhiking in uniform. "Oh shit," he said, "Did he say where he was going? We're on leave and I've got to see him; been chasing him all the way from Vancouver."

My co-worker overheard the conversation and asked, "What do you want with Al?"

He explained that he was Doris' nephew and wanted to see us before steering back to Halifax. He couldn't believe it when he discovered we were camped up a mountain forty miles away. He looked as if he'd lost his last lifeboat. But he was tough long before the navy chiseled him down. He looked at my co-worker and said,

"Can you draw me a map?"

"I can do better than that," he answered. "I was just going out the door to join him at the lake. Jump in my car. I'll take you right to his campsite."

They spent the rest of the weekend with us before getting the same ride back to Kamloops. His five-year stint was almost over, and he did not want to move back to Sault Ste. Marie. Having joined up at seventeen, he'd essentially grown up in the Navy, and it showed. We assured him he could come and stay with us until we considered him ready for Civvy Street. Once out of the Navy, he cut a course straight for Vancouver. He hadn't been kidding about needing help adapting. As a gunner in the Navy the only training he'd received was how to blow things up. He'd also majored in drinking, fighting, and whoring at every port. We had our hands full.

Doris' job was to teach him manners and how to behave. My job was to teach him how to drive a car and find a job. It was a toss-up who had the more difficult task. I saw an opportunity while installing a new switchboard at a Volkswagen dealership in Burnaby. A couple of the mechanics in the garage were Swiss. One of them was the foreman. I told him about my nephew—the good, the bad, and the ugly—with the good being an exaggerated rendering of Reggie's mechanical ability.

"I could use another mechanic," the foreman said. "He'd have to go to night school for three years on the government program to become certified," he cautioned. "If he's interested, send him in. Tell him to come into the garage and ask for me."

Reggie was already nuts about cars. Going into a government sponsored training program to learn all about them was perfect. The next evening he looked discouraged. I asked him how it went.

"Naw, nothing doing there," he groused. "They're not hiring."

"What?" I asked incredulously. "Did you talk to the foreman?"

"Talk to him! They wouldn't even let me see him. Some broad wearing a headset sent me to another crotch in personnel. All she did was get up my ass with a bunch of questions before telling me they didn't need anybody. F***'n' waste of time," he griped in his less than polished Navy lingo.

"Personnel," I shouted. "You don't want to talk to them. I told you to go in the garage and ask for the foreman by name."

"Oh shit! When you said garage I thought you meant the dealership. Isn't the whole place a garage?"

"Hell no! The front is the showroom and office. Go back there tomorrow and go around to the back. You'll find him under a rack or in a pit somewhere."

He did and he got the job. He became great friends with the Swiss guys whose hobby was going to a fast track where they raced

Volkswagen Beatles. In three years he was a top mechanic, married, and a father twice over. But he was still a piece of work.

Our third child, Leonard, was born on a Thursday night in August of '62. Doris' mother was there again. She and I were watching TV when Doris came out of the bedroom, saying, "The baby is coming." It was about time! By our calculations it was ten months. Her North Vancouver doctor had died during the pregnancy, leaving his partner struggling to keep up with all the additional patients. I realize now that it was a mistake to stay with him. We should have gone back to our former doctor in Vancouver who delivered the first two at Vancouver General. Instead, I ended up rushing her to the hospital a few blocks away only to find it practically abandoned. She was hurting, could barely walk, and wanted me to carry her. One look at her and I knew I wasn't up to the task. I assisted her into the hospital yelling, "Get a wheelchair, she's having a baby."

A girl behind the counter looked up, startled. "We don't have one here," she said.

Dumbfounded, I yelled back at her, "Well get something, get a gurney, and get a doctor."

She stammered, "There are no doctors on staff at this hour."

Now I'm really upset. "Then get a nurse. The baby is coming right now." A young nurse appeared right away and took charge. They disappeared while I waited. It didn't take too long before an older, lean, and hard-crusted looking nurse showed up. She was all smiles and carrying Leonard wrapped up in a blanket.

She opened the blanket, saying, "You have a beautiful healthy baby boy." I thought it odd that I got my first peek in the waiting room, instead of through a window into the nursery as in the case of Leslie and Daniel. But, sure enough, he looked wonderful. A short time later I visited Doris. She wanted to know how the baby was.

"Terrific," I answered, "he's a real whopper. How are you doing?"

"I'm okay now," she said, "but the young nurse was all alone and didn't seem to know what she was doing. She was yelling for assistance. She was panicking when the older nurse showed up, saying, 'He's turning blue. He has the cord around his neck.' The older nurse told her to shut up and took over, telling her what to do. I was really scared."

I wanted to reassure her. "Well, she just showed him to me in the waiting room and he looks fine; another perfect specimen. Damn good thing she showed up when she did."

Daniel, Leonard, and Rosa Bisson – 1962.

Moving into management or engineering at BCTel was going to be difficult. I'd already lost out on a mobile radio position. When I applied for an opening in Marketing and Sales, it went to a young fellow who a couple of years earlier, just out of high school, wanted a job in PBX installation. Instead, he was hired to drive the truck delivering material to us. There was a lot of competition for this sales job and his selection surprised all of us. Obviously he had the right stuff and we didn't. I could see that my decision to quit high school would continue to haunt me. In spite of all the courses I'd taken, I was going nowhere. My former apprentice had already transferred to maintenance. He said, "Al, what are you wasting your time for? PBX maintenance is a soft touch." I took his advice and requested a transfer at the first opening.

He wasn't kidding. Some installations of Automatic Electric's Strowger switches took months to complete. Imagine a hospital, a high-rise, a corporate headquarters, or a hotel where there's not only the switch to be installed, but miles of cable and wiring to be pulled through ducts and conduits. Many jobs took months, even with several crews. I enjoyed the challenge of completing a job on schedule, along with the satisfaction of cutting hundreds of phones into service without a glitch. This was something that only a few years earlier had been completely incomprehensible to me. On the other hand, in maintenance you cruised around in a company car with little more than a screwdriver and burnishing pen in your pocket. I also had ample time to pursue other interests and various courses. This was as good as it was ever likely to get.

Something had resonated with me back when we first started training classes. My first instructors had said something that stuck: "We don't come by our habits naturally. They exist because of repetitiveness that eventually becomes ingrained by hooking up neurons in our brain. Bad habits can only be broken by forcefully breaking that connection and replacing them with something else." He was referring to good study habits in place of goofy things that people get addicted to instead of keeping their eye on the ball. It struck a chord that went far beyond a commitment to studying and doing a little homework.

I got interested in metaphysics. There was a plethora of information and books on the subject. I became fascinated with subjects related to life after death, reincarnation, hypnosis, and mental telepathy, as well as Greek philosophers and Hindu yogis. I wasn't interested in signing up or joining some cult, it was just a fascination—voyeurism—without sex. The avatars, gurus, and yogis of India held too much sway over their followers to catch my attention for long. Reincarnation and karma, however, stuck for life.

I wondered what made people so dedicated to one religion or another, and why some were so liberal while others were so conservative. How could they be so committed to one, to the extent of being so violently opposed to the others? Psychology was interesting too, but I was more interested in life itself. I wanted to know how the subconscious mind worked. Was there a super conscious mind, an immortal soul, a fourth dimension, a fifth, or a sixth? I wanted to improve myself. Meditation helped, I even tried sleep-education as a way of reinforcing a positive image and gain self-confidence. Basically, I was not happy with who I was. I was searching for a way to change.

I had plenty of bad habits, but it never occurred to me that they could be actual physical connections—sticky neurons. Even if not connected, they could transmit to other neurons and tell them what to do according to past behavior. Nobody needed to keep repeating the same old routine, beliefs, or job, just because of some silly neurons. Behavior that seems to be normal, abnormal, or necessary can be broken. I'd come to believe my life was like an LP record stuck in the same old groove. Or maybe a ditch I was digging deeper and deeper every year until it was ever more difficult to climb out. My brain needed rewiring. Escape didn't seem as difficult when I compared my brain to a switch board. It was merely a matter of yanking out a cord to break the connection, and plugging it into a better circuit. All it took was motivation. Of course, it wasn't that simple. Back in the time when the company was offering new courses, I was willing to give up anything in order to do the homework and succeed. Now, having reached the top of the PBX pyramid and the end of the road, I needed a new plan.

The first step was to eliminate all the excess baggage I'd been accumulating along with three houses—two in North Vancouver and one in Lynn Valley. Then I needed to move to a good jumping-off spot. I wanted to be ready mentally, with no material attachments, to be able to move on short notice. We moved into a Burnaby townhouse complex with an indoor swimming pool temporarily. By any measure it sounds insane and difficult to pull off. It was made easier by Doris not being happy in British Columbia. All her family was back east. But that wasn't part of the plan. My goal was California. Leslie and Daniel were too young to know the difference, but they were old enough to know that California meant sunshine. That was good enough for them. I used this argument on Doris as well. She knew that even if everything went sideways in California, I'd never go back to British Columbia. I even convinced her it may be the quickest way back east, without even knowing where the thought came from. I suppose I figured if I screwed up in California, why not? But I wasn't planning on screwing up.

All that hocus pocus and mystical stuff may seem like a lot of crap to you, but something must have worked! By the time I got the California bug, I was fearless. The next step was to find a job. I made no secret of it when I advised my supervisor that I was taking a two-week vacation to go job hunting. I told him, "There's no future for me here. I'm going to California to find a job."

Leslie and Daniel at Yosemite National Park, CA.

Chapter 5

1963-65

Palo Alto, California

Start-ups

Even as a young teenager I was drawn to California. I'd often study the coastline, wondering where the best place to live would be. Monterey Bay always looked good! That was before I gave much thought to working for a living. Now, work was everything. I'd have to go where the jobs were unless I wanted to start all over again. Not just any job, it would have to be tied to communications, which covers a lot of territory. No matter where I went, there was bound to be a telephone company, but anything at the operational end of the business would likely be starting all over again. I already knew how to climb a pole and install a telephone. If a telephone company wasn't going to offer more than I had already, what was the point? Maybe the companies that supplied them, the manufacturers, could use my experience? If so, I'd have to go to where the factories were, and that wouldn't be Monterey Bay.

What would make a twenty-nine-year-old father of three, with ten years of seniority toward a pension, pull up stakes and move to a foreign country? The risk of being unemployed was staggering. The answer of course was opportunity—or insanity. If someone is chasing you with a gun, as in the case of refugees fleeing war or revolution, it's an easy decision. But immigrants do it all the time with little provocation. The majority of immigrants are looking for a better life. That's where I fell in. Nobody was chasing me. I just thought the United States would offer more opportunity. I needed to emigrate, and I was full of confidence. I'd done it before on much flakier grounds; now I was more up to the task.

I knew of someone else who'd done it. Monty was a former BCTel employee who had moved to the international division to install Strowger switches in Venezuela. Then I heard he was a manager in a start-up microwave radio company, Farinon Electric, in San Carlos. I called him at work and gave him my pitch, telling him

I was driving down the following week and would like to talk to him. Unsure of what my qualifications were, he invited me to his house in Palo Alto. At the end of the evening, he said, "Okay, come on in tomorrow morning. I'll introduce you to Bill Farinon."

I said, "How about after lunch?" I was staying at a hotel in San Francisco's Tenderloin District and had just bought a new suit that was being altered. I wanted to make a good impression; this was going to be a whole new me.

Farinon Electric, San Carlos CA – 1963.

A few weeks earlier I'd visited a psychic called Omar. He was retired and living with his wife in Vancouver. I knew there were a lot of phonies out there, but I'd read enough to believe that some authentic psychics did exist, or at least seemed reasonably credible. Curiosity got the better of me. Omar didn't look the part, if you're thinking baggy silk pants and a turban. He was an affable old gent who could have been anybody's grandfather. Already faltering, and under his wife's close supervision, he welcomed the conversation as much as he did the small fee he charged. He told me stories about the amazing people he had known and "read for" during his Vaudeville days. One friend in particular was Mandrake the Magician, who he claimed was living in New Westminster, British

Columbia. I knew of Mandrake from the comic books I'd read as a child. It never occurred to me he was a real person.

    I decided to tell Omar nothing, not even if he was hitting close to home. If he was going to tell me my future, he would have to do it on his own. I soon found out he didn't need any help from me. With his crystal ball he could see the American flag waving vigorously. He immediately told me I was moving to the United States. Among other things, he could see I worked with wires, "thousands of them, all mixed up together in a confusing mass" that he couldn't understand. But then he surprised me by saying my roots were also strongly attached to Canada. I would return to what looked like back east. At the same time, he said the American flag continued waving away in his crystal ball. Perhaps, he suggested, the move to Canada was not permanent. I would likely have gotten more out of him had I been more forthcoming. Then he asked me if I'd ever had a near-drowning experience.

    "No," I replied. I thought about the bathtub incident from my childhood, but that was not even close to drowning. It was just water on the back of my head. Yet, in a way it was worse, since I believed my father was *trying* to drown me. I didn't mention it.

    He shook his head, and asked, "Are you sure? I definitely see very strong indications of suffocating and drowning, or something like that." I'd always been able to swim and never even had a close call, but he kept insisting he was seeing something that indicated drowning.

    I said "No" for a second time and wished he'd get off it. But maybe he was on to something. I'd occasionally had claustrophobic nightmares until I was about thirteen. I'd be suffocating in a mass of indescribable, red fleshy substance. For years I couldn't even think about it without slipping into near panic before forcefully discarding it from my mind. Then, recently, I'd drilled down on it with meditation. I went all the way back beyond memory to when I was born, until I found the horrible sensation was no longer there. I couldn't bring it back no matter how hard I tried. I'd outgrown it, but still I wondered if it could have been birth trauma. I realized later that I should have been more open with Omar to see if he could confirm it. Instead, to change the subject, I asked if he could tell me anything about my future health.

    He studied his crystal ball and said, "No, nothing significant, but wait, yes, there seems to be a problem in the right lung." Oddly, at that exact time I was developing a pain in my lower right lung. Not wanting to give any clues, I refused to move in case I gave something away. When I couldn't stand the discomfort any longer, I sat up a little straighter to shift my weight, which stopped the pain. I'd no sooner done that than he said, "No, it appears to disappear and is nothing to worry about. Maybe it was just some gas or something." That's what I thought too. Or maybe it was something else: Twenty years later I did have a pulmonary embolism in the right lung that hospitalized me for weeks. It was a blood clot from a recent broken leg that found its way up to the lung on its way to my brain. No, that's too much of a stretch. It had to be the gas. But how the hell did he know?

Omar also gave me the initials of someone who would play a very important part in my getting a job in the United States. At the time, I discarded it all as the old hit-and-miss game that psychics were known to use in order to draw out information. It's hard to imagine how someone could see into the future unless you accept some scientific theory that time and space do not exist, at least as we understand it. Some say past, present, and future all happen at the same time, but don't expect me to go there. I settled for the simple probability that Omar, by narrowing his concentration on his crystal ball, was somehow able to read my mind and pick something up: thoughts, images, who knows? I would never dispute that all of us have the same ability, no matter how latent. Maybe we could do whatever he was doing and much more. I left his apartment thinking, how'd he do that? I should have been thinking about the initials that he gave me. When I arrived in California, I needed to find that person.

Bill Farinon was a middle-aged man of Italian descent. Having played baseball and hockey during his college days, he was still someone you didn't want to mess with. We went one-on-one in the conference room for my interview. I was sure I'd blown it with one knee going into periodic spasms. On a couple of occasions I almost knocked my coffee off the table with spastic wrist syndrome. It didn't get any better when he brought in Ed Nolan, the chief engineer, along with Wes Fisher and Herb Sutton, both VPs of sales. Wes was tall and slim with a gray suit and blue tie. He was a man well satisfied with himself and wanted others to share that view. They did! Many years later he ended up as president.

Herb was short and chunky with his sleeves rolled up while chewing on a cigar. He was a bit crusty and didn't give a hoot what anyone thought about him or his appearance. He continued to be a major contributor in the company for another decade until the company went public in the early seventies, whereupon he cashed in and retired. Herb had a way of cutting to the core without beating around the bush. After an hour of grilling by the four of them, Bill thanked me and said he'd let me know.

That's it? I'd heard that old brush-off before. I asked, "When?"

The best I could get out of him was, "In a week or so. We'll let you know by letter." I'd shown up thinking I might get this job. Now I was sure I'd blown it. Before the meeting it wasn't all that important; I still had a lot of stops to make. Now I wanted it so badly I didn't want to look any further.

I called Doris. She was uncharacteristically understanding, even relieved. "That's okay, why don't you just come home. Maybe we can move back east?"

With little enthusiasm I made an appointment at PT&T, Pacific Telephone and Telegraph. An odd name now, but not then. They said they'd hire me if I had a green card and lived locally. In all probability I'd be back on residential installation again. Why should I talk to some human resources clerk about my career when I'd just finished talking to the entire board at Farinon? To hell with it, I thought, he has to hire me. Omar said so.

Rather than burn up energy on fruitless interviews with large companies like Western Electric or Stromberg-Carlson, I decided to wait. There weren't many start-ups in telecommunications at that time. I wondered why I thought *my* experience would be so damn beneficial. Why would they need to hire someone from Canada who didn't even have a degree? Even with a degree, I'd need a green card; but how could I get a green card without a job? Negativity was getting to me until I stifled it—screw reality. It wasn't all that bad; I still had my current job. My time would be better spent visualizing getting the letter, moving, and working at Farinon. I took the long way home along the coast. Come on Omar, work with me here.

I knew it would be a tense couple of weeks once back home. I could see the smirk on their faces at work when I showed up empty-handed. *Oh! Hi Al, I thought you moved to California—ha, ha, ha.* But the letter did come. It took a week and contained a solid offer including a moving allowance. That was all I needed to get our visas. Thirty days later we flew to California with Leslie holding her budgie bird in a cage on her lap. Like a canary in a coal mine, I expected it to explode or drop dead at any moment. If not, we were good to go—green cards all around.

It was a great feeling to know I was talking directly to the president. What a contrast to BCTel or Bell Canada! It was also a contrast of cultures. I felt as if I'd jumped ten years into the future in terms of freedom and opportunity even though it was long before the days of Silicon Valley. In between Palo Alto and San Jose, it was mostly apricot and plum trees, an area once known as the prune capital of the world. A few housing tracts were loosely scattered around, as homes were built ever closer to Santa Clara and Los Gatos. Bill said, "Take your time, a few weeks if you need it. You'll want to look into schools and find a place to live."

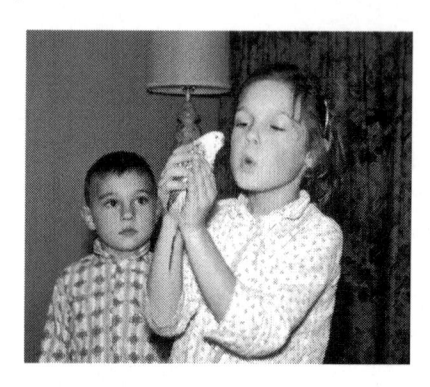

Daniel and Leslie – 1962.

Monty and his wife Joan had just bought a house in Palo Alto. They advised that the best schools were there and people rarely locked their doors. There was a "residents only" park in the Santa Cruz Mountains where people could walk and picnic in the midst of forests and wildlife. Downtown was next to Stanford University where we could join the students riding bicycles everywhere. It was hard to resist. We moved into Monty's old apartment in a low-rise building with a pool. There was even a swim school next door where the kids could learn to swim properly. After a year we bought a bungalow on Southcourt, about a mile from downtown. I wish I still owned it. Had I stayed there, this story would be a lot shorter and I'd be a millionaire by virtue of property alone. But read on. This story has a lot more meat in it than that.

The kids weren't the only ones needing an education. I started night school at Foothill College studying microwave theory. When I signed up for a course in transistor theory, the classroom wasn't large enough to contain us all. The teacher had a unique way of thinning us out. To a standing-room only audience, he demonstrated what the curriculum would be like. Soon, the blackboard was filled with formulas of the most advanced mathematics known to man. There was plenty of room the next night, or at least that's what I heard.

I was employee number 67 in a start-up company manufacturing microwave radios. The products were narrowband tube-type radios and a solid-state 12-channel carrier system. There was nothing new or exciting about that; the multiplexer (carrier system) was solid state, but both were analog. This was before digital technology would dominate the industry, but I knew nothing about any of it. After the Second World War, a lot of individuals had used their wartime communications experience to develop new products in their garages. Many start-ups would grow into large successful corporations. Hewlett Packard was one. When they outgrew one of their first buildings, Farinon moved in, having outgrown its own garage. Lenkurt was another start-up. Len Erikson and Kurt Appert started building some of the very first commercial microwave radio products.

Bill Farinon had worked with the Federal Communications Commission (FCC) and was at Pearl Harbor when the Japanese attacked. After the war he joined Lenkurt as they developed a wideband product for the telecommunications industry. He also saw the need for a low-density product for private corporations and utility companies. When he couldn't convince Len or Kurt to go after it, he said he'd start a company and do it himself. He envisioned a PT150 to 450 MHz line of radios. They laughed at him, and said, "Sure, and who's going to buy it?"

The PT prefix on the product line was Bill's wife's first name. She did all the bookkeeping and wrote the checks. The question of who was going to buy his radios was soon answered when Lenkurt bought some of the early systems. They didn't have a 1-kilowatt narrowband transmitter for long reaches in Alaska. Now I, too, was working with him one block away from Lenkurt's plant.

Breaking into any market is always a problem. By the time I joined them, Farinon had already developed a reputation in the industry for having a high-end quality product. It was a niche market, but that would rapidly change when they started competing directly with Lenkurt for Bell and military projects.

Me, Mario Padavan, Roger Leader, Frank Hind, Jim Hung, and Ken O'Neil – Farinon Electric, 1963.

Bill Farinon was the kind of boss who'd say, "I'm going to lunch, anyone coming?" Then he'd jump in the company's oversize wagon and say, "Somebody else can drive." It was the same way with the parking lot. Many companies spent money on elaborate fountains in front of the main entrance as though it would enhance the product. Bill said, "There'll never be a fountain in any parking lot of mine." In fact there would never be a name on any parking space either. He also said, "If you want a spot close to the front door, get here early." It was his humility and honesty combined with toughness that made everyone feel obligated to perform.

In a telephone operating company like Bell or BCTel you rarely met anyone above your first-line supervisor. This was due to a stringent pecking order. If you did, you'd get shut down for going over someone's head. And forget about lunch with upper management! That might be a privilege for first-line supervisors, but not for craft personnel. Structure and hierarchy was everything, right up to the president at the top of the pyramid.

At Farinon, Bill was the guy working next to you with his sleeves rolled up. The company was growing fast, and within a year I was in charge of the systems assembly department. Before long I had a small, eclectic crew of wiremen, technicians, and engineers working for me. One engineer, Dinshaw Hakamanishi, was an Iranian Zoroastrian. He would have been deported with his family, had Bill not seen his plight in a newspaper article and given him a job. I found his religion interesting, having read up on Buddhism, Hinduism, and Zoroastrianism while living in Vancouver. I saw commonality between all of them and early Christianity. There were a couple of South American brothers, and a Hopi Indian as well. I'd read up on the Arizona Hopis and lent him my book on Hopi anthropology. Another was an engineer from China, who, during the Japanese occupation in the thirties, had seen babies being bayoneted and dropped head-first on a concrete sidewalk. I added to the diversity by hiring a German immigrant who'd witnessed World

Tom Russo. Rene Cortez, Jim Ingham (center), and Dinshaw on right.

War II from inside the other side. He'd completed a Telecommunications Certification Course at BCTel, and I knew he'd be a good candidate for advancement. Years later, he would end up in charge of quality control and responsible for powering up systems all over the world. But in 1963, when most of us were racking up systems in San Carlos, JFK was shot in Dallas. That day we all shared the same tragedy no matter where we came from.

It was my German friend who held two-year-old Leonard on his lap as we rushed him to Stanford Hospital with convulsions. Leonard had survived being born with the umbilical cord around his neck and was seemingly a healthy baby. As he grew older we could see he was not developing as fast as his siblings. We remained in denial and continued to believe he was just a slow starter. Anything else would have been to give up on him and more than we wanted to think about. The doctors at Stanford told us he'd had a grand mal seizure as a result of brain damage at birth. Now it was confirmed. Leonard was mentally impaired and there was no cure. In order to live he would have to be on drugs to control seizures and hyperactivity for the rest of his life. There was nothing else they could do. We would have to cope with it by ourselves. Many would have to resort to a state institution for help, a horrifying thought and prohibitively expensive.

At McGill University in Montreal, Dr. Wilder Penfield was said to be one of the world's leading neurologists. He was in the news for making impressive discoveries into the mysteries of the brain. I asked the Stanford doctors if these discoveries held any promise for Leonard. Their answer was restrained, to soften the blow. They only suggested that Canada was far more likely to be of assistance for this kind of problem than anywhere in the US. They were referring to long-term care. We were still looking for a cure. I'd moved to California for opportunity. Now I was being told it was in Canada. Was I supposed to give up all that we'd gained, just when everything was going so well? The kids loved California, and Doris was making new friends. We all got together with our families and had wonderful times together. I was a shareholder in a company that would one day go public. Imagine! Me, watching the Big Board on Wall Street and playing the market! Even with the war escalating in Vietnam, the future looked bright. This new development threw a dark cloud over everything just when it was looking so good. I couldn't imagine anything worse.

It was a time of martini lunches and compelling work. Boys' night out was typically at some drinking hole along the El Camino Real. The Atherton Club in Menlo Park was an after-work favorite. At other times it could be at any one of many beer joints. One night, a number of us were getting a little more rambunctious than usual when the waitress cut us off. The bouncer was intent on kicking us out. Monty calmed us down and elected himself as spokesman. He stood before the six-foot-six bouncer and proceeded to tell him off. He quickly tired of talking to his belt buckle and said, "Just a minute." With a serious and determined expression on his face, he placed a chair directly in front of the bouncer before climbing on top of it. Now, looking straight at the bouncer, he continued to rag on at him. It was too funny! No one could resist cracking up, including the bouncer. Even the waitress got over someone pinching her bottom and agreed to serve more beer.

Occasionally, I had solo outings on Sunday mornings. I'd drive around with the top down on my car looking for different churches to compare beliefs. The Quakers were interesting! They'd sit around in a circle giving everyone a voice at condemning the draft, including ways and reasons to avoid it. Other people did too, but more discreetly; it was thought unpatriotic to advocate it so blatantly. But sitting among the Quakers, with their unrelenting anti-war stance, I wondered who among us might be a government spy. The Unitarian church was pretty gutsy, too. They had a more universal and liberal approach to issues such as divorce, abortion, and euthanasia over dogma and literal translations of the Bible. These subjects were the firestorms of controversy that dominated politics and religion. Even today the same issues confuse and divide, except now a few more hot coals have been added to the fire, like LBGT and a host of other previously ignored issues.

I had other interests as well. In the RCAF, Monty had just graduated from flying school when World War II ended. Now he had a Cessna 182. Four of us flew up to Vancouver in 1964. Others had planes as well. Even I was thinking about getting a license. If we moved to Canada, I would miss these activities. Most of all, I had an interest in what was best for Leonard. He was now at the center of what all of us did.

It was around this time that Bill Farinon appointed a president to start up a subsidiary company to manufacture a new microwave system for Bell Canada. Vacuum tube type radios were being phased out, and Farinon had developed a solid-state 2000 MHz product. The newly appointed president was an ex-Bell engineer from Montreal

Back: Me, Tad, Monty with Barb and Marny Montgomery, & Roger Nelson. Front left - Daniel, Laurie Nelson, Leslie, and Laurie's two siblings in front of Roger.

and a graduate of McGill. He'd had a lot of success in selling the PT line of radios in Venezuela and the Caribbean area. He also sold one of the first SS2000 systems to Bell Canada, but there was a catch: It had to be manufactured in Canada. The company was formed, and he had the responsibility of setting up a totally independent factory complete with development, manufacturing, and sales. I was asked by the new president if I was interested in heading up the production department.

Naturally I was disappointed that he'd located the factory in Quebec, instead of my home province of Ontario. Toronto would have been my preference, particularly with all the conflict building up in Quebec after decades of English control. I agreed to make a quick trip to Montreal to set up some work benches and instruct a few people on assembly methods. My interest in doing it was exploratory. I needed to see if I thought living there would work for us. Stepping off the plane at Montreal's Dorval Airport, I was hit by the overwhelming heat and humidity of the place. Obviously I'd been on the west coast too long. The building selected for the factory was in a nearby industrial park where the president had already hired a few people for the fledgling operation. This was a ground-floor start-up even if it was a spin-off.

Upon my return to California, Doris and I talked it over. The issue with Leonard was on our minds. We thought the close proximity to Montreal Children's Hospital would be of benefit. The other incentive, for her, was to reconnect with many of her relatives. For me, it was a good career move. But nothing came of it. There was still plenty of time before the field trials were scheduled the following year. With no word forthcoming as the end of August approached, I announced that I would not be interested in moving the kids after school started. I thought it was put to rest. Then Farinon landed a contract to supply PT radios to Hydro Quebec. All stops were removed. The PT radios could be shipped to Canada as modules to be assembled, racked up, and tested as complete systems before delivery and installation. Now I was needed more than ever. This would make the new operation profitable from the very beginning. It would take longer for the new SS2000 line—it had to be built from scratch in Canada; and after that, the rigid approval process toward standardization by a very demanding Bell Canada evaluation team would begin.

I was a systems guy. My crew and I took tested radios as well as carrier and auxiliary equipment off the shelf and wired them into complete systems mounted in relay racks or cabinets. When completed, we moved them to the test department where alignment, performance testing, and compliance with all end-to-end system specifications for the field environment was ensured. When completely aligned they'd come back to my group for packing and shipping to the customer. Either the customer or our EF&I (engineer, furnish, and install) guys would do the installation.

Production was largely assembly line work. I would also have to do all aspects of production planning and control, parts explosions, purchasing, storing, and kitting before assembling and wiring panels, shelves, and power supplies. A large part of this was stuffing printed circuit boards (with capacitors, resistors, transistors etc.) before soldering by means of a wave soldering machine, solder pot, and hand soldering. All this resulted from a simple forecast from sales as to how many systems they thought would be needed in the next three to six months. Once in Montreal I'd be on my own, albeit with support from San Carlos. I needed to do a quick study.

Since production was labor-intensive, most of the employees in the near future would be working for me. It was important to maintain the Farinon policies introduced by Bill in San Carlos. He believed that everyone should have a stake in the business and wanted them to feel like owners. He did this by offering stock options and profit sharing. And he often said, "We don't have an organization chart but we *do* have an organization." To reinforce that feeling he'd remind us, "We're all in this together." It worked, and there was no need for anyone to feel less important than anyone else. With this mindset there was little need for a union. Everyone was on salary; there was no overtime, but you could work as long as you liked. In San Carlos a number of us always worked Tuesday and Thursday evenings. We also worked Saturday mornings, but it was up to the individual. It was usually lead-hands, technicians, and engineers who were that motivated, and not the ordinary assembly line person. Still, these were practices unheard of in a union shop or anywhere that I was aware of.

I never heard anyone complain in San Carlos. If they wanted to finish a job that they were working on before going home, they did so rather than dropping tools and running at five o'clock. Similarly, if you had to take some time for personal business, you were free to do so and expected to make it up later. There were no titles, and it wasn't expected that you had to move up the ladder. Naturally, some were more ambitious than others. Most assembly line workers were women, who were more interested in having a workspace where they worked on the same products day in and day out and then went home to look after their families at five sharp. They were good at it and rarely made mistakes. Cooperation among them was remarkable and totally in line with Bill's message and company objectives. It sounds like brainwashing, or numbing down to the level of robots, but if you had a family and you needed a job, especially one that gave you a lot freedom and choice while amply rewarding good performance, it was a worker's paradise.

Selling the concept in Quebec would be more challenging than building the radio products. Unions were stronger there, and I'd be raiding union companies like Northern Electric, RCA, and CAE (Canadian Aviation Electronics) for employees. Many would be bilingual, but some would be French-speaking only. French Canadians were a definite majority but at an extreme disadvantage in Quebec's predominately managed financial and industrial sectors where promotion above low-level management was difficult to achieve. This was about to radically change. Also, start-ups were rare, especially ones like Farinon Electric.

With the start of Quebec's "Quiet Revolution" in the sixties, Anglophones were held in contempt and Americans were often viewed more favorably than the "English." Even so, US corporations were often suspected of taking over too much of what was thought should be Canadian. In other words, their first impression of this American company would be one of skepticism, viewing it as run by US Anglophones offering limited opportunity to French Canadians while the profits went south. Most production workers would be happy to have a good job and give little thought to any of this. But they'd be bombarded by friends, family, and the media with local opinions that had little to do with Bill Farinon's personal philosophy of inclusiveness and sharing the wealth. Was I up to the challenge of convincing Quebecers that this was the opportunity of a lifetime?

It was a huge gamble, and too much to ask of my family. But then there was Leonard. This could be the best solution to help him while reducing the burden on all of us. It would make a difference to Leslie and Daniel's lives forever, but they were still too young to have a say in the matter. Doris and I shared the same concerns over them as we did with Leonard, but we each had our own selfish motives for wanting to go as well. I was thinking of career advancement and she was thinking of relatives. Maybe we were just using Leonard as an excuse to satisfy our own appetites. Or maybe it was inevitable. After all, Omar had said we'd return to Canada.

For better or worse, I accepted the job.

Doris, Daniel, Leslie, and Leonard – 1964. Middlefield Apartments in Palo Alto, CA.

Daniel, Leonard, and Leslie – 1962.

1961 Buick Electra 225.

Part II

1965 – 1977

Château Frontenac in Quebec City.

Chapter 6

1965-72

Montreal, Quebec

A man in full

With the kids starting school, there was not enough time to travel by car from California to Quebec. I advertised and found two guys who wanted to return to New York City and were only too happy to drive my car across the country. I restricted them on the number of miles they could put on the car, and would fly down from Montreal to Manhattan to pick it up when they arrived. How trusting can you get? I also wondered how trusting Bill Farinon was. I'd never worked in production.

That fall I found myself ordering modules to be assembled, racked up, and tested as complete systems in Canada. I did everything but the testing before loading the entire system in the company wagon and delivering it to Hydro Quebec's Outardes-3, North of Quebec City. A young assembly line worker and I installed it. The first hurdle was over and already the components were on order for the solid-state radios. At New Year's, I took the family to the Château Frontenac in Quebec City to assuage the trauma of moving to Quebec.

The first Farinon PT 150 Radio System assembled in Canada for Hydro Quebec – 1965.

Religion and language have always been major factors in Quebec politics. Both were guaranteed by the Quebec Act of 1774. The school system was a fully funded dual system based on the Roman Catholic and Protestant religions. Standards were high, and uniforms were common in both religions although losing favor in the Protestant/ English system faster than in the Catholic/French system. Where you lived determined which would be available. The Island of Montreal sits downstream from where the Saint Lawrence and Ottawa rivers converge. The further east you go, anywhere in Quebec, the more French you'll find. This was also true of Montreal where West Island was predominantly English, particularly from Westmount toward the west. Even places like Pierrefonds, Dollard-des-Ormeaux, and Baie-D'Urfé were largely English-speaking due to the increase of new subdivisions, and immigrants like us and those from New York, the UK, and Europe.

Pierrefonds P.Q. – 1966.

We bought a house in a new subdivision in Pierrefonds. Leslie, Daniel, and hopefully Leonard would all go to a Protestant school. They'd have an easier time speaking English with no necessity to speak French. Of course, speaking both anywhere in Quebec would be a great asset. The religion issue had been settled in

Vancouver. Since their baptisms, the kids had never been inside a church. Several years later, I took control of saving them from eternal damnation by putting Leslie and Daniel in Sunday school at the closest United Church. It was a geographic rather than a sectarian decision. I had a great deal of respect for the biblical Jesus, but it didn't matter to me if He was a rabbi, a prophet, a mystic, a revolutionary, or the Messiah, He's been categorized as all.

His basic message resonated with my concept of some sort of omniscient intelligence that governs the universe. Whatever that means, I'm sure it's beyond human comprehension. Many who claim to know would argue with that. But the never-ending history of war and bloodshed in the name of religion is also beyond comprehension. Others claim He was none of the above, if He existed at all. I leaned toward prophet, possibly revolutionary. It was either an ancient message, or one way ahead of its time. Either way, it was badly received. Even today it's a tough sell as religions, entrepreneurs, and believers all strive to claim Him as their own. The one thing they have in common is searching for more creative ways to market Him.

I didn't expect the kids to understand any of it. If you accept another's interpretation of anything and hear it often enough, it becomes reality. The kids deserved better. They needed to think for themselves. I just wanted the United Church to introduce them to a few Bible stories with a nice message. Catholicism didn't bother me, but if we couldn't set the example, why try to sell it to them? Even without accepting a faith, there are many benefits to being a member of a church. They do an excellent job of serving communities, and for that I congratulate them. I never felt the need for religion, a club affiliation, or even a social life. Job, work, and family were all I could handle. That doesn't mean I was lacking in faith. A more spiritual person might say, "You just need to learn how to think for yourself. Let your conscience be your guide. All you have to do is shut up, turn down the volume, and listen. Everything you need to know is buried inside." Maybe, but it sounds like another sermon. Besides, I wasn't very good at that stuff either.

Leonard had it down better than any of us. He was the sweetest child on earth when not convulsing or running around wildly crashing into things or falling down stairs. At other times he was blissful and distant—a mystic in his own right. Like the time in the middle of the night when we couldn't sleep because he was giggling and laughing in his bedroom. I entered his room and turned on the light to find him sitting up in bed with a big, euphoric smile on his face. I looked around the room to see what was going on. Who was entertaining him? Nobody! Nothing! At least that I could see. I shook my head and said, "Leonard, you'll have to tell your little friends they must leave now. It's time for you to go to sleep." It sounds crazy, but that was exactly how I felt, or at least what I hoped. There had to be something in this world that Leonard could relate to. He clearly could not master speech. I never knew how well he took in the spoken word. At any rate, he understood and went to sleep, or maybe they were more discrete. Like so many things, we'll never know. This was the Leonard who has stayed with me in my dreams over the years. He's always the same age.

The Montreal Children's Hospital knew exactly what we were faced with. That sounds positive, but in reality it meant they could do nothing other than offer us a psychologist to talk to. They were more intent on treating us, than Leonard. The public-school system had no intention of taking him on, either. We tried a Sunday school solution where we could escape to sit through a sermon while someone else took Leonard. There was a new Unitarian Church in Pierrefonds. I thought it might be a safe haven for him and a temporary reprieve for us. We dropped off the kids. The teacher for Leonard's age said, "No problem, he'll be fine." The sermon that day turned out to be a rather aggressive lecture on raising money to pay for the church. We needed relief, not grief. It didn't matter: When we went to collect Leonard, the teacher was at her wits' end with grief. She told us never to leave him in her class again. We didn't.

In 1961 President Kennedy introduced his sister Rosemary to the world. It opened a huge door toward acceptance of mental health issues by the public at large. Joe Kennedy had insisted on a lobotomy, which caused her more problems than her original behavior. President Kennedy announced a more enlightened view: *"Mental retardation ranks with mental health as a major health, social, and economic problem in this country. It strikes our most precious asset, our children."* A more acceptable term today would be "intellectual disability." Call it what you will; funding was needed for the care and treatment of those afflicted. Clinics and community centers were needed as well as research centers to study the causes. Funding was needed to train teachers of all handicapped children. He started a movement that spread awareness across the country. JFK Schools sprang up all over until even reaching Pointe Claire, close to us. We registered Leonard and it lasted two days. Two hours into the third, I received a call at work, saying, "I'm sorry, you'll have to come and take Leonard home. He's too disruptive. We're not able to handle him." The Catholic Church was another option, but we were more concerned he'd be buried in the attic of a convent than we were of living with him. I'd heard too many stories.

The Douglas Mental Hospital in Verdun was receptive to take him for "observation." He didn't need observing. Doris needed a break! He was slowly killing her. When I visited him there was one young man supervising about thirty children. I took Leonard outside to the playground and sat him on a swing. The gentle swaying movement delighted him as he pensively clung to the ropes. Without any warning the attendant joined us and pulled Leonard back, and pushed him forward as you would any kid. With Leonard, it sent him into an arc projecting him forward into a free fall five feet above the ground. He landed on his face and immediately started crying in pain. I was incensed! Did the attendant know anything at all about who he was supervising?

Inside, other children had the widest range of disabilities I'd ever seen. One hapless individual had the distinction of being what is termed an idiot savant. He could tell what day it was on December 9, 1537, or any other date, but little else. Two children were eight-year-old identical twins. They were good-looking blond boys, well built and strong as if from an Aryan master race, except for the behavior of a pair of wild coyotes. The sight of them was unnerving. I thought they looked predatory and aggressive. They constantly scanned their surrounding for places to pounce. It was confirmed when I visited Leonard the next day. I picked him up to give him a hug and he started to cry in severe pain. I looked at his shoulder and saw teeth marks delineating a mouth outlining every tooth. Someone had clamped down and punctured the flesh in a manner that could only be described as a wild animal attack. I left but quickly broke down. Now it was my turn. I started to cry and couldn't stop. But I couldn't leave Leonard. If it was that difficult for me, what was it like for him? I went back and took him out, never to return. We had exhausted all avenues. Doris was a wreck and now I was cracking up. Something had to be done. Quebec had much to offer, but nothing for Leonard.

As he grew stronger, he was more than anyone could handle. It was a full-time job. The strain on Doris was unbearable, far worse than for me. I was at work wrestling other problems. She needed to get away occasionally, if only for grocery shopping. At the same time, she'd developed an intuitive instinct. She knew exactly where he was at all times, enabling her to avoid most disasters. With me babysitting, he was vulnerable to hurting himself by taking a fall or some other mishap.

Once, he ran across the living room floor to give me a hug, only to trip and bury his teeth into the edge of the coffee table. The damage to his mouth was so extensive I didn't think a doctor would be of any help. When Doris came home, I said, "You'd better take a look at Leonard. He's just cried himself to sleep." His mouth was so swollen that she ran back screaming, "What's the matter with you? Why didn't you take him to Emergency?" I felt like a fool and went immediately. They said there was nothing they could do, and told me to take him home to let it heal by itself. Even the hospital had no idea of how to treat him. On another occasion when he was in for observation, a nurse showed up while I was visiting him. She was making temperature rounds or some such nonsense. At any rate, she marched up and stuck a glass thermometer in his mouth, which he immediately chomped down on and cut his lip. Glass was all over the inside of his mouth as he screeched in pain. How much of this can you stand by helplessly and watch?

Through it all, Leslie and Daniel remained stoic. I never heard them complain, but they were affected by his disability as well. They were far more subdued than they were in the land of fun and sun. They'd been in California long enough to make good friends and become fully integrated. None of their friends ever gave Leonard much thought. Now, as he grew older, just taking him around the block was challenging. Even I was reluctant to take him to the neighborhood park to watch a soccer match. Once there, he'd insist on running onto the field to chase the ball, squirming and crying to get there. Restraining him only made him try harder, causing much disruption in the sidelines. Invariably I'd have to take him home. The harsh reality was I'd torn Leslie and Daniel away from something they'd learned to love, only to find them struggling to cope in a land more foreign than California ever was. Leonard had become an overwhelming presence in our home. He received the attention. Leslie and Daniel carried the burden. Putting it bluntly, the two able ones were being robbed by the disabled one.

Ontario had facilities far more consistent with what I expected from Canada. Doris and I were both born in Ontario and felt a sense of entitlement. Smith Falls was close to Montreal. I could have commuted but living there would be a death sentence for Doris. She had no connection to the place. On the other hand, Oscar and Anne lived in Sarnia, and Cedar Springs Hospital School for Children was close by in Blenheim. After the first interview, they informed us that they had the proper resources, but we would have to be residents of Ontario for at least a year before they could even consider it. It was a ray of sunshine illuminating a path forward even if the destination was questionable.

Me with Leonard – 1967.

What kind of people would consider institutionalizing their child? Let me tell you. In Pierrefonds, I'd watched Doris reduced to a humorless shrew deprived of a life she'd known and loved. She was being deprived of *her* family, *our* family, and all the friends we'd ever known. If I tried to take her out to dinner on a Friday night, we'd be in an argument before we got three blocks from the house. Each altercation was building a wall between us, one brick at a time. Babysitters wouldn't know what to do and couldn't be trusted with him anyway. Leslie and Daniel were responsible children, but it put a huge burden on Leslie to be in charge. I'm sure it added to the pressure on both of them and contributed to friction between them. Not only had they lost the California life they loved, but they'd also lost their mother to Leonard. When he was younger she had more time to care for him and look after the others as well. Normally a seven-year-old requires less care than when he is aged two or three, but not Leonard. With him it worked the other way around. Everything was upside down. None of us were the same.

The same thing would have happened anywhere. Other parents may have been more successful or committed; I'd seen them and would continue to see them. They looked lost and empty with bleak expressions to match their bleak futures while anchored to a disabled child. I admired them; my heart went out to them with compassion. I knew that for us to continue would leave us void of any semblance of a normal life. Already, we eyed each other with short tempers, sad resentment, and little hope. We had to do something.

We made the decision for the sake of everyone. Doris would be the primary beneficiary of such a move. She couldn't do it! How would that look? It wasn't easy for me either, but someone had to take the initiative. I saw no reason why the other children should continue to be held back no matter how much they loved him. We needed something to look forward to, not look back with guilt. I needed to look strong and committed to leave no doubt in anyone's mind that we were making the right choice. I'd learned early in life how to control my emotions. Now, I was becoming an empty shell to ensure I never broke down again as I had in the parking lot outside the hospital. I didn't want to see Leslie and Daniel become so pathetic. At the same time, I didn't want them to be apathetic toward Leonard. We all cared deeply about him, but they in particular deserved to be happy. Doris and I agreed that Leonard needed to be cared for by professionals. I had to make it happen.

We sold the house and set up two residences. One was a high-rise apartment in Sarnia for the family. Everyone was registered for golf and tennis lessons. The other residence was mine; a small studio apartment in Dorval where I'd be close to work. Doris took the car and I would visit by train at least once a month. People said it would never work and they may have been right. It didn't matter. Nothing else was working. We had nothing to lose except a faltering marriage and a dysfunctional family.

Doris soon vacated the high-rise when she discovered the apartment was infected with "fleas." Everyone was being eaten alive. They left and moved in with Oscar and Anne who had opened a second variety store. Oscar rented a trailer to move them. They removed all their personal stuff but were shut down by the owner before they could remove the furniture. It was rumored around town that the building was owned by an ex-Nazi. He had the furniture locked up in the basement and wouldn't let it go until the standard three months' notice was paid.

I took the train to Sarnia to break the lease, fully expecting to have to pay three months' rent to retrieve the furniture. With the car and trailer I went back to the building to have it out with the owner. Doris still had the keys, so I went into the apartment first to see if I could see any sign of these bugs she was going on about. I must admit, I suspected she just wanted to move in with Anne. The apartment was pristine and obviously just cleaned. On my hands and knees, I started searching for bugs in the carpet. She hadn't exaggerated. Dead bodies were everywhere. I'd never seen such long legs on fleas and I still wonder what they really were. They must have been imported from some tropical country. I didn't need tweezers. I just picked them up with my fingers. This was a deal breaker! I went to the penthouse where the owner resided. He was there with his ever-present attendant, the *Oberstabsgefreiter* (corporal), standing silently off to the side of his master's desk ready to pounce at the first command—a human German Shepherd.

I introduced myself and said. "I've come for my furniture."

"*Jawohl*, and when the rent is paid you may have it." With a sinister sneer he added, "Your wife forgot to give her three months' notice."

"Not in this case," I said, "the place is infested and unlivable. The whole building may need to be condemned."

"*Nein, nein,* my building is perfectly clean. We have no bugs."

"Not according to my family. They suffered from bites all over their bodies. Otherwise they wouldn't have had to leave."

He leaned into his desk and said, "I guarantee you cannot find one single bug."

"Okay," I gladly acknowledged. "But if I do, I get the furniture and we're square. Agreed?"

"Yah, yah, no problem!" he voiced confidently. Nodding to his henchman, he said, "Ve go!" The employee looked as if he was going to click his heels, but quickly recovered and rushed to open the door. Inside the apartment, the owner strode across the carpet waving his hand one way, and then the other. "As you see, my building is perfectly clean."

"Yes," I agreed. "The exterminators have done an excellent job. Let's have a closer look." I got down on my knees and started to search through the matting. It didn't take long to find one. I presented it to him, with the comment, "This should suffice. Shall we go and get the furniture now? I've got a 6:00 p.m. train to catch."

"Bah! One bug means nothing. It could have come in after she moved out."

I continued to search and then stood up and said, "You can keep that one. I'll keep these for my lawyer and the building inspectors. I'm sure they'll want to look at the entire building."

He looked at his man with menace. No doubt he'd deal with him later for neglecting to vacuum up all the evidence. Back to me, he smiled the same sinister sneer with which he greeted me in his office, and said, "That won't be necessary. Back your trailer up to the basement window behind the building." Without further comment, he turned on his heel and stormed out of the apartment.

I took his advice regarding the trailer and found him personally passing furniture out the window where I could easily load it. This wasn't his first confiscation by any means. I never saw his *Oberstabsgefreiter* again although I believe he was feeding the furniture to his boss from inside the basement. No doubt more punishment would come later.

Shortly, he said, "That's everything."

I said, "Thank you. Here are your keys," and quickly left.

I parked the loaded trailer for Oscar to unload. Doris drove me to the station with the kids. "How did you get him to give you the furniture?" she wanted to know.

"I beat the crap out of him," I said, largely for the benefit of the kids. Little did they know how happy I was to get away from the creep? She said, "You did not! You'd never do that. You didn't give him any money, did you? You'd better not have. That place was awful and he was worse. How did you do it?"

"It was just diplomacy, strictly diplomacy." I left the conversation up in the air—a mystery—like everything else in our life at that time. Communication was sparse; so was I, dropping in and then disappearing for another month. We were growing ever more distant, but growing all the same. All of us were growing. We just didn't know where it would end.

Living with relatives is handy for the short term, but never successful in the long run. I was not above asking my brother Bill to rent me a unit in one of his low-rise buildings. When one became available, Doris and the kids moved in. It was still months before the time when Cedar Springs could accept Leonard. When we finally admitted him, it was a very sad day. It broke our hearts to see him frightened and crying when we left. Cedar Springs had numerous wings separating residents by age and disabilities. As I'd seen in Verdun, many had horrible disfigurements or physical impairments consistent with cerebral palsy. All suffered from brain damage, as in the case of Leonard. But the place was clean, well-staffed, and managed by professional administrators. They had training and exercise sessions for the patients, as well as an indoor swimming pool and outdoor activities for picnics and camping. Farm animals lent an atmosphere of normalcy. Still, it was a mental institution and every parent's worst nightmare.

In the long run we had to accept that he was better off there than suffering the frustrations of living in a world he had no capacity to understand or cope with. With every visit I was always impressed with the patience and compassion of the staff at all levels. They always accepted our rights as parents to come and go freely with Leonard whenever we wanted. He loved car rides, parks, and hamburger joints. He was mad for sports and tried desperately to catch and throw a ball. Eventually, our pain went away and Leonard adapted to his environment. In its wake was a family torn apart with little likelihood of ever being the same again. The guilt plagued me for years, but actually we were lucky. I could never have imagined Leonard's life would be as fulfilling as it is today. But that, too, was off in the future, like all my other plans.

Nothing was the same anywhere after the sixties. When we first arrived in Quebec, schools were spotless. When drugs made their way onto school grounds, even the buildings deteriorated. By the seventies, lockers, sinks and toilets were being trashed. Graffiti was everywhere. On a brighter note, Montreal was on the world stage with Expo 67. It hosted countries from all around the world. Mayor Drapeau cleaned up the inner city and reinvented Saint Helen's Island for the World's Fair. He introduced the first Canadian lottery to pay for it. At the same time, a social and economic revelation was taking place with Quebec's nationalization of rural electrification, health care, and education. Quebec wanted control of social benefits, financial institutions, industries, welfare, and language. They'd had enough of Ottawa's domination.

In 1968 Pierre Trudeau was elected Prime Minister. He favored individual rights over those of the state, making him an opponent of Quebec nationalism. But things would continue to escalate until the early seventies when he had to initiate the War Measures Act, giving broad powers to the government to maintain security and order during war or insurrection. That was after the Quebec separatists kidnapped Pierre Laporte, a provincial politician, and James Cross, a British diplomat. It amounted to a declaration of war after they murdered Laporte. There was no peace anywhere in Montreal. Mailbox bombs blasted away any sense of security. Radio talk shows constantly fanned the fire with French/English language and culture arguments.

Earlier when JFK was assassinated, I wondered what would happen to the United States. Where did such hatred come from? I was going to night school with an engineering manager from Lockheed. He assured me nothing would change. "The US is governed by a huge machine," he calmly explained. "It keeps running no matter who sits in the White House."

I wasn't comforted. I equated it to a train running down the track. It'll keep going no matter where the conductor is. But if he's not on board, that train had better have a replacement quickly. I didn't want Johnson on board. And I didn't know enough about Nixon to know I didn't want him. As it turned out, both ended as train wrecks. There had to be some meaning to a presidential election, or we would be ruled by dictators and corporations. Maybe a combination of many odious liaisons ruled anyway. Devious minds constantly undermine the good intentions of citizens to elect politicians. Campaigns between elections are never-ending and only won by such means. After JFK, the sixties were not America's best decade. Two more assassinations were yet to come: Martin Luther King and Bobby Kennedy. The Vietnam War intensified, protests amplified, and social values plummeted. Still, by the end of the decade, I wished we had never left California.

I survived in Quebec by immersing myself in the tiny world at Farinon Canada. My obsession was to turn thousands of tiny components into working modules that morphed into microwave systems. Solid-state radios were my purpose in life, my salvation. No matter how much I grew to detest commuting through snow, slush, and blizzards, once there it was my place. So much so, that it was years before I realized how little else I had. The success of the product was gratifying, and growth was rapid. At times, sales were intermittent. In keeping with Bill Farinon's philosophy, we never laid off anyone when things were slow. We optimistically planned for the next quarter. I often kept production workers busy building more work benches or laying floor tiles, while building up inventory for the future. When contracts came in, we delivered systems within the usual three-month period.

The production manager from San Carlos came up for a meeting in the late sixties. He could see I was completely consumed. "Al," he casually asked, "what do you do for recreation?" He had a trailer in California and took his family to Clear Lake every chance he had.

I had nothing! Not even a family since they were in Ontario. I'd forgotten what a normal family or social life was like. I fumbled, embarrassed to find myself without an answer. But I did have a membership to Vic Tanny's gym on top of Place Ville Marie in downtown Montreal. It was a joy to go there on a winter night in sub-zero weather. After a workout I'd go for a swim in the outdoor pool next to the rooftop cocktail bar. If slaphappy bar patrons looked my way, they would have seen the head of a walrus-looking object sticking out of the water with hair and eyebrows covered in white frosty icicles. When I was not there, I could be found making wine in my tiny studio apartment, eating the wheat germ and fried liver recommended by Vic Tanny. More often, I'd be drinking beer at the tavern one block from the factory. My kitchen cupboards contained little except gallon jugs of homemade white wine and a wheel of Oka cheese, just like any other monastery. The tavern stood out against my bohemian lifestyle. That's what saved me! In Quebec, noisy workmates, beer, and rib steaks were normal by any standard.

I also had a number of Air Canada pilots working part-time. They'd left the RCAF to join Air Canada where wages were low, initially. I also paid low wages, but it helped them through their own start-up period until they gained enough commercial cockpit time to make the big money. One of them was a friend of Bob Pearson, who in 1983 gained notoriety as the captain on what became known as the Gimli Glider Flight #143. (It's worth Googling, there's even a movie.) He'd built a summer cottage on Lac Gagnon. Others were following him, and I had to look into it. I began searching for lakefront property with a beach; they were getting rare. The experience of building a cottage would also rebuild our family, bring them back, and hold us together.

Me on deck at Lac Gagnon, PQ.

The lots were on Crown land and free to anyone improving the property by building a cottage. It wasn't long before I was hauling logs across the lake and building one of my own. I couldn't have done it without the help of others. Many volunteers from work joined me, and even the kids pitched in. It was exciting to be looking forward to a weekend away from the plant. Doris shared our enthusiasm. I particularly relied on a local farmer who possessed all the pioneering skills of a *coureur des bois*. He had a wife and twelve kids to feed from what he grew and slaughtered on his small farm. Other sources of seasonal income from people like me helped him, and I couldn't have done it without him. He taught me tricks about building a cottage that would hold the place together for centuries.

The studio in Dorval was exchanged for a three-bedroom apartment in Lachine. It should have been easy with just the four of us, but the separation had changed us. I thought Doris and I had both become more independent, but once back together I had less freedom and resented it. She resented my absences and needed attention. Arguments ensued. We bought a French Poodle and named him Angus in the hope of uniting our French/Anglo differences. Before long she found a fourplex development in Dollard-des-Ormeaux which she encouraged me to look at. I was a sucker for real estate and she knew it. We bought one and now we had a home of our own, plus three.

The cottage was our second home. It was among friends in a string of cottages on the far side of a lake where no roads or power existed. It became our getaway and a major source of recreation. I bought a ski boat for summer and a couple of Skidoos for winter. It was a life away from work and the all the discord of Quebec politics. We were a family just like thousands of other normal cottage-going Canadians. My enthusiasm for production work was being shifted to recreation.

Nothing is static! Even as life assumes tranquility, undercurrents stir. Dissension bubbles to the surface, like a simmering pot of water waiting to boil over. Even at Farinon, people were clamoring for more. Bill Farinon often stated, "There's nothing wrong with maintaining the same job," as opposed to upward mobility. It didn't matter whether you were an assembly line worker or an engineer, you were all equally important. In theory, it was true. Being a partial owner with a share of the profits was supposed to be incentive enough. Had I stayed at Farinon in California, no doubt I'd be appreciated and one day have a nice portfolio for early retirement. It would likely be larger than the BCTel pension I'd already forfeited. But would I be happy? Would it satisfy my insatiable need to improve myself? I didn't give up telephone switching just to become another type of technician. I still had issues with inadequacies that continued to convince me I wasn't as good as I should be. I was not yet fully baked!

Before the move, Bill had sensed my impatience. One day when I was lacing up a cable harness he approached me. After a small discussion, he asked, "Al, I'm not sure you fully appreciate and understand what it means to be a stockholder. Do you?"

The question surprised me. "Yes," I assured him, "of course I do."

Adhering to his own philosophy of *don't be too quick to judge*, he walked away mumbling, "I wish I were convinced."

Me too, I wanted more.

Another kernel of wisdom is *be careful what you wish for*. I should have listened. I'd received a promotion, and then another with the assignment in Quebec. It wasn't just about money, I was driven, always searching, searching. The next step up was going to be more difficult. Farinon Canada was growing fast. By the early seventies a general manager was needed. Someone had to take charge of all the rapidly expanding departments: Purchasing, receiving, shipping, test, quality control, production, drafting, documentation, engineering, and the lists go on. It had to be someone who could provide the leadership to maintain a cohesive and efficient factory. New technologies and computers were being introduced. They were increasing efficiencies in all levels of forecasting, just-in-time planning, budgeting and production. I'd taken a three-year night-school course in supervisory management at Concordia University, but it never prepared me for this. I should have been studying computers, microwave technology, or even accounting. Accounting would be a piece of cake. I wouldn't have to make anything happen; I'd just count beans after others spilled them.

The chief engineer and I met in the tavern for a chat. He was frustrated because I wasn't interested in taking the GM job. Being an engineer from the old school, he was an intractable sort who created a lot of animosity. Inevitably, his cantankerousness would lock horns with someone, but for some reason we generally got along. When I refused to consider it, he asked, "How old are you Al?"

I told him. He shook his head in disgust, saying, "Jesus Christ! A failure and you're not even forty."

I laughed, and said, "That depends on how you define failure." At the time, I was hoping to succeed at something else, not something I was sure I'd fail at.

It hurt just the same; there was too much truth in it. I felt socially inept, naive at in-house politics, technically incompetent, and already stretched to the limit. Without the necessary skills it would be difficult to gain the support needed for resources such as floor space, personnel, automated production methods, and test equipment. There were complicated decisions regarding budgets that everyone had to justify and fight for. If any manager tried to economize and make do, others would blow him away and demand the lion's share. They'd expand their own mini-empires through confrontation and disputes. In this environment, a GM would have to be tough, and do what was best for the company. I hated conflict. I was a pussy!

Soon after I'd arrived in '65, the president hired a young engineer from Jamaica. He had nothing except a new bride from Germany who'd graduated with him from the University of Edinburgh. I lent him my convertible until they got settled. Many years later he acquired a master's degree at Berkley and then a PhD. He became chief engineer, general manager, and president of Farinon Canada before ending up as president of Farinon Electric in San Carlos. I was proud of him. Over the years we would both see enough inept management to justify my concerns about taking the position. The best I'd come up with was lending him my convertible.

It was cottage life that won me over. I'd found my niche. It was the pristine lake, surrounded by virgin forests equally inviting in both summer and winter. In fall, the trees turned into a blaze of color while we waited for ice and snow to transform Gatineau Park into an open highway for snowmobiles and cross-country skiing. In spring we waited in anticipation of again reaching the cottage by boat. I wasn't alone in wanting to escape. Millions of people all over America had taken to the roads in search of adventure and relaxation. It started with backpacks and grew to tents and sleeping bags. It saw no end until the highways were jammed with trailers and recreation vehicles. RVs provided the luxury of five-star hotels. State parks filled up early from previous-year reservations. Private campgrounds competed with swimming pools and electricity—all trappings generally shunned by nature-loving park goers.

Franchise operations got involved. Kampgrounds of America (KOA) surged forward catering to travelers. They designed a successful formula around an A-Frame building complete with convenience store, gift shop, Laundromat, hot showers and clean washrooms. A highly visible swimming pool invited travelers to pull off the highway into drive-through sites with electricity and sewer connections. Smaller sites accommodated tents and tent trailers. Firewood was available for a sense of roughing it. Franchisees flocked to buy the recipe. They paid for the expertise, the coolers, freezers, store shelves, pool tables and souvenirs, all sold by KOA. In return franchisees received professional guidance and exclusivity in their region of choice. KOA's best advice was, "Build it in the middle of the freeway."

I'd found just the spot. It was an intersection of two major highways on a freeway system (#55) that connected IS 91 in the State of Vermont directly to Montreal on #10. Mont Orford, a popular ski mountain and provincial park, was only minutes away. My good friend, the comptroller at work, briefly looked at my meager business plan, and said, "Go for it." I thought it was too quick, but RV travel was really hot in the early seventies. He may have even envied my quirky dream.

My Sherbrooke accountant, the real one who would do the financials, had no comment but was happy for the work. He also was on the board of the credit union that was financing the operation. He must have had some confidence in the venture. The best advice came from my Sherbrooke lawyer. He advised me to just buy land and clear-cut it—by cutting down every tree to sell the lumber off—before reselling the land. He was doing it and laughing all the way to the bank. I was appalled at the suggestion. I thought it criminal.

My realtor showed me a twenty-acre farm in a small community. It had a house, a barn, and a virgin hardwood grove that sloped down to six hundred feet of waterfront. I loved it, but RV highway traffic would never find it. I asked him to show me something where there was lots of traffic, and he did. I was torn between the two locations. I wanted to satisfy my yearning to make a living doing something I loved. Visions of offering outdoor living to others filled my head. My heart said go with the farm—an easy spot to develop. It had buildings in place, woods to roam, and a lake at the back. KOA scoffed at the idea; they knew what they are doing. To make money you had to be near a freeway where there was traffic. My mind said to go with KOA. Greed won. Romance died.

    I still think about the twenty-acre farm by the lake. Over the years I've spent endless hours ruminating over what I could have done with it: Campground, trailer park, par-3 golf course, residential subdivision, public storage, tree farm—the potential was endless. But always, no matter how many sleepless nights and fanciful schemes, I'd come back to *do nothing*—just do nothing—leave it as is. Instead, I did something quite different.

Magog Orford KOA.

Chapter 7

1973-75

Magog, Quebec

A man in free fall

Charles Dickens best described it in the opening lines of *A Tale of Two Cities*, his novel about the French Revolution: "It was the best of times, it was the worst of times, it was the age of wisdom, it was the age of foolishness, it was the epoch of belief, it was the epoch of incredulity, it was the season of Light, it was the season of Darkness, it was the spring of hope, it was the winter of despair, we had everything before us, we had nothing before us, we were all going direct to Heaven, we were all going direct the other way ... "

I wish I could have written that. It would definitely be over the top as an opening for this confessional, but to the point nonetheless. Maybe it was more simply put in the words of Robert Burns: "The best laid schemes o' mice an' men gang aft agley" (often go awry). Yes! That was it. There was no revolution. It was just my own naiveté. Although I did get some help from OPEC. Coincidentally, I opened my KOA campground in 1973, the same year as the "first oil shock" when the Organization of Arab Petroleum Exporting Countries declared an oil embargo. Overnight, oil supply diminished and the price rose. But that was later in the year. I had enough trouble without OPEC.

In '72, little more occurred than breaking ground and starting a foundation for the A-Frame before winter set in. With the help of my son Daniel and friends, along with others from work (two bucks an hour and beer), we planted three thousand trees to create a future buffer between the campground and the highway. Part of the forty acres was slated for a future subdivision. Oh yes, I had a dream! But like so many dreams, it wasn't long until the dream became a nightmare.

Most of the work would have to be done the following spring in time for opening before summer. I'll always remember that spring as the wettest in recorded history. It gave me much insight as to what farmers have to contend with. Language was a problem, too. Doris, my interpreter and reluctant partner, was perfectly bi-lingual. The more I tried to involve her, the worse it got. I'm somewhat insular by nature, but she was beyond that to the point of reclusive. I encouraged her to do some marketing and spread the word around by checking out all the tourist sites—talk to people and distribute brochures.

"The Benedictine Monastery on the other side of Lake Memphremagog," I suggested. "They make cheese, and all kinds of people visit to hear their Gregorian chants. It would be a great place to send campers. Maybe they'll send customers to us. Give them a pile of brochures and strike up a relationship with them."

She left with Angus, our French Poodle, and came back in a funk. Throwing the brochures down, she said, "I'll never do that again, so don't ask me."

"What happened?" I wanted to know after she'd settled down.

"I wouldn't send anyone over there. That darn priest was so rude. He stuck his nose in the air and said, 'Madam, this is a place of worship, not a sideshow.'"

"I know," she'd replied in her very best French. "But in the summer you get visitors from the US. They come to buy your cheese and listen to the beautiful voices of the monks. If they pick up one of our brochures, you may help them find a place to camp and stay longer."

"That's good, that's very good," I clapped my hands in praise. "What did he say to that?"

She lit a cigarette and said, "You don't want to know."

"Come on! Tell me," I insisted.

"He practically threw me out. '*Sss'iiilll-vous-plaît, Madame*, we are monks. We're here for worship and quiet contemplation. We are not a tourist attraction for people to come and goggle at,'" she dramatized by way of imitation. Dealing with the public was nothing she ever aspired to. Supplier, customer, or employees—it made no difference; it just wasn't her thing. It was insane of me to think she would enjoy any part of the operation.

If I was going to continue working for a paycheck, I would need a manager. This was when Oscar and Anne Landry, Doris' brother-in-law and sister, came back into our life. After losing his variety stores due to overreaching enthusiasm with minimal planning, Oscar worked at Ontario Hydro until retirement. With his construction experience and Anne's expertise running a store, we gained some much-needed help. Best of all, I didn't have to ask him; he wanted in and Anne went along as usual. He could manage the campground while she took over the gift shop and registration. I also had a government grant to pay for two local laborers, which added to the in-house slave labor from Leslie and Daniel. Slave is a term relative to their paycheck—there wasn't one, other than the usual allowance from mine. Oscar and Anne lived off the proceeds from the campground. I never made a nickel. We were all in this together.

Gilles Bisson, Doris' nephew from Timmins, was spending the summer with Daniel. Since he was experienced in the ways of northern cottage life, I put him in charge of the firewood that I purchased from a local farmer. It drove the poor old fellow to distraction to have a boy reprimand him every time he dropped off a load of what Giles considered poor wood. He wasn't going to let him get away with anything. There was always something: too small a load, split too thin, not split enough. At fifteen, Gilles was already displaying the leadership and audacity of the future member of parliament he was to become seventeen years later.

Our first customer was a young couple in a VW Beetle. Since we were empty, I told them to pick any site and come back and register later. I rose the next morning in time to see them racing past the office and out the driveway. Throwing on my pants I ran to my car and chased them. Had I caught them it might have been the first time anyone was attacked over a three-dollar registration fee. Not a very inspiring opening. The next customers were three young men from upstate New York. They came equipped for roughing it in the north. When Oscar told me they were chopping down badly needed trees on the knoll behind the campground, I put the run on them as well.

A larger crowd would arrive on Victoria Day on May 24, but we still had a lot of work to do. The next long weekend was the US Memorial Day on the last Monday of May, but it got rained out. I took some solace from seeing another campground near Mount Orford get completely washed out by a flood, never to reopen. Memorial Day in Quebec was nothing anyway; the big celebration was Saint-Jean-Baptiste Day on June 24. In Quebec they euphemistically call it a national holiday, but it receives little attention anywhere else in Canada. It's a feast day that dates back to ancient France and was first brought to North America in 1606. French-speaking people are likely to continue celebrating it anywhere they settle.

I had Quebec folklorist André Lejeune show up with his guitar and Winnebago to attract a crowd for the grand opening. I'd previously heard of him at Lac Gagnon when he and a number of his RV followers showed up for a March snowmobile event. The local club was called *Les Maraudeurs*. In late winter and early spring, they'd have sugaring-off parties in the middle of the lake. Sugaring-off is traditionally done in a sugar shack, deep in the woods and surrounded by maple trees, where the sap is boiled down to syrup or toffee. In Quebec, the parties typically include bacon and eggs with pancakes buried in maple syrup. Snowmobile clubs usually drove big machines and with man and wife riding, they needed them. We preferred smaller machines for cross-country. You could lift your way out of deep powder snow from February blizzards, or wet slush when the lake started to thaw. You couldn't budge the big ones, and there's more than one at the bottom of the lake after being stuck in slush. They'd freeze solid overnight and then sink to the bottom on the first warm day.

On one occasion I came across Marcel Fillion, the guy who helped me build the cottage. He had a broken ski and I stopped to see if I could help, but he had it under control. I took a picture and that spring I framed it and gave it to him as a gift. When I pulled into his farm yard the kids all piled out of the house yelling, *"Papa, Papa, l'Anglais est ici!"* I wanted to answer in French, but in my haste I'm afraid I butchered it and it came out as "I am a cake for your father" instead of "I have a gift..." The welcome subsided but I'm sure he appreciated it anyway.

André was a folksinger and songwriter known to French Canadians in the same way that Gordon Lightfoot was known to the rest of the Canada, only on a lesser scale. He was also a spokesperson for Winnebago. I expected him to fill the place. Several of his camp followers showed up in trailers and RVs. Others came too, just to see André and listen to his music. He didn't fill the place—it was too much to ask of anyone—but it was a good opening. Quebec still needed a lot of educating to know what KOA even meant or what it stood for.

Dominion Day, on July 1 (Canada Day), promised to be better. With the stretch to Independence Day on July 4, we'd get visitors from both sides of the border. We had a few more sites ready and new sod placed all around the pool area. One of the ladies from the assembly line had recently joined the Jehovah Witnesses. She made reservations for a couple of dozen of them to experience camping on the weekend. In the interest of repeat business, I assigned them the best sites closest to the pool. Before they arrived, the sky opened up and poured down rain in buckets. None of them had ever pitched a tent before. Darkness descended over a confused multitude of crying kids and shouting women. Husbands and fathers fared no better as they furiously battled the unfathomable mass of pegs, poles, and canvas. Fresh sod was quickly trampled under dozens of feet thrashing for traction as they attempted to raise their shelters amid much profanity. It was a disaster of biblical proportions. Nothing short of Moses parting a sea of mud could have saved the day.

By midnight they wanted their money back. I told them they could sleep in the A-Frame around the pool table and start again in the morning. It was quite generous considering they would have tracked in mud and plundered the store. Instead, they went home, never to be seen again. The lady from work never mentioned the incident, but I fear she, too, lost face among her Jehovah friends. No doubt everyone on the assembly line was just as unimpressed after a thorough re-telling.

The season had barely started and I already knew it was the biggest mistake of my life. And that's saying a lot. It had nothing to do with camping or the public at large. It wasn't the weather, OPEC, or the damn freeway that never got completed through Vermont. It was a bad decision and had everything to do with money. I finally realized that whatever trickled in would be awash by what poured out. From that time on, the campground was for sale. I'd created my own train wreck.

Business was slow that summer. It wasn't until OPEC's price hike kicked in that the final die was cast. People across both countries put their RVs on blocks and stopped traveling. They dumped their gas guzzlers and bought smaller cars. Several US states imposed a fifty-five-mph maximum speed limit. Every patriotic person adhered to it or stayed home. Camping was still popular in Quebec, just not anywhere close to a highway.

Quebecers expected a secluded lake in the middle of the bush. Many of them had never heard of KOA and for the longest time avoided the place, thinking it was a private club. Oddly, a number of locals caught on and started having family weekend parties. The ladies elected it as their home away from home without the housecleaning. The men preferred to pee in the bushes rather than use the inordinately expensive restrooms. Dozens of them, seemingly all related, would sit around huge bonfires—lighting up the entire campground—drinking and singing folksongs nonstop into the night. I'd shut them down until that business died off as well. American travelers expected quiet after 11:00 p.m. Without local business, that's what we had at any hour.

Oscar and I had different management styles. Mine was shoot-from-the-hip. His was scorched earth. We only had a third of the planned sites completed, and for me that was already too many. He thought the way to succeed was to build more, the thing he knew best how to do. But the tourists were not coming and the money was gone. I still had to work through the week at Farinon just to keep the lights on. When Oscar bought more gravel, I refused to pay. He then bought a dump truck and a front-end loader to rearrange the landscape in search of free gravel. This was the same type of enthusiasm that plagued his variety stores. He may have lacked enough money to pay suppliers, but could always buy a bigger car or expand the building. He wouldn't have the funds for that either. It was just a question of booting the can down the road. Why not? From this point on, it was all downhill.

My marriage was on a similar slope due to my insistence that Doris be involved. She felt she didn't need to be there unless I was there, and then only as an owner, which wasn't much help. She was as depressed as I was. Everything we'd worked for all our lives was lost. Worse was yet to come. I'd screwed up so badly the only way I could see out was to continue my decline into obscurity. My mental state was, *Let them come and get me. I'll go to Spain and live on a damn bicycle.* It was a fanciful notion, but a line I would use later on the credit bureau when the end was near.

But I wasn't finished yet. The situation was perfect for Oscar and Anne. They had no other place to go and Oscar was having fun. And I didn't want to leave the building empty over the winter. When I built the A-frame, I winterized it with a full basement and an apartment upstairs. All we had to do was cut a trail through the back end of the forty acres to hook up to the main snowmobile trail between Magog and Sherbrooke. In winter, that trail had more traffic than Quebec's Hwy 55 at any time of year. I could visualize snowmobile clubs gathering in the parking lot to bask in the basement's warmth while we sold hotdogs and beans.

Oscar couldn't wait to get started. Without consultation, he bought a small secondhand bulldozer to add to his fleet of construction equipment. After that, he needed a garage to store everything in. And while at that he gave it a flat concrete roof because it would be needed for the motel we would soon build on top. We were doubling down. Or was it spiraling? My new problem became how to control his enthusiasm. It didn't matter. I was already at the bottom of a hole so deep that all light at the end of the tunnel had disappeared. To do nothing was to be buried, doing something provided hope; not the promise of hope, just perception. It would have to do.

I cut the trail through the brush with my chainsaw while Oscar ran his bulldozer behind. Some of the wood was used for finishing the basement into a rustic decor with a log-faced bar. My son Daniel's snowshoes and a pair of wooden skis attached to the wall affected an atmosphere of winter refuge. A Renoir print of young couples laughing gaily in a garden patio scene, placed elegantly in a cheap imitation of an antique frame found in a second-hand store, added some class. I was doing it on the cheap. Oscar's concept of cheap differed. He moved the classy washers and dryers from the basement Laundromat to a hastily built shack-like cover behind the building. The cover had a balcony at the top of the outside stairs where he could exit the bedroom door to oversee the camp, much in the fashion of a Buchenwald *Kommandant*. He wanted to surprise me. He did. It resulted in yet another argument. "We need more room in the basement for feeding people when they get here," was his logic. I was now convinced he was beyond redemption. He felt as long as I was footing the bill nothing could stop us. It was only his optimism that sustained me. I knew I was adding folly upon folly, but when drowning you'll grab anything.

I used to be an optimist. Back in '72 I'd bought a new club cab Dodge truck with a fancy tape deck for playing my favorite music—Neil Diamond, Tom Jones, Johnny Cash—which I also piped into the washrooms. I had anti-sway stabilizers installed in the suspension system in order to carry a camper on our winter trips to Florida. It was all part of the dream that helped get me into the mess to begin with. The music stopped in '74 when the truck had to be sold. I traded it for an old Chevy Capris which ended up being totaled when I took out a street light while entering an icy underpass in a drunken stupor. Next to be sold was the cottage at Lac Gagnon. It went to an Air Canada captain who bought it sight unseen for $10,000. Forty years later my son, Daniel, visited it and nothing had changed. It looked as though the new owner had never been there—a time capsule. In '75, I borrowed another $10,000 from Rankin Construction. Each succeeding year was peeling off another layer of optimism. The bones were starting to show and Spain was looking good. All previous sanctimonious assumptions about a deck of cards, sticky neurons, good habits, and optimism were out the window. This was hell. There's no way out. Get used to it.

The summer of '74 was a repeat of the previous one. We had more sites, but there was another major addition. Since the basement was greatly enhanced to accommodate snowmobilers, all we needed was a kitchen and washrooms to turn it into a full-blown restaurant. I hauled over a number of items from a secondhand restaurant supply company in Montreal East. Then Oscar bought more stuff from the gas station across the street. The gas station owner had confiscated it for payment from someone else who knew nothing about the restaurant business. That would do it, I thought. But Oscar had another idea (pronounced "idee") of making it into a "Steakhouse." Needless to say, I was again surprised when I walked in to find a brick BBQ pit in the middle of the basement wall. He explained, "When they smell the rib-eyes smoking they'll be busting our doors down." It never happened.

Come fall, a new strategy was needed to survive another year. The previous winter had taught us one thing: If we expected snowmobilers or anyone else to show up, we needed a liquor license. It was not exactly part of KOA's formula, but neither was much else we were doing. Since the Quebec Government was interested in revenue as much as we were, they would comply with the license. When I told Bob Pearson, my airline captain/cottage friend, he said he was organizing a hockey game between Air Canada and Swiss Air. It was coming up in late December. He would hire a couple of buses to bring both teams over from Montreal after the game. I was concerned about how long it would take for Quebec to issue a liquor license, but Bob guaranteed that we'd have it in time. I didn't ask how, I just knew he had clout, or at least Air Canada did. Hockey in Canada is a big deal.

Oscar hired a cook whose specialty was Brome Lake Duck. Doris and Anne pitched in with our new waitress. Oscar served drinks and I ran the bar. We served over sixty-five dinners on opening night. Since there were no wives or girlfriends to keep it civil, things got pretty wild. Bob's two Skidoos, along with mine, offered some distraction. You can likely picture a bunch of inebriated ex-fighter pilots chasing each other around the campground on four snowmobiles even if there wasn't a lot of snow. I wished I could have; my skidoos were never the same again—neither were Bob's—along with a number of trees.

Many ex-military people are notorious for being frugal. It comes from the many benefits they receive while serving their country, and rightly so. Civilian life by contrast is expensive. The pilots I knew often laughed at some of their own stories. I think they alone may have destroyed the US trend of steakhouses offering unlimited free wine with steak dinners. I, too, was fond of the concept, but only as a consumer. I would never try it in any business of mine; not within striking distance of these guys. At the end of the evening, Oscar told me the one who insisted on running a tab all night had got on the bus without settling his bill. All I had to do was tell Bob. In short order he returned with the full amount—minus tip of course. Aside from Quebecers, Canadians were not known as big tippers. In Switzerland, it was practically against the law. Still, it was our most successful night. And then we settled in for a long Magog winter.

If any of the locals remember the winter of '74/5, they will recall the first winter in the history of the Eastern Townships where snow ceased to fall. It was a phenomenon that would continue until after I shut down in '76, when it again became plentiful and remains so ever since. Of course I exaggerate. It always snows anywhere in Quebec, some years more than others. This year, it was far less than the recent carefree winter days and nights on Lac Gagnon. In those days I'd bemoan seeing a snowmobile caravan show up, violating my sanctuary. Now I *needed* them.

Oscar's middle son wasn't doing well in Vancouver, so Oscar offered him a job as bartender. It never occurred to either of us that as a functioning alcoholic he'd never spent any time behind a bar. And since he'd never owned a snowmobile, we never suspected he'd burn up gas until 3:00 a.m. every night while carousing with his newfound friends. When Oscar finally announced he was fed up, I said, "You put him on the plane; I'll buy the ticket." Sadly, a few years later he had some problem and went to Emergency. He sat there for hours waiting for someone to see him. With insufficient staff, they finally sent him off to a second hospital where he waited again. When they eventually called him, it was too late. He died in an emergency waiting room without even having been looked at.

Oscar's youngest son had a sad ending too. A few years earlier he was involved in an arson incident and sent to Kingston Penitentiary. It wasn't the first time he'd been in trouble. Once, on a cold winter night, he broke into a car and crossed the wires to start it and turn the heater on. He was smart at some things, but clueless at others. His last incident could have been accidental but more likely attributed to the lowlife characters he was hanging out with. Maybe they broke in looking for a place to keep warm. It also could have been intentional. Terry wouldn't have known the difference either way. He would have been there just for companionship. Nonetheless, it was a serious offense. His swifter "friends" made him the patsy so they could walk. It was only Terry who was charged, convicted, and sentenced.

Being mentally challenged, he clearly had no business being in Kingston Penn, a maximum-security prison. Some other facility would have spared him the trauma of living among hardcore convicts. It wasn't long before his body was found badly cut up, completely shaved, and wearing lipstick. Terry wasn't like that, but apparently hardcore convicts are. He had been stabbed repeatedly, indicating he put up a good fight. No one was ever punished for his murder. It's still a fact today that those unable to cope in society often become expendable when all that's needed is a little help.

There was no safety net for the campground either. During the summer of '75, the best face I could put on it was that it was only a year away from the Montreal Summer Olympics. As in Expo '67, people would converge from around the world. If not, I too would make myself scarce. Meanwhile, something had to be done to take full advantage of the liquor license. Other than a few local stragglers, the bar and restaurant business was dying. This time I conducted my market research by cruising a few local bars. I discovered the only ones doing business were those with music and dancing. There was no question about it; girls had to be in the mix. I drew the line at pole dancing, but Country & Western music was really hot. Not surprisingly, Oscar was in before I could get it out of my mouth. He immediately offered up a bartender, who knew of a local band looking for a gig. By the next weekend he surprised me again. This time it was a bandstand in the corner of the basement, fronted by a parquet wood dance floor. What a partner!

    I still wasn't sure how this would go over with campers. With little regard, we started packing in the locals. The attraction was a Country & Western singer who played electric guitar and took turns singing with his girlfriend alongside a wicked bass guitar player in front of a totally insane drummer. The first of the week was always quiet. By Thursday you could expect a few people dropping in, impatient to get started. The fun began on Fridays, with Saturdays even better. It never stopped until dying once again on Sunday.

    The cops never came around. I never met one the whole time we were in business. The mafia expressed interest once; their local representative must have reported losing market share. Ridiculous! He could have been concerned about the bar attracting some of his customers, but never his market. I was tipped off by one of my customers who got it from a pizza delivery. "They're going to get a visit from my dealer in Montreal on Saturday night," he'd told my informant. I expected I'd recognize him from the Luca Brasi character in *The Godfather*.

It was a busy night and I was looking forward to it. Around 11:00 p.m. a young man showed up looking very much out of place in suit and tie. It could have been Armani, but I wouldn't know Armani from Yo Momma. He definitely could have been a character out of a Hollywood film, just not the one I expected. This guy looked as if he'd just graduated from Harvard and probably had. At any rate, he was a long way from looking like any of my regulars. After briefly checking the crowd, he slid onto a barstool directly in front of me. It had to be him!

Getting into character, I asked, "What's your poison?" and gave him the first one on the house.

I was excited! Could he possibly be interested in buying the joint? He could buy the entire operation with a month's spillage from pizza deliveries alone. But he wasn't buying. He was selling. Now I was getting nervous. I had never bought smoked or sold any commodity he trafficked in, and I sure wasn't going to start now. I was so green that when he asked, "Do you carry a piece?" I thought he wanted a slice of pizza. It was asked as casually as *how ya' do'n* between old acquaintances sitting over a drink while discussing life…or death. Then I got it!

Thinking of Bogart, I made a joke. "What would I do with a gun? I don't have enough customers as it is."

This guy needed a lesson on what *my* world was like. I explained that what he was seeing was a one-night wonder—a few locals who briefly show up then disappeared for the rest of the week. Half of them were high before they arrived, and judging by the smell the other half lit up before leaving. I needed to convince him we were a campground first and only a bar by necessity. I told him I disapproved of marijuana: "The damn stuff is killing my beer sales."

Once convinced I was no threat to his business, and more importantly an unlikely ally, he left without having touched his drink—vodka, straight, no ice. To my relief it was just a friendly handshake and a goodbye. Bartenders shouldn't drink but I knocked his off before the door closed behind him. The issue never came up again. I could see him reporting to the don: "Forget about it! He's already toast."

Had I been cut from a different cloth, had my parents not done something right, I could have pulled it off. Like Marlon Brando in *On the Waterfront,* I could have been a contender. I could have been somebody. I could have turned it into a money pit. Clearly there was a way to make money: Dancing girls and pizza deliveries with marijuana were far more profitable than any KOA formula. Country & Western paled in comparison. But success comes at a price. I had no idea what that price would be, and I didn't want to succeed badly enough to find out. I'd done a lot of stupid things, but I'd yet to break the law.

For all I knew, the police didn't even know I existed. Inspectors never showed up. I could have been running an opium den for all anyone in government knew. That was the beauty of Quebec. Aside from their obsession over language control, it was the freest place on earth. Yeah, really! You could get a serious fine for advertising *Hot Dogs* instead of *chiens chauds*, or *French Fries* instead of *frites*, but that didn't make them the mainstay of law and order. Marijuana and other illegal drugs were peddled everywhere. They were secretly bought by anyone old enough to find the cash. Money ran up the food chain to the mob, to crooked cops, and on to politicians. How else could it happen? Stepping out of line in that crowd could have serious consequences. I didn't need anyone to remind me of that. Luca Brasi had said it all in just one scene, a knife pinning his hand to the bar while someone strangled him.

I was already pushing the envelope by not carding anyone. The bar was something of a money maker but not to the point of any profit after the overhead. At one point, Oscar delayed paying the utility bill until they cut off the power. I suggested that if we could only turn all these kids into alcoholics instead of drug addicts, we'd have a business plan for an entire generation. Anything more than the current operation would be crossing the line; I'd already pushed my entrepreneurial skills to the limit. Only an eternal optimist would not want to follow Harry's advice and declare bankruptcy. Meanwhile, the bar was putting food on the table and a roof over Oscar and Anne.

Something else was needed to keep the wheels on. I'd long been wishing I'd just started a mobile home park instead of a campground. We had plenty of space off to the side away from campers. Oscar had the equipment to put in a road and dig a sewer line of sorts. Nothing fancy! We could hook up as many as ten units to a septic tank. Water and electricity were no problem—they'd be on meters, and renters could pay their own bills. It was a no-brainer.

Literally! We did it anyway. We got one customer, and then another came along. I didn't pay much attention. At least Oscar picked up some money installing them and selling propane. With no landscaping, it looked more like an abandoned storage yard. The last time I checked Google Earth it was the only thing left standing. At least we did something right.

Doris hated everything about it! Who could blame her? Certainly not me; I was not only responsible but in total agreement with her. She had a small Mazda, and we lived in our fourplex which had revenue from the other three apartments. I was only there when I wasn't traveling through the week. Weekends were always at the campground. If she showed up at all, it was only to visit Anne. Even then she'd end up getting into a fight with Oscar until it spilled over onto me. I needed him more than I needed her, and possibly Anne more than either of them. Anne's attitude was *man-the-walls* in contrast to Doris' *abandon-the-fort*. Leslie and Daniel had long since been released from their servitude after the first season. Still, they seemed to enjoy weekends at the place. Daniel usually brought along his friend Derek Forward. The two of them would torment Oscar while he tried to get as much work out of them as possible. Garbage pick-up and site cleaning were necessary. Since they were boys, I warned them not to be sniffing the Kleenexes behind the tents. They thought it was funny, but having spent a fortune on washrooms, I didn't. What was it about peeing outside that attracted people? Leslie would show up occasionally as well. She was great friends with Anne and always helped her with the gift shop, registration, and whatnot. It was practically the only time I got to see the kids.

One weekend I agreed to spend a Saturday night away from the campground. I looked forward to some family time and watching TV. Maybe it was too much wine, but as the evening progressed the bickering intensified. Doris thought I should spend more time there. I was used to constant grief about what a mistake the campground was and how she was against it from the beginning. She never understood how miserable I was, and how unhappy I was even beforehand; I'd been running on empty for years. But the campground was just plain stupid—an ill-conceived attempt to give us a common purpose, something we could work on together. A simpler solution would have been to agree to a permanent separation. That was another bad topic. The argument intensified to the point of becoming physical.

This had happened once before when she'd returned from Ontario and thought I was running around. I was before she returned, but not after. The phone rang, but an unidentified female wouldn't identify herself, so I hung up. After a couple more times I told Doris to answer it. She did and that put a stop to it. In the argument that followed, she slapped me. I'm not a big fan of violence. I congratulated her on winning a fight but losing a husband. I started packing. Every time I grabbed a shirt out of the closet she snatched it and started ripping it in half—no easy feat. I kept feeding her shirts until she decided that slapping me was easier. I didn't resist until after all the crappy shirts were gone. We were down to good ones and my cheek was smarting. I grabbed her wrist before the next one landed and that ended it. It hurt her more than she was hurting me.

She clearly didn't want me to go. I knew it was not the time, but I wanted to leave from that moment on. A few days later, the wife of one of the guys from work called her and said she was sorry. She explained that they were having a party and after several drinks everyone thought it would be funny. It wasn't, and it didn't help. That's why we adopted Angus, our Scottish/French peacemaker. Angus had his own issues. I wanted to breed him and he was never neutered. A few years later he was run over by a car while "running around," which brings me back to the Saturday night meltdown.

This time it was different. She started taunting me, saying, "You want to hit me? Go ahead, hit me." I walked into the bedroom to get away, but she followed, continuing to say, "Hit me. Go ahead, hit me. I dare you. Hit me." I walked back into the living room trying to ignore her. Still she followed and kept it up. It was almost comical, until I snapped. Without thinking I turned and slapped her—three times from the wrist—front, back and front again. She fell into a chair and repeated for all to hear, "*He hit me. He hit me.*" Aside from the people in the lower unit, the only ones to hear would have been the kids and Anne. They were in bed but not likely asleep. I'll never know. They never mentioned it, and I didn't hang around long enough to chat about it.

It happened so fast it surprised her. What surprised me was it felt so damn good. I'd finally done something. After years of losing everything, drip by drip like Chinese torture, I'd finally kicked some ass. If only she could have fought back and kicked mine in return, I would have wallowed in the exhilaration of adrenalin until exhausted. Instead, I said, "That's it; I've just reached the bottom. Now I'm a wife-beater on top of everything else." I left and drove straight to the campground, cursing and intimidating every car on the way. I still needed to kick some ass. Luckily, traffic was sparse at that hour of the morning. Once there, the anger subsided at the site of the A-frame with a light left on. It never looked so well, the closest thing to home.

Oscar's son, Vince, the former Texas trucker-come-longshoreman had shown up. He had a big cab-over RV complete with wife and step-daughter. The RV looked good on the property. It was nice to know they were coming back—RVs, that is. His wife was ticked off at him for picking up a teenage hitchhiker and having sex with her in the RV before dropping her off along the way. My recent indiscretion paled by comparison. After the fight with Doris, his wife saw herself as a possible candidate for co-ownership when Oscar and Anne left. Vince liked the idea, too. At least, he did little to discourage her. He gave her free rein while still trying to catch her in the act. I didn't know if I was being set up or if it was my imagination. She never let up until cornering me in what used to be the laundry room. What was it Jesus said, "The spirit indeed is willing but flesh is weak"? We went at each other with all the passion of "hell hath no greater fury," until quickly spent on the laundry room table.

I wasn't looking for a partner of any sort, business or pleasure. I wanted out from everything; if this was a new low, my way out had to be up and away from entanglements. When they left, it was the first step. Vince appeared to be doing alright, but you never knew with him. I'd heard stories since last seeing him in Vancouver. One story had him as a bush pilot. Another had him as some kind of enforcer, or maybe a private eye of sorts. You got in touch with him by leaving a message with a bartender in Vancouver's Gastown.

I still wasn't sure what he did for a living. Both RV and wife could have been rentals for all I knew.

Chapter 8

1976

Dorval, Quebec

Back to adolescence

After the first year of the campground, I was next to useless at Farinon. It was the most important job I'd ever had, and I was blowing it. Phone calls related to the campground—inspectors, collectors, suppliers, KOA, and a host of others with issues—continued to distract me. When it got too hectic, I'd go to a nearby park in Dorval. I'd sit in the middle of a soccer field and bask in the silence of green grass and blue skies to calm my shattered nerves. One hour, and I'd be ready to go back to the factory and into the turbulence of parts, people, and problems. At one point, a girl from the production line slipped me some green and yellow pills. I suspected they were Valium but didn't ask. I would have taken arsenic.

It was the same in Magog. Whenever I felt the dark moods of finanicide (my word for financial suicide) descending, I'd slip away and walk among Mont Orford's tall trees to lift me up. Oscar was a power-napper. He could lie down for twenty minutes and bounce back for another two hours. By the end of summer I had a choice to make: Quit my job in Dorval and move to the campground, or keep Oscar and expand. Neither held much promise.

Was this bad karma? Is that how it worked? How many years, or lives, had I been accumulating it? It all started after Leonard's first seizure. It could be for not taking better care of him. I should have paid more attention during the pregnancy. I should never have left Vancouver. I should never have left California only to end up leaving Leonard in an institution. I sent my family to Ontario and got carried away with work, cottage, boats, and snowmobiles. I didn't stop until I buried myself in a campground which stripped me of everything. Wait! That was it. It had to be! Nothing was ever right after that. Forget about karma; this was just a bad business decision. Others had been through far worse. Besides, I was only forty, and it was only mid-game. The first half was just a learning experience. There'd be plenty of time to come back in the second half.

I never realized it, but the road back had already started a few years earlier after the KOA's first season. It was an act of sheer desperation inspired by too many beers at the tavern that caused me to quit. I showed up at my boss's house around 10:00 p.m., too pissed to find the right address until I jumped a fence. He couldn't understand why I was quitting any more than I could. It wasn't that he needed me. I was useless! I tried to explain it to him: "You have no idea how much fun running a campground is over working in a factory." It was a lie of course, but also true. It was the *owning* of a campground that sucked.

He asked, "There must be other things you can do. Why don't you move into sales?"

I was too burned out to understand what he was saying. I hated my job. I was broke and consumed with self-loathing, having committed all my stock option money. As for sales, what the hell was he thinking? I couldn't sell puppies to five-year-olds!

Yet, no matter how much I despised myself, there was something inside that never gave up. Whatever it was, I knew it was essentially me, my essence. Everything else was just dust, if you can consider blood, meat, and bone that simply. It, the real me, was in the control room calling the real shots. At times I could see it laughing and encouraging the flesh-and-blood me to do the same. It always expressed that this was not the end of the world, don't give up. You learn by experience even if it's a bad one. At other times it said, "What the *fuck?*" This was one of those moments.

My boss could see the pathetic creature I'd become. Maybe he'd even had days like this himself. After all, his job was tougher than mine, wasn't it? "Let's think about it," he said. "Why don't you take a couple weeks off until I find a slot? We'll talk when you get back."

Yes! I needed to get away. The restorative power of jumping off the treadmill is amazing. On the way back through Toronto I talked to my friend, Harry Lockwood. Being the owner of the Brampton Credit Bureau, he'd know exactly what to do. "Declare bankruptcy," he said. "And get rid of Oscar." My boss would likely have agreed, but he never mentioned the campground. He had a better idea.

In San Carlos, Farinon had bought a couple of small companies manufacturing products for the telephone industry. I would sell the products in Canada. The first order of business was a one-week sales course at the Ambassador Hotel in Manhattan, and then another week in California to organize products for inventory in Canada. The job itself involved calling on telephone companies from Newfoundland to British Columbia. Once on their approved list, the products could be ordered with a simple requisition to purchase. After eight years of factory work I'd been turned loose. No more Valium. No more soccer field.

One of the US companies was Dracon Industries. They had a unique way of simplifying installations by using magnetic clamps to organize cables. They also had relay racks and a power supply for powering up station equipment. The other company was CB Electronics. It was a cable pair identifier that reduced the time of cable splicing. Bell Canada would buy it if we modified it to make it a one-man job. They wanted more electronics, and that involved development work with field trials until standardized. The product was evolving and so was I. I was traveling far and wide between weekends. Sales were happening. All was well, at least on this end. Phone Man was back but he still had a campground.

The '76 Olympics had been the only reason to stay open for another year. I gave up any pretense of co-existence and took an apartment in a Dorval high-rise. After the dust-up with Doris we tried marriage counseling, but that didn't work. When she didn't show up for her second session, the counselor told me, "You don't need me, you need a lawyer." When Anne found out I was having an affair with a recently divorced barfly at the campground, it wasn't long until Doris knew about it. Then things really got ugly. As if anything previously was a cakewalk.

We discussed a legal separation. I wanted her to pick a lawyer for both of us. Her choice was a feminist with the sole objective of leaving me in a state of perpetual servitude. I quickly hired my own lawyer to have room for negotiation. Doris upped the ante by getting a full-blown downtown divorce lawyer to level the playing field. It only divided us more. I wanted her to have everything we could get out of the fourplex. I'd already tapped it for $10,000 to get the KOA through a previous year, and she wanted it back. Everything we owned for the last twenty-three years was half hers. I felt, rightly or wrongly, that if we rose and fell together then we both crashed with the campground. Her lawyer advised her to disappear until after the sale of the fourplex. I knew her aunt in Montreal was the only place she could disappear to. I called and asked to talk to Doris. Of course she wasn't there. I told her aunt, "Just tell her she'd be better off talking to me than her damn lawyer." It didn't convince her. She'd already gone to ground. This was going to be war.

After the closing of the fourplex sale, we all rode the same elevator down. Her lawyer rather flippantly said, "Why don't you guys just get divorced?" He wasn't satisfied with handling the separation, now he was pushing for more. We'd never talked about divorce. She answered, "No, of course not. We don't want to do that."

I found her response interesting. By all indications she hated me, but that had little to do with it. From her point of view a bird in the hand was better than turning one loose. Her lawyer could see we'd never achieve an amicable separation. Why would a separation work if the marriage didn't? Any love we had for each other was long gone. I couldn't recall either of us ever saying, I love you. For her, marriage was more of a career move. It gave her the security she'd never had as a child. Even when she was twenty-one she couldn't face leaving Oscar and Anne to live on her own. She moved with them to Kimberly, then Vancouver, and would have stayed with them when they returned to Sarnia if she hadn't moved directly in with me. I could see this going on for another twenty-three years. I would be in the grip of her hand for the rest of my life with her lawyer doing all the squeezing.

I had to admit he was giving better advice than my own lawyer. We both needed a push if we were ever to have any happiness. We'd had disagreements before; I'd walked out a couple of times, but always after a phone call or two it was back to the same old thing. We co-existed for the sake of the kids, security, and appearances. It was a sham with very little communication. Something had to be done or we'd be back in the same position where both of us felt empty and chained together. I needed to burn the bridges and build a wall; to move on and render retreat impossible. Otherwise, I would cave in and return as soon as the whining started. I needed a reason, something or someone, to pull me in the other direction. I called my lawyer and told him to forget the separation and serve divorce papers in the morning. Lucky she was staying with her aunt; she hated change, and this was a big one. She would need consoling as much as I needed a change.

The '76 Olympics came in a flash and were gone in two weeks. Olympics or not, there still wasn't enough oil to keep Americans traveling by RV. Even Oscar could see it was all over, and that wasn't all. I started another relationship with a camper who'd become friends with Anne, who actually encouraged me. She thought I'd need a new manager when they left after Labor Day. Then my barfly friend started seeing the "bouncer." We didn't need a bouncer. He was a just a young amateur wrestler who said he'd work for free beer on Saturday nights. I thought his looming presence might eventually be required. The only time he saw any action was when he got in a fight with his younger brother who showed up drunk. The two of them were rolling around on the dance floor in a couple of strangleholds while an older brother was kicking and yelling at both of them. It provided a level of entertainment I hadn't counted on. When I fired him, meaning I cut off his free beer, I asked him what was going on between him and our mutual friend. He knew she was seeing someone but insisted he didn't know it was me. "I'll stop seeing her," he said.

 I said, "No, if that's what she wants to do, I'll stop seeing her." I needed an exit and he would serve the purpose well. She'd given me a watch, thinking it odd that I never wore one. Several years earlier I'd found I didn't need one. While confined to factory work, there was no time; I was a caged lion. My clock was in my head. If I needed to sync up, there were plenty of clocks around. For the most part, I winged it with no problem. With the campground, I had no time for her either. I was tired of winging it. I gave her the watch back and told her I realized it must get lonely through the week and that she had far better prospects locally.

 Then the bouncer's girlfriend started calling me. She was upset over him seeing someone I was supposed to be seeing—there are no secrets in a small town. The only thing to do was to see her as well. But then the barfly showed up again on the following Saturday and passed the watch back to me. It became a symbol of whether our relationship was on or off depending on who held the watch. And still nobody except Anne new about the camper. Are you keeping up? What had started as a little fling had escalated into a three-ring circus. Like in musical chairs, we all needed the music to stop in order to scramble out of the game.

When Doris' brother Conrad visited the campground that summer, he jokingly said, "I should punch you in the nose." I told him he'd have to get in line, and that was no joke.

It was time to clear my life of all frivolous relationships. I needed someone compatible with what I'd once been: someone who needed to make a break from the past and start a new life. I wanted to reset the clock and regain the life I had so many years ago; to go back to simplicity and start again. I wasn't looking for someone to marry. But if I was, what would she be like? She'd be full of optimism and hope for the future as if making the first steps into adulthood. She could be my director of quality control without taking control; a partner able to straighten me out when necessary. I'd still be me, but she'd know when to holler *bullshit*.

I'd been running loose for too long. Yes, I was a loose cannon, self-absorbed and unfeeling. I drank and partied too much; even my clothes sucked. A friend from work was another one. I'd hired him when he was in college and needed part time work. When he graduated I took him on full time and later encouraged him to move to the test area where he'd have more opportunity for advancement. Later he was working in international sales. Then, one day he joined a dating service. Suddenly he was hooked up and totally centered while I was still bogged down between factory and campground. "Call Nadine," he said and gave me her card.

Nadine wasn't impressed when I told her I was not looking for a wife, the entire premise of her business. I would have been happy if she'd just given me a list of all the young ones. But she didn't work that way. She firmly believed that a couple should be in the same age bracket in order to be compatible. I decided to play along with her for three months; anything longer would get in the way of my exit plan. She had files on all her clients that somehow gave her the power of matchmaking. Each week I'd receive three names in the mail; no pictures, just phone numbers. My name would be circulated to the women along with the names of two other aspiring optimists. This was not only to give the women a heads-up but also the ability to call us if so inclined. All were searching for someone, whatever their method.

The objective was to go through all three names in one week. It became a daunting challenge because you received another three names the following week and every week after. I quickly needed to learn the art of telephone interviewing in order to cull them. When in doubt, it was best to suggest a quick coffee to get acquainted, but really to make a quick exit. No matter how inept, suddenly you had a stable of beauties to pick from. No longer was it necessary to go to a bar, a church, or wherever one went to seek companionship other than work. They came from all walks of life and places you'd never find under any other circumstance. A profusion of them were right there in your mail box. They were school teachers, flight attendants, headhunters, lonely and abandoned wives, and many others with no other sensible way to meet people. Mostly they were recently divorced mothers looking for a way forward.

My first call landed me in front of a frumpy German *hausfrau* with sad, droopy eyes and a mottled complexion. What was expected to be dinner out quickly changed to coffee at the nearest corner for a brief introduction. I was pissed off and told Nadine she had to be kidding. The second one had resorted to knitting her way through life with macramé. When I arrived at her house, I had to part yards of it just to enter the living room. It was strung all over the house and I assumed her bedroom as well. It was as if I'd entered a gigantic spider web and she was the dreaded black widow spider. I never took my eyes off her as I backed out the door, forgoing coffee.

Things picked up with improved screening. There was a well-funded school teacher who found me trainable, if not educable. That was worrisome, too. She had three children. One was a teenage girl who expected to receive expensive gifts every time I returned from a trip, as had been her due in better times. I was old-school and believed kids shouldn't be pampered. How could I shower gifts on her children when I didn't on my own? It would never work! I was already a father and not doing well at it.

There were other candidates too. Some were totally out of my league and others not even on the farm team. A more promising candidate was a registrar of student records at one of the local universities. We connected but she had children, too, and was planning on going back for her PhD. She suggested a contract whereby I'd look after her for five years until she graduated, and then she'd look after me for five years while I went to university. What could be better? Nothing, except I was already struggling to keep my own kids in school. Besides, I was leaving. I'd be gone within a year, never mind two back-to-back five-year plans.

Nadeen couldn't understand why I wouldn't sign up for another three months. She was sure she'd hook me up eventually. "Well," she finally said, "I'm sorry it didn't work out. But there's a nice lady who just joined. I'll send you one more as a bonus. Her name is Lesley Oliver."

She was in my mailbox on Monday. It was 6:00 p.m. and this was my last shot. I decided to forgo all caution. After a boring weekend at the campground I needed to go out and do something, have some fun. On weekends, I was usually sober. Well, okay, it was only a couple of days, but that's when most people kicked back to relax and enjoy having a good time. Four years earlier, my life had flipped upside down. I'd developed the habit of having a good time through the week, instead. I was already into my second martini when I called Ms. Lesley...or was it Mrs. Oliver?

"Have you been drinking?" she wanted to know.

"No! No," I insisted, "hardly at all." It was a contradiction but nobody had ever asked me before. I didn't want to lie this early in the relationship.

"Yes you have. I can tell. Maybe another night this weekend would be better?"

Well, I thought, isn't she the picky one. "No, weekends don't work for me. It has to be through the week…" was as far as I got. I could tell what she was thinking. *This guy is married!*

"Oh! And why is that?" she replied coolly.

"It's a long story…" I started again, intending to make it as short as possible, but she made it shorter.

"Okay, I like long stories, but maybe you should call me when you haven't had a drink? Bye."

This would never work. I had no intention of being rebuffed by anyone that stuffy again. It lasted until Wednesday. After my first martini, I had to show her who was boss. Steady, take it slow, I cautioned myself as I dialed the number.

"Hello?" she answered.

Yes! She's in. "Hi, this is Al Rankin. Did I talk to you on Monday night?" I thought, If she doesn't have a sense of humor, to hell with it. At least she laughed. Okay, let's see where this is going. It had to be now; by Friday night I'd be back in the barrel.

"Yes, I'm free tonight. What did you have in mind?"

"Anything," I said. "The thing is, I have this campground that keeps me busy on weekends. The only time I'm around is through the week." That ought to clear the deck.

She sounded a little more relaxed when she replied. "The Olympics have just finished. Did you get a chance to see any of the events?"

"No, I haven't even seen the Park. Did you?"

"No, but I've seen some of the buildings, especially the pool. My friend's husband owns the company that built it."

Wow! I thought. Move over Oscar! This gal knows some real construction people. But I said, "No kidding? Why don't I pick you up and we'll drive around and have a look at it?" When she agreed, I gave up any thoughts of a second martini.

She answered the door. I looked and saw a fourteen-year-old girl. She had long, wavy reddish-blond hair. "Lesley?" I asked, thinking Nadeen must have lost her mind.

"No! I'm Wendy, her daughter, but come on in," she giggled. I looked down the hall and saw a Wendy lookalike putting some finishing touches on her face in front of a mirror. It brought back visions of my first fantasy from twenty-five years ago—June Allyson—she had the hair. I'd never seen anything like it. We got through the introductions under Wendy's watchful eye and headed for the Montreal Olympic Park.

Wendy and Lesley Oliver.

An amazing transformation had taken place in the city. During four years of my own Olympian efforts I'd never seen any of the Park's construction, not even on television. But I heard plenty of bitching about the escalating debt on the car radio. The pool became known as *The Big O* and was often called "The Big Owe." While vying for the Olympics, Mayor Drapeau had announced, "The Olympics could no more lose money than a man could have a baby." How profound, yet erroneous nonetheless. The city was left with one billion dollars of debt; all of it his baby. Cost overruns on this place made the campground look like lunch money. Had I known how little money would come my way, I would have shut down a year earlier.

I kept my mouth shut as we drove around. She explained how her friend's father came to Montreal from Italy. He started a construction company with a telescopic preform solution for long concrete beams. He made a fortune. Swell! That really helped. Switching subjects, she asked, "Would you like to see the Botanical Gardens?"

"Yes, yes, by all means. Where is it?" I knew nothing! It was across the street and I'd never even heard of it. We talked while walking until 8:00 p.m. My stomach was growling and I needed a drink.

"Would you like something to eat?" I asked.

"Oh yes, that would be lovely. I had to skip dinner."

Damn, why didn't I ask earlier? She must be thinking I was never going to feed her. I asked, "Do you like Greek food? I know a nice place downtown." She did, so off we went.

We wined and dined and then danced to a small but gregarious trio. When they quit at midnight, I used five-dollar bills to keep the bouzouki player until three. I don't know why, I hadn't danced in twenty years. I think it was my way of keeping the conversation going. How often do you find someone interesting to talk to? Or listen to? At times it seemed as if there was no need to talk. We were having the same thought simultaneously, sometimes bumping into each other and then laughing. What the hell was going on? This wasn't supposed to happen. I was the original Gone Boy. She did little more than bat her eyes when I said I was going to California. But I heard it.

"California," she said incredulously. "What's *there?*" She clearly wasn't impressed.

I told her about the Mediterranean climate of the Bay Area. How the mountains blocked the morning's ocean fog tumbling over the hills to be burned off by brilliant year-round sunshine. How the wind-swept bay to the east of the Peninsula acted as a natural air conditioner, with changing seasons barely detectable. And how nobody ever said "San Francisco," it was known only as "the city."
Her eyes were glazing over with confusion. Suddenly she lit up. "The city!" she cried, "Tell me about the city."

I had her attention again. They used to call me *old silver tongue* at Farinon when I was trying to convince production workers how good it was going to be. Here, I was on shakier ground. The only parts of San Francisco I really knew were Broadway and North Beach. In the sixties, during Carol Doda's reign, Broadway was the topless capitol of America. Topless shoeshine girls, barbers, bands, and waitresses were everywhere. Tits were in! But I couldn't tell her. She was a lady. I'd already said too much anyway. Why the hell did I have to tell her I was leaving? Was this the lost innocence I was searching for? And if so, what made me think I could survive anywhere in the United States after the sixties?

On the way home, we talked. It was more of a mutual interrogation by probing to see who could glean the most out of the other. We thought it interesting that her name was Lesley and I'd picked the same name for my daughter, spelled Leslie. The symmetry never ended. We'd both left high school before graduating. Our first jobs were at Bell Canada; she worked in the library, I worked in the field. She took a commercial art course by correspondence. I'd only thought about it, but I did give a painting course complete with art kit to my ex. We both immigrated to the States. She went to Boston before marrying; I went to Palo Alto after. We'd married too young, had kids, and stuck it out for twenty-some years. Our spouses had the same birth date in the month of October. She and her husband moved to Ontario and later back to Quebec, to the town of Montreal West. Doris and I moved from Palo Alto to end up a few miles away from them in west Montreal. We both went into travel businesses with our spouses—they had a tape-travel-guide tour business; we had a campground for travelers. In '73 they almost visited our campground to give a pitch on using their services. Both businesses failed. So did the marriages. We both liked searching for antiques in Montreal's secondhand stores. By the time we met in '76, we were both divorced and totally confused about what we were doing. Desperation had driven us both to Nadine. Who the hell was this person? Was she stalking me?

In Dorval, the VP of international sales offered me a job. He was Austrian and had his own Germanic way of running things. It often conflicted with California's international sales, rendering them constantly at war over countries. He demanded a lot of autonomy and usually got what he wanted, with or without consent. I had reservations about his audacity, but I admired his style and jumped into the wake of his turbulence.

His current obsession was a proposal for a major project in communist Poland. I was working exclusively on this when we flew in three engineers, along with their director whose penchant for politics exceeded his interest in technology. The director stood in stark contrast to our previous client who was an engineer from Hungary and traveled alone. The three Polish engineers were great guys as well. They could have accomplished more without their director. We wanted them to visit the Canadian and US factories, along with a number of working sites in Canada. The director was a member of the Communist Party whose only purpose seemed to be spying on the other three in order to avoid defections. His favorite saying, often repeated with a laugh in search of a laugh, was, "There is no ruder pest than a man from Budapest." He should have met the Hungarian.

Their government had given each of them a Canadian $100 bill for all personal expenses, which I believe they took home with them after three weeks in North America. We installed them in the company apartment with some basic supplies, mainly vodka. They put it in the freezer, along with a bottle of Canada Dry which exploded all over the freezer. We all had a great laugh over that one. You could say the Canada Dry broke the ice, but I think it was the other way around.

After wining and dining for several days, we started the tour at the Department of Defense (DOC) in Ottawa. The day ended together with some DOC engineers at a Japanese restaurant. A crowd was being shown to a nearby table when I heard, "Al? Is that you?" I looked up and there was Mike Lockwood, Harry's son. Talk about serendipity! I hardly recognized him. The last I'd heard he was driving a cab in Yellowknife, and now he was going to university, or was he teaching high school by this time? As an infant, twenty-some years earlier, he'd lived at our house in North Vancouver for a while. Moments like this were heartening after years of factory and campground.

The next stop, at the director's insistence, was Niagara Falls. I rented a car at Toronto airport and we crammed all the luggage and gear into the trunk. They were amazed at the size of the car. It even had an automatic transmission. After the tour with boots and raincoats, they wanted to take some pictures but had left their cameras in the car on Niagara Parkway. I made the short walk back; traffic was light, but tourists were everywhere. When I got near, I could see the trunk was wide open. All their clothes, passports, money, and luggage were locked in the trunk—at least they were supposed to be. I raced forward and almost dove into the trunk, fearing the worst. The cameras were right on top. Everything was untouched. Apparently, I hadn't closed the trunk properly. I grabbed the cameras, slammed down the lid, and never said a word to them. Silently, I thanked my lucky stars for all the honest people of Ontario and tourists everywhere, before kicking my ass all the way back to the falls.

Next, we visited microwave sites in Edmonton and Vancouver. On the flight to Edmonton the director wanted to sit with me. Private conversations with the others were always watched and guarded. One of the engineers had an unpronounceable but distinctly Polish name. I'd mentioned to him that there were a few of them in Edmonton, and did he want to check them out to see if they were long lost relatives? He was eager, but the director was not. He asked me to drop it. He was more interested in discussing corporate America, exploitation, and the evils of capitalism. I told him nothing could be further from the truth. Not only was there no exploitation, but with stock options every employee had the potential of retiring comfortably at an early age. Normally I would have enjoyed waxing on to applaud Farinon virtues, but at the time I was poor evidence of it and totally depressed. I couldn't tell him I'd lost every cent by squandering it on another enterprise. His gloating satisfaction would have driven me to an early exit at 35,000 feet over Saskatchewan.

He persisted in finding another flaw. While driving back through Edmonton from a microwave site, he offended our host by commenting on the houses: "With all this land, why are all the houses built so close together?" Having already lost patience, the Edmonton engineer looked at me in despair. I took a shot at explaining: "In Canada everyone owns their own house. All the service—electricity, gas, and telephone—are provided economically by public utilities which are usually private businesses. This part of the city was built seventy-five to a hundred years ago. Newer subdivisions tend to spread houses out a lot more. If we had more time I'm sure we could show you better neighborhoods where people of your level would live." He dropped it.

In Vancouver we rented a large Ford station wagon. I took them to Stanley Park where we drove around the seawall. He'd never driven an automatic, so, in a large empty parking lot I offered to let him try it out. He wanted to do it on his own. Off he went around the parking lot, grinning like Alice's Cheshire cat, while his engineers looked on enviously. After he made his maiden loop, I offered the same ride to the other three in turn. Afterward, they mutually agreed that it was dead easy and no big deal. Bragging rights over driving a big "American" car went awash.

The flight to San Francisco was canceled due to fog. After a long delay Air Canada transported everyone to Abbotsford airport, where we encountered another delay waiting for a new crew. Finally, we arrived at SFO around 1:00 a.m., an hour at which all Customs and Border Protection (CBP) staff had gone home. There was a third long delay with all the passengers left standing in a holding area waiting for admittance into the country. None of us knew what the delay was. This was the Poles' first introduction to the United States of America and our director was not impressed. The more I reassured him that it had nothing to do with them, the more he insisted it was political. With little success at pacifying him, I couldn't resist needling him. With a concerned expression, I looked up at the ceiling and asked, "What's that hissing sound?" I was thinking *gas* and knew he would get it. After all, with the invasion of Poland he was a lot closer to it than I ever was. He looked up, startled at first but then shook his head in mock disgust. Imagine such a thing happening in America! It was tactless, but it was late. A little levity wouldn't kill him.

When the CBP officers arrived, the director rushed to the front of the line. He flashed his passport and credentials only to get stopped cold. The first question stumped him: "Where are you staying?"

"San Francisco," he said, having nothing else on his mind since leaving Poland.

"Where in San Francisco?" the officer replied, already looking annoyed at having been pulled out of bed in the middle of the night.

The director was stuck. The entire line was held up, with him looking more suspicious with every passing second. I was further back, following the engineers. I was sure something would come up when they flashed passports from a communist country. I quickly pushed to the front to tell the officer who all of them were, what we were doing, and where we were staying in Palo Alto. He understood immediately and cleared us through. At last, they'd arrived on American soil, the envy of every Pole living under Russia's thumb.

Our first meeting in San Carlos was cut short when the director got bored with technical talk. He wanted to go to San Francisco. The others were interested in the presentations being given. I suggested we leave the engineers there while we went somewhere to discuss business issues with our Canadian president who was in the room. He was wearing his white Caribbean shirt untucked and open-necked as though dressed for cocktail hour in Granada where he had a house. Everyone else was in suit, shirt, and tie. The director was suspicious that this was not the president of Farinon Canada. He wouldn't have left his engineers alone, anyway, not even for Jerry Ford, President of the United States.

After a quick tour of the factory, the rest of the trip was spent sightseeing. High on the list was a trip to a shopping mall to see if the alleged cornucopian variety of goods was actually real. The tour ended with a Chinese dinner near the airport where the president joined us for the wrap-up. With minutes to spare I put them on a plane to New York where my boss met them. Not to be outdone, he continued taking them all over Manhattan, the Bowery, Chinatown, Little Italy, and the Empire State Building. I chilled out in Palo Alto for the long Labor Day weekend. I'd like to have heard the director's debriefing when he returned to Warsaw. I wouldn't recognize his version any more than he would mine, but we got the contract anyway.

It was the first weekend I skipped the campground in years. It didn't matter at this point. Soon there would be no more campers anyway. Oscar and Anne were leaving for Timmins and another place of refuge. When I returned from California, I showed up for the keys and the week's receipts before closing down for good. Oscar was chomping on a cigar and anxious to get going. We never discussed salary. He just took what he needed. With little money coming in, I knew it was less than any hired manager would want. In parting there were no tears or hugs; just handshakes with the customary good luck and drive carefully platitudes.

There was nothing emotional or unpredictable about Anne. She was always there, quick to laugh and never complaining. I valued her friendship more than her dedication to the campground. Oscar always called her "my honey"—an understatement in my opinion. I often questioned Oscar's judgment, but never about her. I watched them leave the entrance, never to be seen again.

Suddenly the place was ghostly quiet—empty—with no life. I shuddered at the thought of living there without them.

Anne and Oscar Landry.

Chapter 9

1977

Nowhere and Everywhere

Gone boy

Vultures always circle over near-dead bodies. They wait for death and then claim a carcass before other predators move in to clean the bones. The campground was breathing death rattles. The deader it got, the more I lived. Word gets around! Nobody knew what I'd do next. Even I didn't know. I just needed space and stopped showing up.

The first vulture to land was one of the regulars who kept a trailer there year-round. He never let a month go by without visiting. At one time he wanted the entire campground. But he wanted it for nothing and had no idea it would take so long. For years he had Oscar convinced he'd buy it one day. I'd long since given up on him and would have cut ties earlier had he not continued to play the same game with me after Oscar left. His only purpose was to keep Oscar informed—a spy lurking in my midst. He'd call feigning interest, but it was only to inform Oscar if there was a secret buyer about to throw money at me to the exclusion of Oscar.

Oscar was the second vulture. It was he who was encouraging the other guy to string me along, pretending interest in buying. When I learned they were communicating regularly I shouldn't have been surprised. After all, Oscar had more sweat-equity in the place than I did. Unfortunately, the only thing to recover was a mortgage held by the credit union, and nobody wanted that. I felt betrayed when I realized they were circling together, and cut off all contact with both.

Others moved in, sniffing the body. Old regulars wondered what happened to the bar. Winter was coming and they needed a hangout. Music was needed to resuscitate some life, if nothing else. A young couple showed up needing a place to live and work. He was an organist; she was a singer. They made their living while others listened, danced, drank, and spent money that should have been mine. I wanted no part of it. I leased them the building, wished them luck, and watched from afar. The further the better; the stench of decay was invasive.

Lesley and I had struck up a close relationship. I think she thought I was different than other men she met. She just didn't know the extent of it. In spite of our commonality, we were almost direct opposites. She'd come from Westmount and loved cities like Boston, New York, London, Paris, and the ocean beaches of Maine. I came from the south-western Ontario and loved small towns, mountains, and lakes. She was an artist and a micro-manager, living in the present while obsessed with details and tidiness. I was a reader and looked to the future; a dreamer and macro thinker who only saw the big picture while ignoring the clutter of the present. She was quick to laughter, as well as anger which rapidly abated. I was slow to both and even slower at dismissing the latter. Revenge was not in my nature, but dismissal was easy. We had nothing in common except our capacity to make each other more functional. They say opposites attract. If so, we couldn't have missed each other if we'd tried.

Some nights we'd meet at the tavern and drink beer with friends from work. When I had a yearning for a canoe trip, she was there even though she'd never done it before. When I wanted to see the cottage she came too, insisting we camp on a tiny island in the middle of the lake. It was thick with trees and covered by rocks; nobody ever camped there. We pitched tent and cooked steaks on a makeshift BBQ before canoeing around visiting old friends. Later we went again in the fall before the lake froze over. This time we slept in the old cottage, which was never locked. It would be the last time I'd see it. The new owner had yet to see it.

When I said I was going to Portugal to visit an agent before taking a vacation, Lesley came too. This was more familiar ground for her since she'd recently toured Italy. We spent the weekend in Lisbon and then rented a car to drive down the coast to the Algarve, staying at Pousada castles on the way. The country was full of refugees and void of tourists due to a military coup in Angola. The beaches were left to us. We stopped in Faro, went to Spain, saw bullfights in Seville, enjoyed a country fair in Zafra, and visited Évora's Roman temple of Diana on the way back to the airport. Sharing new experiences brought us closer together. In late December when I had to go to the campground, she came too.

Someone had left the door open and a water line froze. It burst and flooded the basement, destroying the dance floor with no little damage to the organ. The entire place was rundown and neglected. Anne would have been appalled, but nothing compared to Lesley's reaction. At last she'd seen the one thing she couldn't endure. The couple wanted it put back in shape so they could continue business. We didn't stay long. I had a meeting in Sherbrooke and told them we'd talk later on the way back. And then I showed Lesley something else she couldn't endure.

I'd borrowed money from a bank to get through the summer, and needed to pay it back. The bank manager was the third party in my musical-chair escapade, now over for some time. Lesley sat in the car and watched through the passenger's window. She saw me render a quick kiss goodbye, seen in silhouette through the frosted glass from backlighting in the hall. She insisted it was longer. I suggested it may have been a distortion from condensation on the glass. She acknowledged it was steamy but wondered what was behind it. I insisted it was a gentleman's farewell. She wondered what else needed severance. I told her we'd soon find out. I had to stop at the campground.

On the way, she asked, "Are you serious? You want to go back to that horrible mess?"

"NO! I hate it," I tried to explain. "But it's my responsibility; I can't shake the damn place. It's my albatross."

She said, "If you don't want to go you don't have to. It's up to you, not them." She had three children besides Wendy: an adult son, Trevor, who was already a disc jockey on Montreal radio, and two identical redheaded twins, Derek and David. She appeared to see the campground as merely some high-school prom party gone badly.

"It's not them I'm worried about," I explained. "All they did was cause the flood and a lot of damage. The entire campground is my problem. Even if I default, I can't just walk off and leave it. There's no easy way out."

She persisted. "Of course there is. Just do it. You've done everything you could possibly do."

I'd been wrestling for a way out for years. Bankruptcy was not an option. After resisting for so long, I wasn't settling for a bunch of lawyers and bankers controlling my life. It was incorporated, didn't that account for something? The fork in the freeway was approaching fast. To the left was the campground and Buchenwald;

to the right was Montreal and freedom. "Screw it," I said in harsher terms. I swung hard to the right and took the freeway to Montreal. I never looked back. Could it really be that simple?

The bank was no problem. They held all my Farinon stock and had loaned me the money to buy the land, to build, and rearrange the landscape. I never made a payment while the interest accumulated. Enough was enough! I told the bank to sell the stock and clear the debt. Then there was the local credit bureau. I'd waited for them to come after me. Then I realized why they'd been paying the taxes. They could see where I was headed. They made sure they'd own the land and everything on it. Both my lawyer and my accountant were members of the board. Their inactivity loomed like an unseen elephant in the room. Still, it would be an issue next spring when I failed to open.

We had a meeting and I laid out my intention. There was no upside to this mess unless they wanted a campground. While they chewed on it, I asked my lawyer if his being on the board was a conflict of interest. He said he could always resign but suggested I might be better off with him on it. I agreed and fired him. Let them have it. I faded into the night. If they got greedy there was always Spain.

The VP of international sales was opening an office in Salzburg, Austria, and wanted me with him. This would be a great opportunity for anyone, let alone someone who may have a reason to leave the country. That's not what I had in mind. My mind was on California. Another offer was calling. I'd been away too long and was anxious to return. The consulate lady advised I had two avenues to getting a visa. She could rejuvenate my previous one, or issue a new one on the basis of an employee returning to continuous employment. She suggested the first option should be easy.

Lesley knew it was over. I called and suggested a final dinner, but she already had a date. Fine, I thought, I'll go out on my own. We had a customer in from Venezuela, so I joined the rest of the group for dinner at the airport Hilton. Five of us walked across the dance floor to a table. Who do you think was sitting at an adjacent table? Lesley! She was there with her date. What are the odds? It wasn't long before I received a note written on a cocktail napkin. I was preoccupied and stuffed the note in my pocket. A few minutes later she got my attention again and motioned for me to read it. It read, *Can I join you guys?* I looked at her and indicated, *Sure, come on over.* After apologizing to her friend, she came over and livened up the party. Business and car talk was off the table. Later, we were dancing when the combo played "Feelings." To this day, whenever she hears it she stops everything and pokes me to get my attention. I hate that!

My exit time was approaching, and I was concerned about giving notice on my apartment. In early September I told the superintendent my situation. I wanted him to know he could expect a vacancy sometime soon in case he had a renter wanting to move in around November. He agreed it was acceptable. Without further discussion he went ahead and signed a lease with a young lady, expecting me to move on her date, not mine. When she showed up, I said, "Wait a minute, I haven't left yet. I haven't even given the superintendent a date. How can he sign a lease with you when my lease is still valid?" The superintendent was brought in. He was put off. He couldn't admit he'd misunderstood or made a mistake; so much for a heads-up. It got nasty. We had an agreement and now he wanted three months' notice. He thought he was holding all the cards, but I held the wild card.

I put on my poker face, smiled, and said, "Well then, I guess I'll just have to stay." With nothing else to say I shut the door and wrote them off. I never did like renting.

I began dumping what little furniture I had. In October the time had come. On the last night, I took my two Les's, Leslie and Lesley, out to dinner and explained my clandestine escape plan. I'd arranged to have someone show up with his pickup truck before midnight. He would take a couple of items and also deliver the mattress to one of Lesley's friends. Like Oscar, the girls were all in. They helped me clean out the apartment, but under the circumstances I left the cleaning *up* to the superintendent. All was quiet when we loaded the elevator and squeezed in amongst furniture, mattress, and lamps. By then the girls were giggling so much it was getting out of hand. I tried to control them without much success. I was at the back of the elevator with my arms loaded. Leslie 1.0 was holding the cutlery tray. Lesley 2.0 was closest to the controls. She missed the lobby button and hit the red one. It set off a bell loud enough to wake the entire building. Finally, she hit the right one and we descended to the lobby. We convulsed in laughter.

When the door opened we fell out as one, causing Leslie 1.0 to drop the tray and spill cutlery all over the lobby with a loud clatter. My driver was ready. We loaded his pickup and made tracks.

Leslie 1.0 and Lesley 2.0.

It wasn't over yet; I still had the border to cross. On the way I visited my son Daniel at Ryerson University in Toronto. Leonard at Cedar Springs was next before saying goodbye to other family members. Then I crossed the bridge. After twelve years of trials and tribulations, it was over. But not so fast! Something was amiss. I needed to return to make things right. Was I finally doing the right thing? Don't count on it! It was an immigration officer's decision, not mine. The visa was no good. I argued, but they said if I wanted to dispute it I'd have to make an appointment with the immigration judge in Detroit. It would take about three months for a hearing. When would it end?

One moment I was on top of the world and the next I was in the same boat as a couple of hapless Mexican kids making their way home. At least I wasn't put up against the wall and frisked. I don't know what became of them, but I was sent back across the bridge. I'd given up my job in Montreal and had no intention of returning to ask for it back. My job was in California, but without a green card I had nothing! I drove back with visions of sleeping in my car while job hunting in some far-flung destination like Calgary. This needed to be straightened out, and what better place than the closest bar? I ordered a double scotch and called the consulate in Montreal. While quaffing my scotch, I told her what happened. I didn't tell her that maybe she'd screwed up and immigration was right. I wanted it fixed and only she could do it. She said, "Come back to Montreal and I'll expedite a new visa on the basis of a returning employee. It should only take a couple of weeks."

Meanwhile I was homeless. I called Lesley when I arrived. "Hey, it's me," I murmured, thinking how things had changed since the first time I called her with a martini in hand.

"Oh my god," she said. "Are you in California already?"

"Nope, not even close."

On her invite I moved in for two weeks. Trevor was long gone and married with a daughter, Jessica. I slept in his room with Nutmeg, his orange tabby cat, who liked sleeping on my head. Wendy left me notes in the bathroom if soap, toothpaste, a towel, or anything was left out of order—another micro manager! The twins, Derek and David, were rarely seen.

David and Derek

We did all the things we never had time for previously: picnics on Mount Royal, Italian markets on St. Denis, and dinners at numerous cheap but delicious Eastern European, Greek, and French restaurants. All too soon the second visa arrived.

The consulate said, "It's best to fly. You're more likely to avoid confusion at the border. Airport immigration people are more used to this kind of documentation."

Flying was a luxury I couldn't afford. Lesley contributed that between Montreal and New York, everyone goes through Champlain. Naturally, she came too; no, not to California, to Vermont where her parents lived. It was an opportunity to visit.

At the border she insisted on coming in with me when I presented my papers. "Just in case they give you a bad time like the last time," was her reasoning. I wondered what she thought she could do, other than easily scuttle my plans and keep me in Montreal. Apparently, I wasn't that much in demand. She was charming to the point of annoyance. The immigration official paid more attention to her than me. I was merely rubber stamped while they had a nice chat. Then I realized her game: She cared enough to set me free.

I met her parents for the first time. Her mother noticed my complacency and remarked, "My, this is quite an adventure for you. You don't seem to be too excited about it?"

I wasn't. And I wouldn't be until I reached California. Even then I couldn't be sure what would happen. But I'd spent too long getting this far to look back now. "Don't worry," I said dryly, "I'll get into it when I hit the road." They both thought it was hilarious. So did I; my twelve-year exile was over.

Twelve years earlier I'd arrived in Montreal on a winning streak. I became over confident, then disillusioned, if not delusional. I got too far ahead of the wheelhouse and totally lost. I'd raised the stakes, only to lose everything. But what had I lost? I still had my health. The rest of it was just history—a living experience. Why do people jump out a window after losing their life's savings? There may have been times when I felt like cutting my throat, or couldn't have cared less if a tree or overpass pillar suddenly appeared in front of me while driving. I'd never aim for one; life is too important to throw away. It's easier to just take on a new life. For me it felt as if it were the sixth: After Brights Grove there was Sarnia, Vancouver, California, and Quebec. I needed another.

Part III

1977 – 2013

Stanford University, Stanford, Palo Alto.

Chapter 10

1977-79

Palo Alto, California

A whole new ball game

It's the fourth quarter of the twentieth century and a whole new ballgame. The score is 0 to 0—as far as telecommunications is concerned—and there hasn't been a lot of action yet. That's about to change. The stakes are high. Nobody knows how this game will play out or where it will end. Not even the best of fiction writers could have seen this one coming. It was all-out war; a civil war within the industry. The older players were playing the same old game. Why should they change? They're the champions, the giants of the industry. Unstoppable! Or so they thought.

The competition had a lot of new players. They sat out the third quarter itching to get in the game but had yet to learn the rules. They were young, green, and full of energy. At the same time, they were hungry, mean, and looking for blood even if it required throwing out the rule book. Who would the winners be, who will be the rising stars? No doubt you never heard of them. There will be a lot of losers this time around. Will Phone Man be one of them? Can he play in this league? Can he even get in the game? If so, he'll have to play a better game than he did in the third quarter.

My first stop was Nashville. It was too far after a long day, but nothing less would do. Everything I owned was in the trunk of my Mercury Montego. After years of driving over salt-laced winter roads, it was rusted to the point of disintegration. I'd had an accident in Montreal while making an illegal U-turn and got broad-sided on the passenger side by a taxi. The whole side caved in without leaving a mark on his car. After the body shop it looked good—on the outside; what was hidden was another story. The radiator, muffler, battery, and parts of the fenders were still held together with tie wraps and coat hangers. The headlights shook to the extent of creating a strobe light effect that magically cleared the road in front.

I arrived around midnight. The downtown area was in a state of ruin and urban decay. Hookers walked the streets looking for one more client before retiring for the night. The Grand Ole Opry House was deserted, closed, and neglected; a building long since past its prime. Nashville had grown up and moved out, but this was still a good place to start. Music was big business, and recording studios were now uptown and around the beltway. The new and much improved Opry House could be found on Opryland Drive in Opryland, USA, nine miles east of town. I could have driven right past it and not even known. I didn't care. It was old Nashville that I wanted. I found some sparsely populated honky-tonk bars. The first had a tired emcee cracking bad jokes and beating up his audience because he hated them more than he hated his job. The second was more promising. Music blasted through the closed door. This was the Nashville I was looking for.

Four guys were on a stage making the kind of sounds Nashville was known for. They didn't need to sing; their Blue Grass music said it all. But they were nothing compared to the fifth guy, barely noticeable to their right. He looked as if he might have been an Ozark throwback from generations of inbreeding. A twelve-string electric guitar was lying flat across his lap. The only sign of life was in his fingers where the real music was coming from. When the others took a break, he kept on playing. He could produce any sound including voice and he never once lost his audience. His guitar could carry on a better conversation than the guy in the first joint.

Nashville was merely a one-night stop. When I arrived in New Orleans I found that the Bourbon Street bars never closed. The booze blended nicely with the jazz, and my spirit lifted even further when I saw a young tap dancer making a living from tourists. When things slowed down he'd approach someone and say, "I'll bet yo a dollar I can tell yo where you got dem shoes."

The target, I like to think from New York City, would take him up on it. Then he'd say, "Yo got dem on yo feet." That was New Orleans. But I had a job of my own waiting for me in California. But first, Galveston, Houston, and Dallas were on the itinerary, as were El Paso and Juarez. I just wanted to see these places for myself.

After New Orleans I stopped in Houston, only to find a national woman's conference taking place. Thousands of feminists from all across the country had come together to hammer out their issues, and they had plenty. Liberals had different issues than conservatives. Democrat or Republican, it didn't matter, both had issues among themselves just like men. The very thought of that many women organizing was unthinkable. When they find out they're smarter and better at everything than we are, we're in trouble. What the hell did they want? And what made them think they could agree on anything? Men had been trying for years without success.

This was going to be a world-class, take-no-prisoner meeting. All the hard-asses were in town. It was no place for me even if I could have found a room. They wanted recognition and gainful employment—equal pay and a seat at the table—they were tired of being kicked around. They wanted power. Frightening! I didn't get it, and I wasn't alone. We'd need another generation or two, maybe never, but sooner or later it would sink in. At this time I'd have a better chance of surviving on JFK's lap in Dealey Plaza, where I quickly fled. It was time to get out of Dodge.

This was my first visit to Dallas, and after fourteen years the sight of Dealey Plaza left a strange feeling in my gut. Something terrible went down that day. It was more than the loss of the life of our president; we lost a voice that America badly needed at a crucial time. A quick drive through was more than enough. I was more intent on seeing Juarez, across the Rio Grande from El Paso. Mexico's border towns are interesting, but I wouldn't want to live there. I stayed just long enough to buy a Clint Eastwood leather spaghetti-western hat and take a quick walk around town.

There was no point in buying the hat without passing through a few swinging doors. I took my first swig of Tecate before noticing a lady sitting quietly at a table. She looked out of place and really pissed off.

"Just visiting?" I asked.

"Humph," she grunted, "Yeah, visiting."

That didn't go far. "Where are you from?" I persisted.

"El Paso," was all she muttered.

I tried again. "What brings you here?"

"My husband," she answered, with a little more passion bordering on testy. That was okay; I had no intention of moving on her.

"Where's he?" I asked, trying to get a little more out of her while taking another sip of beer.

        She looked up for the first time and spat out, "At a whore house."
        I choked on my drink and lost my voice. California, here I come.

        I knew things had changed since my departure in '65. I'd seen and created enough of my own while in Canada. There were changes everywhere. Elvis had died and so had a lot more: Groucho Marx, Bing Crosby, and Charlie Chaplin to name a few. These were people I'd watched in movies all my life. In the late sixties, San Francisco's Haight Ashbury district became home to the flower children. They gave birth to a hippie generation of dropouts that spread around the world. It was a movement fostered by ex-Harvard professor Timothy Leary. His message was to change society by turning on, tuning in, and dropping out. It boiled down to: Join a commune for free love, sex, drugs, and crazy clothes while growing pot and vegetables in the most remote place you could find. What was he smoking? As a psychologist, you'd think he'd have known better. It might have been a good plan for one night, but what about tomorrow? Whatever happened to find a job, stay in school, start a business, or join the Peace Corps?
        The entire country had been in turmoil. Between 1965 and 1974, it's estimated there were over 1.3 million deaths in Vietnam, including military, VC, and civilians. While the body count and casualties accumulated, Martin Luther King and Robert Kennedy were assassinated in similar fashion to President Kennedy. We'll never know how many died in the carpet bombings of Cambodia that lasted four years. The world watched as civilians resorted to drugs, sex, and anti-war demonstrations that ended in riots. Peaceniks, flower children, hippies, rock stars, and radical groups were all fighting for a cause, often at odds with each other. It left me thinking our only hope for the future might be with the ladies gathered in Houston.
        It took until the end of the Vietnam War to start turning the tide. Gerald Ford was the last of the Nixon administration and even he suffered two assassination attempts. He didn't see Jimmy Carter coming, either. Jimmy was a former executive officer in the Navy, associated with the nuclear submarine program. He was also a former State Senator and a Governor of Georgia. Most people only called him a peanut farmer, but he got elected anyway. Someone else

won an election that same year: Harvey Milk came out of San Francisco's Castro District to be the first gay person elected to the Board of Supervisors. Both Milk and Mayor Moscone were shot dead in City Hall by a disgruntled former supervisor. And I thought I had a hard time in Magog?

Coupled with the race riots, it seemed as if violence was everywhere and getting worse. Additionally, thousands of returning drug-addicted vets faced unemployment and public scorn from a frustrated population. The majority of people carried on as always. They worked hard in the quest for a better life and still believed in the American Dream. But minorities were everywhere, and so were the disadvantaged and disabled. They could dream, but only Washington could change the course.

We were sitting on the cutting edge of change and nobody saw it. Some knew, but few knew how big it was. It was a change that would sweep the world in the last quarter of the century and define the next. It came out of nowhere and was based on nothing—zero. Well, almost nothing; there was also that *one* thing. Don't underestimate the power of two bits of information. Recorded in binary combinations the two digits, zero and one, digitized information could represent endless words and images. The sea-change transformation about to be unleashed was digital technology. This was the birth of the Information Age.

I started my new assignment at Farinon Microwave in Mountain View. There'd been several new spin-offs and this one offered wideband microwave systems. Bill Farinon had retired by now. One thing he hadn't thought enough about was building a management team strong enough to replace him. This was no small task because he was one of a kind. When the current president was no longer up to the task, it fell to the comptroller to take on the presidency. It was a sign of times to come where moneymen would take over companies and treat them like bargaining chips for take-overs and spin-offs. Everyone had a different opinion about what was wrong and where they should be going. Digital radios were taking over, and fiber optics was a new emerging technology. Neither would be a smooth transition. Radios were the backbone and couldn't be ignored. Fiber was thought by many to be the future, but microwave aficionados didn't agree. Farinon Electric was in a mess. The last thing Bill wanted was to come back in and take over, but it had to be done. One of the first things he did was to hold a stand-up meeting of the type that always proved effective in the past.

A large crowd was gathered in the production area to receive some much-needed motivation. From where I stood the air was rife with marijuana. Bill's voice, scraggly from years of shouting going back as far as his college baseball and hockey days, was largely sucked up by the mass of bodies. He barely reached the disinterested crowd at the back of the room where they were more intent on their own conversations. For them it was an unexpected break, an excuse to toke up and shoot the breeze.

Standing near me was a lanky, long-haired youth dressed in T-shirt, cut-offs and sandals. He asked another of similar ilk, "Who's the old guy?"

I was appalled that the question should have to be asked. I turned to them and as though speaking the obvious, I answered, "That's Bill!"

I knew the company was in trouble when he replied, "Who the hell's Bill?"

I couldn't imagine anyone not knowing who Bill was. When I'd left in '65, I knew practically everyone in the company by first name. The number of employees had not only grown but also changed in content. I believe it was Bill's last stand-up meeting. I could see he was disappointed and didn't want to be there.

It took a special talent to do the tough slogging required in a start-up, and he was a master at it. He had a lot of patience, but he also had a temper; not the out-of-control kind that was often destructive, but rather, a positive force that he used effectively to get things done. He never used it on little people, but no matter how high up in any organization you were with, you wouldn't want to be on the receiving end of it. Even customers were intimidated if they suffered his wrath while procrastinating during negotiations. He was a force of nature capable of removing any roadblock. It took quite another skill to manage a large corporation.

My new boss was a Texan. He had a pot belly and wore cowboy shirts and boots. His feet pointed outward left and right, but he knew exactly where he was going. Many didn't like him or where he was going, especially when he was promoted to general manager. This caused a revolt by a gang of four sales engineers. They threatened to quit if Bill didn't reverse the decision and find another GM. If they knew anything about Bill, they should have known he'd never back down from a fight. Instead, he fired them all, saying, "Nobody's going to tell me how to run my own damn company." It wasn't long until Bill hired an experienced executive from somewhere else in the industry to be his CEO. His mission was to straighten out the company, make it profitable, and look good on paper. Bill's mission was to sell it. Nobody knew that, yet.

I was too entrenched to know anything of the plans taking place. I knew nothing except how to sell the same old product that I'd sold in Canada. I was traveling coast to coast pushing cable pair identifiers to Bell companies. By now, both ADC and Hewlett Packard had state-of-the-art products that competed directly with CB Electronics. They were multi-national companies with sales forces all over the United States. I was a gang of one. CB Electronics' days were numbered unless new products were introduced, and that would take another division. But there were already too many acquisitions and spin-offs. Many were failing, being sold, or shut down. I wasn't sure what part of the company would survive and who would be eliminated. A year passed and I still knew nothing.

This was the shaky ground I found myself on when I invited Lesley to come and visit. She left snow-covered Montreal to be embraced by the smell of California's bougainvillea and eucalyptus trees. On the surface it appeared as though I hadn't exaggerated the beauty of it. A closer look would have revealed I was living in a tiny room in a sleazy Mountain View hotel. It had to go. I rented a studio apartment in one of the Oakwood complexes with a swimming pool and recreation center. We toured the peninsula, the coast, and the city, and I introduced her to friends and threw a New Year's Eve party. It was standing-room-only cocktails in my apartment and then over to Oakwood's party in the community center. She loved it! I'm sure she wondered when I was going to say, come on down. But it wasn't that simple. She still had three kids at home and didn't need another one. I was just getting started and not sure where I was going.

After she returned to Montreal there was no need to keep the apartment. I was on the road too often for that kind of luxury. I rented a room from an elderly couple in Menlo Park and found it much more suited to the situation. They even had a room for my daughter, Leslie, when her turn to visit came up. We went to Disneyland and Las Vegas where we saw the Olivia Newton-John Show at Caesar's Palace. When Daniel visited, he showed up earlier than expected, and I found him playing chess with my Texas landlord before I even knew he'd arrived. We went to Santa Cruz and Carmel—our playground back in the sixties—before skiing at Tahoe. Both of them were getting their lives together on their own. Still, I wanted green cards for them.

I asked Lesley if she'd like to move too. Her twins were old enough to go solo in Montreal, but sixteen-year-old Wendy was too young. If she wanted to come she was welcome. It only took three months for them to get their green cards. Anticipating a more stable lifestyle, I found a two-bedroom apartment in Palo Alto. Since she was supposed to be traveling light, I furnished the place by plundering garage sales before her arrival. My taste leaned toward Mediterranean, which she immediately dubbed Spanish Torture. My favorite was a high-armed hexagon chair with red and black velvet embossed upholstery. She called it the "whore's chair." I said I wouldn't know. It was first to go.

She'd been working at McGill in the Educational Research department. A new job was found with a marketing group at the front end of selling the credit card concept to banks. Like most everyone else in those days, they worked, played, and drank hard. Being a new enterprise, it was difficult to know what it was all about. When she asked what they did, the explanation was, "We make money. And we do whatever it takes," followed by howls of laughter. Sitting at the front desk she didn't have to know the ins and outs, but one thing was clear: "Don't get the wives' phone calls mixed up with the mistresses'."

When a young family member of one of the principal owners got in trouble in Texas, they offered him a job with the firm. He arrived without a car, so I sold him my Montego. To celebrate, he joined the others at the "Library" in Los Altos to drink until midnight. On his way home he pulled onto the Bayshore Freeway and got creamed. The Montego disintegrated into pieces scattered all over the freeway. Fortunately there were no injuries, but he'd neglected to register the car. It took months to convince the DMV it was not my car.

Wendy's integration was also challenging. Her expectations of California leaned more toward Timothy Leary's Utopian dream. It seriously conflicted with ours, which resulted in a frustrating summer for her. With no friends, while contemplating a school to which she had no connection, she opted to live in Montreal with her father. He also had a new spouse. The frustration continued, but Wendy was nothing if not a survivor.

I was still concerned about my own survival. I had a place in the sales department, but it hardly represented the new life I was looking for. With all the difficulty and competition over new digital radios and fiber products, I wanted out. I was a country boy at heart, and yet, I always found myself in cities because of my work. If I wanted to live in the country, why didn't I just do it? California had everything: beaches, deserts, mountains.

The mountains! That's where I needed to be. I had always loved the Sierras. All I had to do was find a way of making a living. I had a solution. I quit. I was going into real estate. Yeah! I could do that. I could do anything I wanted to, couldn't I? Couldn't anybody?

You decide.

Chapter 11

1979-82

San Francisco, California

Into the light

I longed to live in the Sierras. With no telecom factories, the best way to make a living would be to sell real estate. I took a course and passed the exam for a California Real Estate License. Now, any office could take me on. Why not? There was no salary. It cost them nothing and they collected a good part of any sales commission before I received what was left. I signed on with the Milpitas office of a rapidly expanding Santa Clara firm. As soon as I gained the necessary experience, I would make my break to the mountains. But first I needed to see if I was up to the job. Milpitas and San Jose would be a good test. If I could make it there, I could do it anywhere, I thought.

    My first lesson was that there is only one *a* in realtor. To this day I still hear realtors saying "realator." Some also say Ti*a*juana for Tijuana, Mexico, and they are not alone. The second lesson was about the "farm." In real estate parlance, a farm is a neighborhood several blocks in size that you regularly attend to. I staked out my farm and sent notices to everyone. The more people you knew, the greater the possibility of getting a listing. I also knocked on doors, wanting them to know I had a buyer for the area. If they weren't moving, did they have any friends, family or neighbors who were? Since nobody was ever home, except what sounded like vicious attack dogs, I left pamphlets and optimistically marched on to the next house. Raffles were popular. Those who responded became your customer base after filling in the blanks in the hope of winning a turkey or something.

    Miracles do happen—I got a listing. It was from two young fellows who'd been buddies since high school. They had a four-bedroom bungalow very much like every other one in Milpitas. In keeping with the times, they lived with their girlfriends. We settled on a price, and I estimated the closing costs. Since it was going to be a four-way split, they wanted to net as much as possible. A seminar had taught me the average cost of repairs after inspection was about $250. This was in 1979, remember. In less than a month another realtor from a Santa Clara office had a buyer and negotiations started. We settled on a price and she called in the inspector. The dry rot and termite damage to the back deck and kitchen was estimated to be $2500. The sellers turned on me like a pack of wolves, and then they turned on each other. The buyer's agent and I watched with open mouths as it almost came to blows. I suggested they settle down and do the repairs themselves.

"We don't know how," one protested. "Do you know how to do that, Earl?"

"I don't know. But it doesn't matter anyway. We don't have any tools."

I suggested it was a good time to learn and showed them where to start cutting, and what kind of lumber to buy. All they had to do was make it look like it used to. I was prepared to help them if necessary, but held back until they digested the first part.

One of the girls said, "You can do it honey. I'll help you."

Not yet convinced they had the skill, Earl said, "Er...yeah, I guess so. But will they allow it?" Obviously, the buyers would hope to have professional repairs.

The other agent and I looked at each other, and then back at them. Neither of us was sure. I looked back at her and said, "I won't tell if you won't." She agreed.

The guys took it on. Considering their inexperience, they did a very good job. They not only sold their house but they also learned an important new skill. It probably even improved their love lives since the girls decided they'd never live together again. The two couples went their own way and bought separate houses, but not from me.

Finding a seller was easier than finding a buyer. If you have a client you have to drive them all over the county to show them properties. After weeks of work, they're likely to buy one of the properties you'd introduced them to from another realtor; a friend, church or family member. A month later I did find a house for a young couple and the transaction was completed. Another trick I'd gleaned from seminars was, after the deal closed, remind the client that they'd just rendered you unemployed, and could they suggest someone among their many acquaintances who may be able to use your professional services. I tried it. Their complete silence was not comforting.

Another sign of trouble occurred when the interest rates went through the roof and the market switched overnight from being a seller's market to a buyer's. In a climate of sixteen to twenty per cent interest rates, buyers were few and far between. They simply disappeared while houses sat on the market waiting for any decent offer. The only realtors likely to survive in that climate were the well-established ones. Another realtor in my office had been after me to join the Masons, meaning a Masonic Lodge. "You'll never make it unless you belong to every church and lodge in the county," he exaggerated.

He sponsored me and I underwent a period of scrutiny. They even came to our apartment to see where we lived. With the exception of one humorless old gent on the panel, I thought I was doing pretty well. The fact that we were not married must have driven him over the edge. I could see he disapproved of my divorce. Even worse was leaving my family in Canada. The fact that Lesley and I were living happily together in a nice apartment complex with a patio, courtyard, and pool was of little interest to him.

I had better luck with Pope John Paul II, many years later. Lesley and I visited the Vatican where the Pope shook our hands and said some very nice words. To clarify, this was no private hearing; we just happened to be there when he was receiving a large group from Germany already seated and waiting for him. A Swiss Guard, capable of speaking every language in the civilized world, told us where the Pope would be entering from. We stood front and center along a rope line. It eventually grew to a couple of hundred people vying for the same position. I had to stand behind Lesley to allow others a place on the rope. Most people wanted to kiss his ring and receive a blessing of some sort. Just seeing him, being in the same room with him, was more than all of us expected.

Finally, he arrived. When he reached us, he paused to hold our outreaching hands amid the noisy frantic crowd. During the brief encounter he said something to Lesley which we later assumed may have been in German. Had we shouted out "American!" above the commotion, I'm sure he would have switched to English. But there was little time for anything with people groping from both the side and back of us for his attention. Through it all, he continued to smile and touch as many visitors as possible. And he did this for the entire rope line while cameras, including Vatican photographers, continually shot off flashbulbs in his angelic-looking face. That night I found the Vatican's photography shop and bought our pictures. They were among hundreds lining a wall for people to find. It was all there in color—the crowd, the Pope talking to Lesley, the handshake, my diffident smile, Lesley's excitement.

Pope John Paul II.

What a contrast to the Masons where I was blackballed. In the polling, I got eleven white balls and one black. It was obviously the old curmudgeon who dropped it. He stood out in stark contrast to Pope John II, a humble man with power over kings and empires. "Don't worry about it," insisted my sponsor," I know a guy who's been blackballed three or four times. He just kept moving from one lodge to another until he made it."

"Thanks, but no thanks," I replied. I thought him very brave to discuss this, considering he was likely in danger of revealing secrets. What was it—disembowelment, beheading? I wasn't sure. I did learn something, though: I was cut out to be neither realtor, nor Mason. I was a phone man.

Lesley knew it before I did. "We never go anywhere anymore," she complained. "When the kids come to visit you won't even go into the city with us."

It was true! The last time the kids were in town, I was focusing on real estate when she called from a payphone. "We just sat down at Il Postino's in North Beach; if you hurry you can join us for dessert."

I was tied to my job more than I was to her. Now, she was after me to go to London with her on vacation. I asked, "What do you expect me to do, tell my clients I can't show them a house because I'm off to London to see the Queen?"

"Yes," she said, "exactly! That's what I intend to do with or without you." Then added in a softer, more pleading tone, "You too, if you'll come."

She was obviously getting fed up with my ridiculous hours, working nights and weekends. I couldn't afford to leave. I needed another contract and needed it soon. Even if I was successful in the long run, it could hardly be considered a normal life for either of us. Who was I kidding? I would have to return to telecommunications.

All it took was a phone call to one company. The owner and I had worked together in San Carlos in the sixties. Now he had his own spin-off in San Francisco's Chinatown. He'd been after me since I left Farinon less than a year earlier. At that time I had my sights on the mountains. Now I called him and asked if he'd found anyone yet. He hadn't, and. I could see him on Saturday morning. I took Lesley with me so we could have a day in the city. To hell with real estate!

The plant was on Mission Street but he was already building new headquarters in North Beach, the Italian district. Over the years, Chinatown had been crowding the Italians out, but Italian restaurants were not going anywhere. I'd soon be trying them all when I wasn't traveling all over North America peddling products. But first I had some personal business to attend to. Lesley's trip to London was not going to be just a vacation. It would be a honeymoon. After the interview, I took her to a hole-in-the-wall Italian restaurant and proposed. It was not the most romantic setting, but nobody had ever accused me of that.

"Marriage?" she said. "No. I don't want to get married. Why would I want to get married?" It sounded like Hamlet's mother when he asked her how she liked the play: *"The lady doth protest too much, methinks."*

I thought she wanted me to beg. Maybe even get down on one knee. "I don't know," I puzzled, "Isn't that what all women want? So, why don't we just get married?"

She laughed. "That's silly! No, I don't want to marry you." I should have been relieved. But now I was getting pissed off. Salesmen don't like rejection, but if you plan on staying in the game you learn how to handle it.

"Look," I said, "I've just proposed to you twice. I'm going to do it one more time and if you reject me I'll defer to your better judgment. The subject will never come up again. Will you marry me?"

"Yes," she said without hesitation. "I thought you were joking. Does this mean you're quitting real estate and getting a real job?" I ignored the implication

A week later the wedding plans were underway. Since we were on our way to London I wanted to keep it short and simple. She wanted an Episcopalian Church. I'd already been married in a church and it didn't work. I suggested Las Vegas which she immediately rejected. To break the deadlock one of our friends said, "Why don't you get married in our garden in Palo Alto?" We jumped on it. It was agreed we'd have a few guests from both of our work places, and then go to the Bourbon Street Bar in the Old Mill Shopping Mall for the reception. The rental judge from San Jose was invited but respectfully declined. After a couple of hours of libations and dancing, the one left standing would drive us to the airport. Now we needed to find an apartment in San Francisco. In our haste, we found one in a jazzed-up Victorian on California Street. It was occupied by three girls. The landlady assured us they'd be out by the time we got back from London. Perfect! What could go wrong?

We did get to see the Queen although there was no close contact as in the case of Pope John II. We saw her while she saw thousands of us as her carriage trotted by with President Suharto of Indonesia on route to the palace. By coincidence, we'd arrived during a state visit. All of the Queen's horses and all the Queen's men were turned out for the occasion. Humpty Dumpty couldn't have planned it better. It would not have been difficult for the Queen to pick out Lesley with her frantic jumping up and down while everyone else just waved and screamed with boisterous decorum.

Walter Fink, me, Lesley, and the judge – 1979.

It was an unparalleled exhibition of sheer devotion—no demonstrators, protestors, religious fanatics, or assassins. Her guest, however, was later claimed by Transparency International to be "the most corrupt leader in modern history, having embezzled an alleged $15 to 35 billion during his rule." It was no small amount, but almost insignificant by the turn-of-the-century standards; barely enough to cover bonuses handed out to a few CEOs. Politicians have always been vulnerable to temptation if they plan on staying in the game. If not, they don't last long. Royals know how to handle it—they're born to it.

When we returned to San Francisco our reception was more sedate. The girls were still in the apartment. The landlady had not informed them that they were moving. I told her I didn't believe she could move them at such short notice. She said she could. We left and took a place on Nob Hill at the corner of Washington and Jones. From our living room window we looked straight down the hill at the Transamerica Pyramid building. I called the landlady and told her we'd found another place. She went nuts! She was actually successful in forcing the three girls to move. I later learned she hated them and couldn't wait to stick it to them at the last minute by throwing them out. The girls, however, couldn't wait to get away from her.

I called them to apologize. "I had no idea it would come to this. Why did you move so quickly?"

She said, "My dad is a friend of the lawyer for the big-shot owner. We didn't want to cause any trouble."

"Owner," I questioned, "I thought the landlady was the owner. I'd be happy to talk to him. I can explain it had nothing to do with you and that it was entirely my fault."

She said, "No, don't do that. The owner is a rich Japanese guy with nightclubs all over a famous strip in Tokyo. He spends most of his time breeding race horses in Southern California. Nobody is supposed to know who he is or where he lives. I only know because my dad took me there once. Anyway, we've found a much better place and wouldn't move back there for anything."

The plot thickened when I was served notice at work to appear in small claims court for the landlady's lost revenue. A tall, thin, sixty-something gent in a gray suit came to the office and ask the receptionist to see me. I went out with my hand extended to shake his. He jammed the summons in my hand and said, "I've done what I had to do," and darted for the door. I was a bit shaken. This was a first for me!

I went to City Hall and searched the records to find the owner's identity. It was buried in a large legal firm, so I called the girls back and asked if they'd give me the owner's name and address. They thought it would be fun to get her in trouble. They gave it to me but made me promise not to say where I got it from. This guy was not the kind to suffer any sort of notoriety. He certainly wouldn't want his name flaunted in front of a judge. After checking out my legal standing with a free legal service at City Hall, I wrote the esteemed horse breeder (with all due respect) requesting he call his property manager and tell her to back off because she didn't have a leg to stand on. I never heard from him. But she did. He must have been livid. I knew she would be.

I was in LA on the date of the hearing when she won by default. It had slipped my mind, but I remembered when I received a notice to pay the damages. The judge had ruled against me for not appearing. I wasn't finished yet. I went to the courthouse and explained my absence due to pressing business in LA. They granted me another hearing and sent her a notice of the court's reversal with the new date to appear. I could only imagine her rage this time.

At the appointed hour she and her husband stood next to me in front of the judge. I recognized her husband. He was the guy who'd served the papers that brought us all before the bench. She went first. "I'm sick, and this man is affecting my health. Twice now my husband has had to take time off work to bring me here. Now he's in trouble and may lose his job, too. It's all because this awful man didn't…blah, blah, blah." She ranted on about how the owner was threatening to fire her if she didn't come up with the money and get the apartment rented.

I had to admire her. It was quite a performance. At first I thought she may have once been an actress. By the time the judge cut her off, I was thinking a two-bit hooker.

The judge looked as if he'd heard the story a thousand times. He turned to me and said, "Well?"

I started to tell him I was shocked when I came back from our honeymoon to find she had not given the girls their notice. In San Francisco there was no way the girls would have to move in less than three months. She started shouting over me, "Not true, Your Honor, not true. I gave them notice to leave and the place was ready for him. Now my boss is threatening to fire me, and besides…blah, blah, blah."

Good! She just admitted she'd kicked them out without due notice. The judge sat with one eye cocked open a little wider than the other. He was still staring at her when he waved me away. He said, "You can go."

The mallet came down in my favor. She was still pleading her case when I left the courtroom. It was easier than I thought.

This was the city! A place where crazy people lived and bankers commuted. They converged from north, south, and east. Every day both bridges and the freeways were filled with traffic, one-way-in during the morning, and the other way at night. We had two cars in a city where most people needed none. Parking space in a garage could be more expensive than our small apartment. We developed a technique that required circling the block with the window rolled down in order to hear a motor start up. At the first sign of anyone moving, you had to race to be first to grab free parking on the street. It was free, but not ideal. My International ex-school-bus truck was broken into and sleeping bags were stolen from right under our window. My '72 Audi received a bullet hole in the driver's window—obviously a random shot since we were both still around. The Audi was for sales calls, the International for weekends. Lesley drove the International to her new job at the San Francisco General Hospital, and switched to the Audi when I was out of town. After a year we'd had enough of the city and moved to a modern complex in Burlingame to add a third lifestyle. It had a swimming pool and gym and was close to the airport and many restaurants.

She loved the city, I loved the mountains. When I say mountains, I specifically mean Pine Mountain Lake, a development close to Yosemite National Park, in the small town of Groveland. It was formerly called Garret by the Spanish to commemorate the place for hangings. There were two ways to get there. One was the old stagecoach road snaking almost straight up the mountain alongside the once proud river bed. The other was the new highway a few miles longer on the other side. We went stagecoach.

Once there, we would stay at a campground with limited facilities and a small stream running through it to form a nice swimming hole. The stream had a small dam. For part of the year it overflowed into a waterfall for cold morning showers. Further upstream was a larger dam that backed up to a sizeable lake with a couple of good beaches. I started flipping properties; nothing big, just empty lots that I'd finance and hold until I found a buyer. With little demand they were reasonable, and there were plenty of them. Eventually I had one paid for. We waited and waited for the interest rates to come down in order to build.

Through weekends of camping and looking for properties, we'd become close friends with a contractor. He was a mountain man who worked in residential construction. Several years earlier he was in a bar fight at Groveland's Iron Door Saloon. Afterward, when he was walking to his truck across the parking lot, his opponent tried to run him down with his truck. He was hit by the truck and badly injured, leaving his wife and two kids with no money while he was in the hospital for several months. As often happens in rural communities, a church group came to the rescue. The Jehovah Witnesses kept his wife supplied with food and literature until he recovered. He, too, was visited and kept supplied with hope and literature. By the time we met them they were both devout Witnesses. He spent many hours trying to convince us that the Final Days were upon us. He failed, but he was a better house builder. When I couldn't wait any longer, we used the lot for equity to get a bank loan to build on it. We gave him a set of plans and told him to build our dream house. Interest rates be damned!

We loved having our own place to visit on weekends. When my vacation came up, I spent two weeks in the National Forest cutting down trees for fence posts. I'd told the Department of Forestry I was interested in cedar fence posts six to eight inches in diameter. I was allowed to cut trees in a relatively small area alongside a logging road deep in the park. My trees were the ones they'd identified with an orange ribbon. It never occurred to me that many of the trees would have three or four posts in one tree. This became a serious one-man logging operation. Even after cutting one down the branches would cling to others, refusing to part. I had to use the International to pull them out. Cut down to size they would still hang out the back of the vehicle. Some were as thick as twelve inches in diameter. I hauled them to the house—eight feet long, dripping wet, and heavy. On more than one occasion I thought I was having a heart attack. Inexplicably, I was having fun.

Lesley was now working at an investment firm in Burlingame. When I told her what I was doing, she took time off and joined me. She arrived with work boots, gloves, T-shirt, and jeans to make a definite fashion statement suitable to the environment.

Together we cut, trimmed, and hauled more than enough logs to surround the back of our house on a one-acre lot. The last time I looked they were still neatly stacked off to one side. It was never about the fence. It was all about the mountain, Yosemite Park, mining towns, gold rush folklore, and the deer that spilled over our property after the first snowfall in the High Sierras. For me it was about getting out of the city. I was getting closer to making the big move. There must be something I could do to make a living besides going back into real estate.

Meanwhile, I was traveling so much it didn't make sense to have two homes. I only saw Lesley on weekends anyway, so why not drop the apartment in Burlingame and move to Groveland? I even found her a calico kitten, Rosemary, to sweeten the deal. When Rosemary got sick, Lesley had to drive to the closest veterinarian twenty miles down the mountain to Sonora. And Rosemary was really sick. She had to have regular treatments two or three times a week. Lesley learned firsthand what it would be like when we got older and one of us became ill. This was her first indication that living there would be more than challenging. The second occurred when she started hearing noises in the night. Even in the daytime the kitchen door could open on its own with no one there, not even the wind. It spooked her. She asked around to see if anyone else experienced strange things happening. Yes, there was a rumor about a miner who'd been hanged for some offence—claim jumping or horse theft no doubt. Friends living close by confirmed it. One day they were walking by an old well near our house with their granddaughter. The little girl stopped and stared.

"Grammy," she said, "There's a man over there."

"Where?" Grammy asked. She couldn't see a thing.

Her granddaughter said, "There, by the well, let's go see." Grammy grabbed her hand and said, "No, child, it's just your imagination." They quickly departed.

Others were equally convinced of the miner's presence. One lady said, "Oh sure! He used to live in the area and refuses to leave. Nobody goes near the well."

One of our friends was a psychologist who worked with social services in San Jose. She and her husband had built their house a couple of years earlier. When he took an early retirement, they moved in permanently before we did. She was setting up her own therapy business for alcoholics, drug addicts, and others afflicted with various mountain diseases. They were mostly female ailments, like obesity and depression. Her patients loved her; anything was better than driving all the way to Modesto to see a doctor. When Lesley told her about the ghost freaking her out, she said she knew a lady in her San Jose office who claimed to be psychic. When asked about it, the psychic told her to bring a few things from our house, like a dish towel or curtain, in order to pick up the vibes.

It worked! The psychic said, "Yes, no question about it. He's an old prospector who used to live on their land during the '49er Gold Rush—they hanged him after a dispute over claim jumping. But he was innocent. He thinks he's still alive and wants his land back. He resents your friend being there." She could even see a red bandanna around his neck and the grimy, sweat-drenched hat. How much imagination did that take? *Swell*, I thought, *this is all I need! How can I argue against that body of evidence?*

In San Francisco the telecom company soon had three buildings going full steam ahead assembling products under contract for other companies. The owner had visions of manufacturing in China where labor was even cheaper. Aside from contract work from a few companies like Farinon, Western Electric, and HP, all he had were a few niche products of his own. And he only had one salesman—me, the token white guy euphemistically called the VP of sales. He needed more proprietary products and sought guidance from a consultant. The consultant recommended hiring a former executive from Ampex, a San Carlos start-up that had been a leader in tape-recorder products. For many years, Ampex owned the industry worldwide, and Hollywood in particular. By the late seventies the product was too expensive, too large, and running into competition from Sony and others with smaller groundbreaking products using solid-state technologies. The candidate had been a high-level executive with their international division until rehab and finding himself displaced. His new job would be to find products that we could claim as our own as an O.E.M (original equipment manufacturer).

He showed up with a ridiculous platform of "You've got a problem? I'm the doctor!" But he was carrying more baggage than the troubled Ampex Corporation. In my first meeting with him, he came right to the point. "PBX is big. It's the fastest growing end-user product in the market right now." He asked me, "Do you know what a PBX is?" The very question suggested that someone had recently put a bug in his ear about something called switchboards—that they were suddenly hot—but told him little else.

I could see where this was going. "Uh, yeeaah, I've heard of the term. How about you? Are you familiar with the new solid-state versions, and the software technology to drive them? Do you have any idea what the competition is doing—companies like Stromberg-Carlson, Mitel, or Rolm—and how many light-years they are ahead of us? It's a complicated field to get into and would take a lot of funding"

"No! But that doesn't matter. Pacific Bell needs PBXs and they know all about them."

"No doubt they do," I agreed. "But that doesn't mean they want to do business with a company that knows nothing. They have a standards group staffed with more engineers than we have assembly line workers."

"Well, you know all those people, don't you?"

This guy was dangerous. I told him I knew a few, enough to know where the front door was.

"Good!" he shouted with a maniacal look in his eyes while slapping his hands together and rubbing them briskly. "We're going into the PBX business and I want them to educate me. We'll jump right into the forefront."

I told him, "That's not how it works. They're busy evaluating competing products and you don't get to see them unless you have something to offer. They expect us to go in there and tell them why they need our product, and that we actually have something superior to the competition."

He pounded my desk with a fist in his excitement. "Exactly! I knew you were the right man. We'll have the best product. Just go in there and find out what they want."

One of our engineers had seen him in the washroom sipping out of a flask on his first day. At first I worried about him being an alcoholic. Now I knew he was certifiably insane. "No can do," I said, "I'm having enough trouble getting them to take the Acoustic Disturbance Protector (ADP) seriously."

I'd been working with General Telephone (GTE) in Santa Monica on the ADP device. We developed the product in response to their need to protect operators from ear damage and hearing loss. The GTE engineer in Santa Monica had told us he'd seen telephone operators in Mexico with blood running out of their ears. I'd recently had an article on the product ghostwritten by our advertising firm for the December 31, 1981, publication of *Telephony* magazine. I was getting calls from all over the world—mostly debunking the idea. Bell wasn't impressed either. They were more paranoid about litigation from employees with hearing damage than improving the headset.

Plantronics eyed us cautiously too. They were aware of the problem and manufactured a good headset that was becoming the industry's de facto standard. Yet, short-duration, high-impulse spikes could still damage the ear without even being heard or felt. Our device clipped the spikes at a tolerable level before reaching the headset. It was mounted in the switchboard, not in the headset's receiver, but it improved the performance of any headset. Unfortunately, our advertising agency also represented Plantronics, who became incensed. Since they were a much more lucrative account, the ad agency had to fire us as a client or else lose Plantronics.

The "doctor" wasn't impressed either. He said, "I'm not interested in mice-nut gadgets. We're getting into the big league here. Give me the numbers and I'll call them myself."

A few days later I asked him how it went, knowing damn well.

He said, "Rude bunch of bastards, aren't they? To hell with them, I'm going to learn all about these PBXs by myself. There's a big communication expo in Chicago next week. Everybody will be there..." He continued muttering as he headed to the washroom to fortify his unshakable belief in himself. Something was needed to give him a measure of success at bringing in a new product line.

I asked the consultant why he'd recommend him to us. "Who advised hiring this guy for marketing?"

"I did," he said, proudly.

"Did you interview him before hand?"

"No, but he had a great resume with many success stories."

No doubt, I thought, *he laid a few on me as well.* "Have you ever sat down and talked to him?" I asked again.

"Well, no, I guess I haven't. Why?"

"I don't know, but I think you should. You might find it interesting."

After getting rid of Doc, a general manager was hired. He in turn brought a VP of marketing with him. Both were from a near-bankrupt company that was acquired by another. Undeterred, they came with enthusiasm and knew how to throw money at a problem! We had more expensive dinners in New York, Dallas, Chicago, and other great convention cities than ever before. One dinner was for a dozen Hewlett Packard procurement people in the private dining room at the top of the Rockefeller Center in Manhattan. The marketing guy was so optimistic he was signing up agents all over the country. Yet, without a product approved by at least one company, I couldn't see any way they'd be taken seriously. The further he ventured from telecommunications, the more I lost interest.

I'd succeeded in getting our alarm and control system in some of the smaller BOCs (Bell Operating Companies), but I wanted AT&T to standardize on it. It would save money whenever Western

Electric's much larger product was not warranted. It wasn't that WECo didn't have alarm systems, but ours would fit in a single rack-mounting space. WECo's equipment generally tended to comprise older products large enough to be used as boat anchors. Bell companies had been compelled to use them for decades. I made an appointment with an AT&T product development VP in New Jersey, hoping to convince him to use our product for their smaller applications. His mind was on something entirely different. He wasn't interested, but he had a lot of interesting things to say.

He was at the front end of AT&T's expansion into a new technology. In fact, he was obsessed with it. "Cellular," he said. "That's where you need to be." I'd never heard of the term in relation to telecommunication. It became clear when he explained: They were planning cell sites all over the country. They would be reached by radio and cover a small area serving customers from each cell site location. I wasn't impressed. He assured me this was going to be a really big deal. "Bigger than Dick Tracy's wrist watch. Cellular technology will give everyone connectivity with complete mobility everywhere," he insisted. It still seemed inordinately expensive to me. How would they afford to install and manage all those cell sites? I discussed it with my employer. We couldn't see any way of tapping into it, other than selling alarm and control systems for remote sites.

Craig McCaw knew what to do. In the early eighties, when the Federal Communications Committee held their lotteries for licenses, McCaw, along with several other well-connected people, won and bought as many cellular licenses as they could. He started McCaw Cellular and was soon taking business away from the telephone companies. In 1994 he sold out to AT&T for $11.5 billion. Then he bought Nextel, when they were having trouble, and eventually sold that operation to Sprint for $6.5 billion. Who knew?

Later, I would be selling digital channel banks to cellular companies for backhauling cell sites to the switches. But that's further in the future and as close as I got. It was only one of many changes to come.

Lesley was getting cabin fever in Groveland. A lot of our neighbors were "flatlanders" and only there on weekends. Most of the locals were involved with the church and various charity events that I'd hoped she'd get caught up in. Trouble came in the middle of the week. She received another unannounced visit from her ghost friend, the dead miner. He set off the security system that I'd installed to suppress her fears, but it only intensified them. This time I was more sympathetic. I knew the problem would be with the alarm system, not the dead miner. A power failure had set off a horn that could be heard for half a mile in all directions. After days of silence, solitude, and creepy sounds, it *really* freaked her out. She called a neighbor who came over and unplugged the alarm system, which did little good until he yanked out the back-up dry cells. Not knowing where I was, she placed a few frantic calls.

"Where's Allan? How can I find him?"

One friend reached me and said, "Allan, for Chrissake, what the hell have you done to Lesley?"

"Nothing I'm aware of, but then I haven't seen her for a couple of days. Why do you ask?"

"She called me in an awful state. Hysterical she was. She's up there all alone on that damn mountain going crazy. She kept going on about some dead miner sneaking up on her all day and keeping her awake at night with noises. I couldn't make much sense out of the screaming horn thing, but I told her I'd find you. You'd better get her out of there before she loses it."

I called. Things had cooled down, but she was obviously still on edge. I dropped everything and took a couple of days off—happy to see me would be an understatement. We had a nice long weekend, hiking, exploring, dinner at the club, drinks and a game of pool at the Iron Door—all the fun things I thought likely to settle her down. But she was a city girl. She enjoyed these moments, but they were not exactly her hot buttons. There was little chance she'd ever learn to accept it as a way of life.

My plan for the ghost was to tell him, "You're dead, so bugger off." I recommended Lesley break it to him gently. Tell him he is no longer among us. He's in the spirit world and should go to the light, or whatever. She tried it and maybe it worked. We'll never know. At the end of the weekend she was packed, loaded, and sitting in the car. There was no way I was getting off that mountain without her.

Something else was going to the light. A significant change was taking place in the telecom industry. In Canada, Northern Electric had been working on their fiber optic transmission products. At the center of this was the need for a fiber optic cable and electro-optical transmission terminals. This became their Optical Systems Division (OSD). After field trials starting with Bell and then other companies, Saskatchewan Government Telephone entered into a contract requiring OSD to build a factory in Saskatoon. By now they were expanding sales to the United States and opening an office in Atlanta. Fiber optics had taken off. In fact it was the latest technology driving the industry.

I knew OSD's director of marketing and sales from our Farinon Canada days together. I called him and asked, "Do you have any openings in the US?"

"Would you be willing to move to Atlanta?" he wanted to know.

"Sure," I answered, thinking, that's exactly what I had in mind.

"Send me your resume and I'll see what we have."

Dave was a one-of-a-kind decision maker; especially if it flew in the face of logic. The more controversial it was, the better he liked it. It always set him at odds with upper management, but that was part of the game. Northern was rife with politics and nobody could play the game better than he could, or so he thought. It was all about breaking the rules, obfuscating, and never letting them know the full story. But he got the job done.

Earlier, in the late sixties, I'd introduced him to a couple of girls who were living across the hall from me at the Royal Dixie apartment complex in Dorval. Actually, I didn't introduce him, I was invited to one of their parties and suggested he show up in my place. Since he was recently divorced, he'd receive a better reception then I would, even if unannounced. I'd met them much the same way. After work one day, when I had no ice in the freezer, I went across the hall and knocked on their door. One of them answered.

I said, "Hi, my name's Al. I live across the hall and I've got no ice for my martini. Do you suppose I could borrow some?" She looked at me in that peculiar way Brits do when they know you're "having them on." Unable to contain it, she burst out laughing. When she regained control, she said, "Okay, I've got the ice if you have the gin."

Anyway, he went to the party. The next thing I knew he was living with one of them on a farm in Ontario and they had three kids. He got her to move there by promising to buy her a horse, something she had always wanted. With Dave, she got the horse and a whole lot more.

So would I.

Lilburn, Gwinette County, Georgia – 1983.

Chapter 12

1983-86

Atlanta, Georgia

LD riding the wave

I've always admired innovators, the creative types with that unique mixture of balls and brains that allowed them to seize an idea and drive it to fruition with a start-up company. Then there are others capable of going way beyond that: to take an existing company with old methods and turn it into a giant of the industry with new technology. Imagine someone taking on AT&T with such fervor that it would end up turning the entire telecommunication industry upside down. At this point in my life, it had already happened. It wasn't a technology breakthrough by engineers, as you would expect. It was more of a legal coup by lawyers— thousands of them—to create a revolution of seismic proportions. It was a battle between law firms and a corporate dynasty—the beginning of the end. Over the next two decades every major telephone company in the country would surge, stutter, and stall, before falling into the hands of strangers eagerly scrambling for scraps. A hundred-year-old industry would never be the same again. Even major suppliers would be wiped out. How could this happen?

    Several years earlier, Bill McGowan took a small communications company, Microwave Communications of America Inc. (MCI), and turned it into the second largest long-distance provider in the country. They changed the name to MCI Communications and went public in 1972. In '74 they filed an antitrust lawsuit against AT&T, and by 1980, MCI had convinced the Federal Court that AT&T was "anti-competitive, anti-consumer, and abusing its monopoly status." A jury awarded MCI $1.8 billion. It led to the AT&T breakup and MCI capturing twenty percent of the long-distance market. It's been said that MCI knew far more about swaying the Supreme Court than anything connected to dial tone. It didn't matter. They popped the lid off the bottle and the genie was out. And it didn't confine itself to telecommunications. Deregulation had opened doors in industries such as airlines, banking, and power utilities as well. It was only the beginning.

By 1983, MCI was building the first high-speed fiber optic network between Washington and New York. They were also burying fiber through cities and cornfields all across the country. Not since the railroad robber-baron days of the nineteenth century had anything jump-started a nationwide race to link the two oceans. After all those years of high interest and energy costs, the country was alive again. Reagan promised smaller government, tax cuts, and "trickle-down" economics. Everyone was encouraged to open a business, buy a house, and get more stuff. In just a few years, barely known companies were taking on AT&T in its own back yard. Start-up companies jumped on board all across the country. Northern Telecom's Optical Systems Division (OSD) had just signed an agreement to sell two hundred million dollars' worth of fiber optic products to MCI. But what did any of that have to do with me?

I was to be OSD's project manager on the MCI contract. What were they thinking? I knew nothing about project management. I had enough trouble managing my life. And fiber optics! What was that all about? I knew it sent light down a stretch of glass smaller than a hair from your head, but how? Where did it come from? How do you stretch glass in such an insane manner; and what about that digital thing? I hated to turn a light bulb on and off for fear of burning out a filament. How the hell can you switch a light on and off millions of times per second and then count it from somewhere across the country? Microwave technology was easy! You just hooked the radio up to an antenna and let it fly.

In Saskatoon, OSD had lots of people who knew all about their products. And if they didn't, they had Bell Northern Research (BNR) and Bell Canada to draw from. They had jointly developed the product in the first place. Northern Telecom was Canada's version of Western Electric Company (WECo) in the United States. Prior to '76 it was known as Northern Electric Company (NECo). The similarity between the two was not surprising when you consider WECo was forced to sell its Canadian subsidiary in 1949. The tri-corporate structure of Northern Telecom, Bell Canada, and BNR was just like AT&T's, with each having their own telephone, manufacturing, and R&D divisions. The Optical Systems Division in Saskatoon was just a tiny division of Northern Telecom. Surely there had to be somebody more qualified than me within that massive structure? Of course there was! And any engineering grad in Canada would jump at the opportunity to work for Northern in any capacity.

Dave did his thinking outside the box. Hiring me was a leap of faith far beyond anything Human Resources was capable of. Strategically, we met at the Velvet Turtle in Burlingame instead of Saskatoon. I asked, "What's the job pay?"

"What are you making now?" he wanted to know. I was making a base pay with commissions. I had to think of a healthy mean average. "Okay," he said. "The job is in Atlanta, when can you start?"

That's it? I wondered. It was too easy! Maybe there was more to it. "Well, this is a big move. I'll have to talk it over with Lesley. You know how it is when you're married and have to break all your ties with friends and neighbors. Then there's family to consider, stability and such." I wavered, searching for a reason why it may be difficult to move. "It'll be a joint decision, of course, and then there's a house to sell. We have an unbelievable amount of furniture to move..."

"Sure, sure," he waved it away, knowing the spoof game better than anyone. "I'll put you in for a corporate move. Northern will buy the house, move you, and pay for temporary housing. Is there anything else bothering you?"

"Nope, I think that about covers it. I'm sure Lesley will love Atlanta."

I did mention a minor deficiency to her. I didn't know squat about the product or what the job entailed. As usual, she knew the simple answer. "Go to the library," she said. "They have books on everything. Just look for fiber optics and they're sure to have it." Now why didn't I think of that? I didn't because I didn't have time. "Later," I said. "Right now we have to start packing." We were living in an apartment in Burlingame. That quickly changed back to Groveland where the majority of the furniture was.

Northern had a relocation contract with Merrill Lynch. It ensured a fair market price by getting three estimates and taking the middle one. They bought our house in Groveland, unseen and oblivious to the remoteness. Our contractor said it was the slickest deal he'd ever seen. It was especially so, considering the amount of time it took before selling at a loss. Northern didn't care about minor real estate transactions during the process of recruiting. They were the world's leading manufacturer of digital switching equipment. Their stock was like gold. If they wanted to buy a company's technology, they just threw a bunch of stock at them and walked off with the entire company, employees and all. In this league, I wouldn't even register on the radar. But I would in Saskatoon.

I asked Dave where he wanted me to go first. He said, "You have to go to Saskatoon in order to get familiarized." And then he said, "No, don't go there yet. You'll screw up. Those bastards will murder you. You'd better go to Atlanta first. You have to find a house there anyway."

Atlanta is a beautiful city. In the eighties it had issues. The child murderers of the late seventies had disappeared, or at least the police had charged a twenty-three-year-old with them. He'd been killing adults, and that was close enough to stop the international press from scourging the city with worldwide reports on the matter. Kids continued to get murdered occasionally, but that was old news by now. A bigger issue was the famous Atlanta Underground that was once the vibrant center of Atlanta's downtown shopping and nightlife. It was shut down in 1980 and stayed that way for much of the decade. It was a small part of the city left abandoned; crime and violence were rampant with vagrants occupying buildings.

On contemplating house hunting, the first thing Lesley said was, "I want to live downtown. That's where all the museums and art classes will be."

Northern Telecom's factory was in Stone Mountain where OSD's office was temporarily located. Everyone was working at getting fully staffed and operational as early as possible. I was rushed through the process of indoctrination as though I'd ridden in on a white horse. The marketing manager had just transferred from Saskatoon and even he installed my multi-featured SL1 telephone that I'd never seen before. Dave's administrative assistant showed me how to use a fax machine I never knew existed.

A customer from Motorola, to whom I sold supervisory equipment, had told me, "You have to live outside the 285 Circle. The entire area inside has been taken over."

Northern Telecom's personnel manager recommended a realtor who said much the same thing in his own coded language. He said, "You don't want to live in Stone Mountain. Gwinette County is the best place to buy. That's the safest and fastest growing area." So we elected to live in Gwinette County where a couple of years earlier a white supremacist serial killer shot Larry Flynt (*Hustler* magazine) and his lawyer. Apparently, white killers didn't count.

That aside, Lesley was not happy about being so far away from downtown. It helped that she was a cat person. We now had room for two of them—adult Siamese littermates named Sammy and Loco; she'd need the company. It was suburbia, but we had a swimming pool. The first night we used it we were enjoying a nice swim when I said, "This is perfect! It'll suit our purpose until we can find a nice piece of property on Lake Lanier to build a new house." She choked on the chlorine-loaded water and almost sank. Didn't she realize by now that I never lived in the present? I already had my eye on something and soon bought it with what was left over from the sale in Groveland. We couldn't afford to build, but we put in a dock for my Laser sailboat. It wasn't Groveland, but it was a nice place for a Sunday afternoon on the lake.

Not long after arriving, I took my first trip to Saskatoon. OSD was working double shifts. Raw material came in one door and complete optical transmission systems went out the other. Glass in the form of cylinders was melted into a tiny fiber to be pulled out for miles in length. It was jacketed, color coded, spun into a slotted core cable, and coiled onto reels for shipping. In the field it needed to be buried, strung through the air, or pulled through conduit before being spliced and hooked up to terminals. They also had an opto-electronic product line that lit up the fiber with gigabits of light to carry hundreds of voice circuits over a single fiber. It made copper look like jungle drums.

There was no red-carpet treatment for me in Saskatoon. I may have slipped in under the radar by way of Atlanta, but just one trip to Saskatoon and I was a blip on everybody's screen. Many in middle management unfailingly resented my sponsor's cavalier style, even before I materialized. The others just wanted my job. The president ruled over a bunch of directors whom he insisted on calling his cabinet. The word "board" was already being used by a much loftier group of Brahmins in corporate headquarters, where he aspired to be. He had directors of manufacturing, engineering, quality control, finance, and more. The manager of product line management also had patent rights to the fiber cable design. He was one of those who wanted to be relocated to Atlanta. I beat him to it.

Project managers and product line managers were working in cubicles. Their tiny little spaces buzzed with activity. Often they could be found in their manager's cubicle, surrounding his desk and conferencing through a frequency-clipped SL1 speaker phone. Others poked away on Macintosh computers—another recent innovation—intently doing things I couldn't comprehend. Such were the first generation of yuppies in the eighties. They flooded the industry with their college degrees, three-piece suits, and insatiable lust for self-serving excellence; all qualities far removed from their predecessor generation of hippies. To my fifty-year-old mind they barely looked old enough to be out of school. They arrived at a time of technological advancement and knew how to reap the harvest. No post-graduate course or seminar was ever overlooked. The larger the corporation, the more opportunities it was likely to present.

The director of manufacturing had a storage yard full of multimode cable reels built for the Canadian market. It was an earlier product with limited speed of light capacity, and incapable of long distances. He insisted it should go toward the MCI contract in order to reduce his inventory. What he really wanted was to increase his manufacturing efficiency on paper. It had taken years for OSD to perfect the manufacturing of fiber cable: first at BNR, then on Bell Canada projects, and later with some independents before the sweetheart deal with SaskTel. Multimode fiber was a mainstay for the Canadian telephone market at the time, but demand was falling. Very little of it was required for MCI's long-haul ambitions. He thought my job was to sell MCI on using his short reels of multimode cable and fought vigorously to have his inventory sent to MCI. Failing that, he fought to have it moved to Operations' or Marketing's bottom line to get it off his own; just another one of the games played in any factory.

The majority of MCI's requirement was for single mode fiber. They needed long lengths on cable reels containing high-quality single mode fibers capable of much higher speeds over longer distances with less attenuation. It was the difference between riding a bicycle and a Harley. My job was not only to make sure they got the right quantity delivered to different routes all over the country, but to ensure it met all the advertised specifications when installed and working. I had a lot of catching up to do, but so did OSD.

Northern Telecom had always enjoyed a captive market with Bell Canada. It was the same between Western Electric and the AT&T Bell Companies. Little selling was required in either; both were monopolies supplying themselves. After the breakup of AT&T, Bell companies were free to shop wherever they liked. The newly formed "Baby Bells" were showing their independence by building their own networks with products of their choosing. With a totally deregulated market, Northern had no end of competition in a market that gave no quarter. As much as OSD considered they were the experts on outside plant, MCI was convinced they could do it faster for less money.

MCI was a small, private microwave system provider grown large and gone rogue. They were not the least bit interested in what Ma Bell was doing. They were ready to kick her ass. Their game was to make money and they were shopping the world for products—especially in Japan, which was leading the pack. Fujitsu had already signed a multimillion-dollar deal for 450 Mbps terminals. And Siecor, a cable manufacturer proclaiming to be the fiber expert in the face of OSD, had also signed a major contract with MCI. For the next few years, advancement in high-speed transmission would happen so fast it would make products obsolete before they hit the market. I needed to keep up with the technology and get ahead of the competition. More importantly, I needed to get in front of MCI.

I flew in to Washington National Airport and took the Metro. The parks around Foggy Bottom and other downtown Metro stops were still populated with 'Nam Vets in wheelchairs. Others, too, had been reduced to homelessness and begging for handouts. But money was everywhere. Hotels were filled, restaurants and bars overflowed, disco clubs howled, and strip-bars did what they did best until the early morning hours. Peddlers, politicians, lawyers, and lobbyists were all drinking from the same well. As in the days after World War II, Washington was the center of the tornado fueling the big engine for the long climb up.

The first meeting did not go well. MCI had set it up with OSD and Fujitsu to test compatibility and compliance issues between OSD's cable and Fujitsu's electronics. The OSD manager of product line management was opposed to sitting at the same table with Fujitsu and insisted we walk out of the meeting. The Japanese 450 Mbps product had beat out OSD's less sexy 135 Mbps, but it wasn't because of that. He was more concerned about protecting his patent rights on OSD's cable. I didn't get it! Fujitsu was not in the cable business. They couldn't care less about his cable design or anyone's patent. The purpose of the field trial was to convince them they could successfully transmit their electronics over our fiber. Eventually we got back together. The next issue quickly topped the agenda. Our reels were going to be about three days late arriving.

"This is outrageous!" MCI's director of engineering shouted. "We have four Fujitsu engineers here, all the way from Japan, and you guys aren't ready. What are they supposed to do?"

The room fell silent. I thought, Uh-oh! An hour ago we'd walked out. This time they're going to throw us out.

My boss, Dave, broke the silence by underplaying the seriousness of the delay. "I'd suggest they extend their stay a few days longer." It was spoken with the casualness of someone examining his fingers.

The MCI director wasn't amused. He ranted on about contractual obligations and the great inconvenience to MCI and Fujitsu, while insisting OSD absorb the cost, suffer penalties, etc., etc. It was an act of course—a negotiating tactic used by major assholes. I'd never seen such abrasiveness from a customer. It was an obvious display of intimidation, and working quite well with me. I wondered, *Jesus! Is this the way it's going to be?*

Again, Dave defused him, this time speaking directly to the Japanese. "A couple of extra days; what's the big deal? You have hotel rooms. Enjoy yourselves."

After much sucking of air, they agreed they could wait. Behind the act, they appeared to like the idea. With $200 million in contracts floating around, the cost of a few extra days in Washington was nothing, no matter how much they spent. Likewise, the MCI director looked pleased about having asserted such great authority. This was Washington, a place that thrived on polarization, controversy, and competition over power. What I came away with was a resolve to let things roll off my back no matter how screwed up they got. And they would.

MCI's rocky relationship with AT&T left them with only Northern to pit against Siecor for their fiber optic cable. Siecor had the advantage of being owned 50/50 by Corning Glass of New York and Siemens of Germany—the same people we had to buy our glass cylinders from. They also had a good cable design, using plastic tubes to protect the fibers within the cable instead of OSD's slotted core design. And they had unlimited resources to provide engineering and installation support in the field.

Northern was the darling of Bell Canada where they could do no wrong. No matter what they came up with, it was accepted as being the best. Most of the product ideas came from Bell and BNR, and were then manufactured by Northern. The OSD division was populated with engineers and managers from within the corporate envelope, which rendered a lot of talent with a high opinion and level of confidence among themselves. They entered the US market convinced they were the best in the industry. MCI knew better. They constantly provided me with evidence to the contrary at every opportunity. This was a new technology, and they wanted to treat it with new ideas unrestrained by any of Bell's tried and true methods, whether US or Canadian.

I went solo to my next meeting. This time it was with a conference room full of project managers. It started off much like the last one. The bellicose director bawled, "Siecor!" as though having solved the world's greatest problem next to famine. "You've heard of them I presume?" In spite of the intended sarcasm, I'd heard plenty about them in the last few days.

He set down his pipe and continued. "They tell me they can supply me with ninety-six single-mode fibers in a tube-protected, gel-filled, armor-jacketed, rodent-proof cable on five-kilometer reels." I wondered, *why not add "self-trenching" to your string of fifty-dollar words, dickhead*. I could just see him telling his disciples, "Siecor's dragging their feet. Watch me trick this greenhorn into making a commitment."

I watched him pick up his insidious looking pipe and take a pull. I thought about the director of manufacturing in Saskatoon who was bitching about being expected to build a one-kilometer reel with only twelve fibers. While pondering how to handle the outburst, I immediately discarded my first thought. I was cussing myself for not realizing he'd play the Siecor card. It finally came to me: Throw some doubt at him. "Yes, I'd heard they were thinking about a 96-fiber cable. I wonder how long it will take them to solve all the problems."

He extracted his pipe with an audible pop, and said, "Are you telling me you're not working on it?"

Damn right we're not, I thought, but told him, "Frankly I'd rather you get it from Siecor. We all want longer reels but if you include that many fibers the cost will kill you. And with high-speed electronics getting faster, you may never need them." None of us knew the upper limits of the laser diode ON/OFF switching, yet. Already it was infinitely higher than the relatively slow light-emitting LED being used as recently as last year. I congratulated myself anyway. If he was going to blow smoke, so was I.

His response was sobering. Pointing his pipe stem at me he said, "Listen Al, we're building the first, the largest, and the most fiber routes in the world. Do you understand what that means?"

Again, *damn right I don't.* Finally, with the same seriousness, I said, "No, at least not yet. That's what this trip is all about. Let's start again. Let's just go around the room and get to know each other better. That way I'll know where I can help you the most." With that, I turned to the guy next to me, and said, "Hi, I'm Al, what's your job?"

After going around the table I felt better about putting a human face on the many projects. Each project manager elaborated, showing his expertise in front of the boss. Most of my technical information had been recently gleaned from data sheets. Many of the project managers were solid Siecor and Fujitsu supporters. Siecor was local and the Japanese were ahead of us. Both were already well embedded, and their sales and marketing people were pros when it came to entertaining. With time well spent and getting on, I suggested lunch. It was time to level the playing field.

Dave had tipped me off about MCI: "After three martinis they don't know fiber optics from smoke signals." He also told me what the director's favorite restaurant was *The White House,* an expensive restaurant where the real big shots went. Lunch progressed to dinner at *La Niçoise* in Georgetown, where waitresses wore roller skates while serving tables. We followed up with drinks at the *Chamber Maids* until 2:00 a.m. A good night on the town could always fix a lot of problems.

Next it was fusion sets. Cable-splicers had been splicing copper wire for a hundred years. It was easy: just twist or crimp them together and slide a sleeve over them. Now, they had to use newly invented complicated electronics to fuse together barely visible strands of glass under a microscope without causing refraction or undue attenuation. Only the younger ones with good eyesight even attempted it. I was under pressure to win the fusion set business.

Being new technology, fusion sets were coming from BNR where they were still struggling to complete them.

I asked the point man at BNR, "Where are the fusion sets?"

He answered, "We subcontracted them out. Every one received so far had problems, and they're already three months behind."

I said, "If you expect to sell any, I've got to have more than a data sheet. MCI already has a school set up at their tech center in Dallas. They may be training the same good-old-boy-tobacco-spitting splicers, but they're using Siecor's state-of-the-art fusion sets. What have we got?"

His answer was more disheartening than the first. "The first two they shipped us crapped out in a week. I'm still waiting on four more they promise to replace them with. I need you to come to Ottawa and light a fire under them." Everyone was passing the buck. If BNR, the research group of one of Canada's largest corporation, couldn't burn their subcontractors without me lighting a fire, we were in trouble.

MCI in Dallas was trying to get our first fusion sets before they were approved by Washington. Big surprise: Texans didn't trust Washington. Regional competition existed throughout the corporation. Our own operations people in Atlanta were trying to screw me by selling them the ones I needed for Washington. At the same time I was fighting off the Northern sales guy for Bell South who was complaining because I wouldn't turn the fusion sets loose. He insisted he had sold some as part of a large fiber project. It was a lie, of course; another fact of life within a corporate structure. I told him any sets coming out of BNR were going to MCI first.

He went straight to Dave to plead his case but was cut off with, "What size is the order?"

"Four million dollars," he insisted. It was peanuts, even with the exaggeration.

Dave dismissed him with a wave of the hand. "F*** off!" he said, "MCI is two hundred million."

If fusion sets got into the field before they were working properly we'd never sell any. On the other hand, if I could get them on the approved product list through normal channels, the entire Northern sales force would be able to sell them all across the country. That would open up the rest of the market to Bell, independents, and anyone else. The sets would have a track record as a working product. In this league, volume was everything.

MCI project managers were always complaining about something. If it wasn't their field guys in Chicago, Wilmington, or Dallas complaining, it was headquarters or purchasing in Washington and Arlington. In between site visits I'd be in Washington smoothing things over. The cable had a flaw where occasionally a fiber would slip out of a slot and get pinched while being cabled. Also, color coding was applied by a hokey arrangement of ink marking-pens where some pens would fade to the point of not being seen clearly. Occasionally I'd take the major MCI's project managers to Saskatoon and let them have a go at headquarters for themselves. I loved making management squirm in order to make them appreciate what I faced every day. On one trip, they told OSD in advance they wanted cowboy boots and gave them all the sizes. OSD bought six pairs of beautiful brown leather boots, and MCI was even pissed at that. The boots were Saskatchewan low-heel style, better adapted to Saskatchewan wheat fields than Washington's line-dancing bars. MCI expected Texas-style ass-kickers with high heels and some in-your-face design and color for their trips to Dallas as well.

I had another problem! Siecor's cable protected the fibers with plastic tubes. Ours were protected by a powder fill in the cable's slotted core. Splicers had to shake the powder loose before splicing and often did so while sitting in a manhole. Here's the shocker. An associate inside OSD whispered that the powder held carcinogens. If MCI had gotten wind of it they would have gone ballistic! If true, OSHA (Occupational, Safety and Health Administration) would have been all over us. At other times, stories were just plain funny. Splicers were often outdoors working in a freezing corn field. On one occasion a splicer sat in the back seat of a rental car with the motor running to keep warm. He had a buried cable coming in one window and out the other. Needless to say, he had to spend the next several hours re-splicing the cable outside in a much colder environment unless he wanted to bury the car along with it.

I soon needed a couple of field technical guys in Washington. OSD hired two from AGT International, the contracting arm of Alberta

Government Telephone. Malcolm MacGregor and Garry Forbes had spent years working for AGT in outside plant and transmission systems. Malcolm knew everything about outside plant; Garry was an engineering grad from Edmonton University. Having worked on a line gang while going to University, he knew all about both cable and electronics. Finally I had some much-needed help and less traveling. Eventually, we usurped them both from AGT International and hired them permanently in Atlanta. Visas were easy at Northern where lawyers took care of everything.

Project management sounds like the job from hell, and could have been if I hadn't enjoyed traveling. I'd go anywhere, especially if I'd never been there before. But every weekend I was home. Friday nights would usually find all of us blowing off steam around noisy extended tables at Bennigans, a popular restaurant chain. Saturdays were more likely a dinner party at one house or another.

Lesley had to drive miles through traffic to get to her downtown art classes. Thick blinding rain, and sometimes snow and ice over Atlanta's hilly terrain, worsened the traffic conditions. She hated suburbia and was getting depressed. Northern, not surprisingly, had counseling services for employees' families. House calls from their psychologist helped, but that was not the solution. She needed the city. Then she remembered something she'd heard or experienced earlier. Depression can be caused by a vitamin deficiency. She loaded up on them and it worked. The psychologist seemed downright disappointed when I gave her the explanation of why she was no longer needed. I think we both knew her problem was related to my job. If so, it would return again sooner or later.

I convinced my other Leslie to move from Toronto. She had her green card and was working for an advertising agency that rehired her in Atlanta. Malcolm and Garry became part of our social life and Garry quickly became smitten with Leslie. At first I wasn't impressed with his desire to marry her. Telephone guys were a lusty lot and engineering students were near feral during university years. He and I spent many days working and entertaining customers while in the field. I thought of him as a fellow worker and a friend, but not a son-in-law. As his fixation increased, I came around to appreciating his potential as a responsible married man. I had no choice but knowing what I know now, I would have picked him myself.

I knew even less about weddings and had little regard for over-the-top spectacles that people made of them. I also knew nothing about how young women felt about them. As usual, I delegated the matter to others while I flew off into the sunset on matters more pressing—holding a job. It was unfair of me to expect the two Lesley(ie)s to agree on such an emotional and important event. What, where, who, and how to accommodate all the out-of-town visitors was beyond any of us. Tension grew until an explosion erupted that took months to settle down. To resolve it I said, "What's all the fuss about? Why don't you just tell me how much money it'll take and go to a church and hook up?" They did. Even I was cut out. I realized what a mistake I'd made when I missed the opportunity to give her away. Not my best moment.

We'd adopted a dog and called her Georgie. What else—this was Atlanta! She was a mix of Golden Retriever and Irish Setter with a little Georgia hound thrown in. This gave her a retriever's sweet disposition overrun by the setter's instinct to run mindlessly at every opportunity. The hound contributed to her feistiness should any other dog question her heritage. I had to catch a flight to Washington, and Georgie was hell-bent on freedom. I just wanted her to pee. I tried to catch her and slipped on a patch of ice, breaking my leg. Now I had lots of time at home.

I started traveling too soon, and after a flight to Washington I developed a blood clot in my right lung. It led to a pulmonary embolism that put me in the hospital. It had to be dissolved before reaching the brain, taking me out for another month. None of it was Georgie's fault. She just gave me a nice long vacation. My new boss was a transfer from Northern or Bell Canada where most of their managers came from. Since I was in the hospital, he gave my MCI job away to Malcolm. Since Garry had taken my daughter, I felt usurped on both counts. And I thought they were friends. As a consolation prize, while still lying helpless in my hospital bed, I was offered the position of marketing manager for all the Independent telephone companies. MCI was now behind me and I couldn't have thought of a better cure. Working with telephone companies would be like coming home.

Heads were rolling everywhere! Between '84 and '86 there were many casualties. Dave was fired and took to sailing the Atlantic to explore the African coast with his kids. When he returned he was soon hired by Telco Systems, a fiber optic company located near Boston. Earlier, Telco Systems had bought Raytheon's optoelectronic division which had an ideal product applicable to the commercial market. Before long they were catapulted into the lead for high-speed transmission products. With a state-of-the-art 560 Mbps transceiver, and 45 Mbps multiplexers, they were winning huge contracts everywhere. As I watched the competition and where the contracts were going, I called him and asked, "How are you guys so successful? You're kicking our ass out here. You must be selling multiplexers faster than you can possibly build them. How are you going to keep up with the demand?"

He said, "That's the beauty of it. We don't build it. We contract our manufacturing out." *Oh, oh, I thought, this is going to be interesting.* I knew enough about manufacturing to know it was hard enough to build newly developed products in-house, never mind outside.

A few years earlier, nobody had an inkling of where this technology was going. Now the demand was staggering. And it would only be a couple more years before manufacturers, including OSD, would be doubling the 560 Mbps capacity. MCI had plenty of changes too. Very few of their management had outside plant experience. They had a high turnover rate of staff working on telecommunications. I'd seen three directors come and go as MCI flourished with profits undiminished.

Lesley's five years of being in the States was coming up. She was excited about becoming a citizen. I helped her memorize the Constitution and anything else required, to the point where I knew all the answers as well as she did. I thought I'd better join her while still saturated with the Bill of Rights and a slew of things. At her hearing, she was assigned to a plug-ugly obese judge who grilled her harshly. When he asked her if she had ever worked as a prostitute it really floored her. It took the bloom clean off all her excitement. I, on the other hand, was assigned a female judge. She merely asked a few constitutional and geographical questions before welcoming me to the fold. Had she asked me if I'd ever been a prostitute I would have accepted it as a compliment. I never thought I looked that sexy. At the swearing in ceremony, we joined a hundred others in pledging allegiance to the United States of America. Now we could vote and that was exciting enough.

In addition to the Bell market, Northern Telecom had regional sales offices in strategic areas serving the independent telephone companies all across the country. It was their primary market, a much more laid-back market than MCI or any of the baby Bells. MCI was the modern Barbarian attacking the incumbent Roman Empire—AT&T. It (MCI) was on a mission to take as much AT&T and Bell long-distance territory and business as it could. Northern dominated the US and Canadian market with their DMS line of digital central office switches. Now, they were starting to do the same in Europe and China. Even Japan was buying, and that was Nippon Electric Company's (NEC) home base. It was a remarkable coup, but nothing could stop Northern at this time in history.

My job was to represent OSD at the independent sales force's quarterly meetings and assist salespeople when calling on their outside plant customers. Transmission sales guys usually sold electronic systems but knew nothing about optical cable products. With the advent of fiber, the two products were combined, requiring them to be knowledgeable about both. I was gaining a whole new network of sales guys and telephone companies from coast to coast. Life was good, but it was only a year before the new director of marketing was replaced by my nemesis, the product line manager who had patent rights on the cable. He always wanted to move to Atlanta. Now he got his wish.

Giving a presentation, or any form of public speaking, was not my forte. In fact, I hated doing it and consequently would avoid it I could. It all went back to my childhood, when I learned very early not to make a fool of myself by doing something embarrassing. At one gigantic conference for all telephone companies in the Northeast, I was thrust on stage with a teleprompter laying out my entire speech. I'd never used a teleprompter and decided not to rehearse. In my mulishness I wasn't going to read a script written by someone unknown to me. I winged it as always. Naturally, I was awful. On another occasion in Dallas, I'd just introduced myself and suddenly my mind went blank. I must have been totally stalled for thirty seconds, which felt like minutes before I could think, let alone talk. The crowd was starting to look at each other. Another thirty seconds and they would have dialed 911. My mind was screaming at me to get back in there and take over my dumb-ass body. It finally kicked in and I continued with my usual mediocre performance.

On another occasion, in Lubbock, a different problem emerged. The air was so dry my throat seized up. I was doing just fine for the first ten or fifteen minutes and then my voice started breaking up. At first it became deep and scratchy, only to end up no better than a tightly bound squeak. I fought to get it back and felt like a fool. It hadn't occurred to me what the problem was until one guy said, "It's the dry air. I'll get you a glass of water." He saved the day. After a minute or two, while everyone patiently waited, I was able to continue. A change in climate can play funny tricks on you. One time in Manitoba I was with four engineers out to lunch after a meeting when my nose started to bleed. Nobody noticed, but I excused myself and went to the restroom to sop it up and apply paper towels with cold water on my nose. It wouldn't stop. After about twenty minutes the engineering manager decided to check in on me. He found me in front of the sink with bloody paper towels all over the place. I asked him to go back and order another round and I'd join them in a few minutes. Finally, it slowed down to the point where I could stuff both nostrils with toilet paper and get the engineers back to their office.

Because of my insecurity at public speaking, I was suspicious that my new boss had an alternative motive when he insisted I give a presentation to a major assembly of all sales and management from across the country and right up to the top of Northern. The president was even going to be there. It was my job to deliver it, but if I blew it I could be out. My speech would be following all the concise-speaking, young, professional product line managers with their smooth orations of the various products under their control. The purpose was not only to impress management, but to motivate the sales force to get out and sell products. I chose to target the later. It was our first introduction of OSD's latest cable offering and there was going to be a prize for anyone coming up with a name for it. After going over all the products, I addressed the contest. I told them the new cable was cheap, easy to make, and readily available. Then I added, "I thought maybe someone in the Western Region could come up with a name for it." Everyone laughed. Then, the Texas regional manager stood up and shouted, "I can think of a couple of names from the back door of the Pink Pony in Dallas, but would it sell?" This time everyone howled. I glanced over at the president and he, too, was laughing. Even the only two women in the room shared a smirk. Today, I would be crucified, but in those days, it secured my job for another year.

When the DMS switching division convinced headquarters they didn't need a transmission division anymore, everyone's job was at risk. Arguments would break out late at night in hotel bars between sales and marketing guys from the two divisions converging on the same customer. With the fiber interface integrated into the switch, the switching division wanted to shut down the transmission division and roll everything into switching. This would also mean dumping the transmission sales force. Nobody took them seriously. I updated my resume anyway.

For some time, Lesley and I were looking to buy in Buckhead, Atlanta's uptown. We found a house that had been on the market for months. It was there as a result of a corporate move, much like the one that got us out of Groveland. Considering how insecure my job was, it was not a good time to be buying a house. A new kitchen was needed, but we were sure we could upgrade and flip the house if worse came to worst. If so, we'd do far better with the older house in Buckhead than the larger one in Gwinette County, even with its swimming pool. That house had barely appreciated enough to cover the realtor's commission. We sold it and bought the old one in Buckhead close to Lennox Square, a super mall complex with many conveniences such as banks and medical facilities along with high-rise buildings. It was a prime property. We thought of it as an investment, and never permanent.

My days with OSD were numbered. With all the changes taking place, not just me, but everyone should have been worried. When my new boss and chief nemesis offered me a three-month severance, I knew it was worth more than that to him. He'd been waiting three years. I told him to make it six months and we'd part friends. We put the Buckhead house on the market and looked forward to returning to California. With the network I had developed while working with the independent telephone companies, getting a job would be no problem. Yeah!

Buckhead, Atlanta, Georgia – 1986.

Chapter 13

1986-92

Pleasanton, California

Back to the loop

California may have been on my mind but I wasn't on hers. My first instinct was to fly there, pick up a job, and start planning another move. It didn't happen. I swept the coast from San Diego to San Francisco and came up with nothing. High-speed toll networks were already becoming old news. Since telephony's conception, last-mile service had been restricted to voice-level frequencies over a copper pair. The big rage at this time was a modem offering low-speed data services over a telephone line. Modem sales guys were making a fortune selling data products. I resented their intrusion into my perception of telephony. Maybe it was jealousy, but I saw them as slick, fast-talking operators who snorted cocaine while driving Mercedes up and down the freeways of LA. Data was hot and I still didn't know why. I'd spent three years learning all about toll and fiber transmission, only to find out it was all happening in the loop where I started thirty-six years earlier. For the rest of the century, demand for higher speeds in that "last mile" service would increase as computers became ever more widespread.

Even the Bay Area, my home turf, was indifferent to me. At one time I had contacts in Farinon spin-offs up and down the Peninsula. Now, I was forgotten. Maybe I was done for. I'd been away too long and everything had changed. It didn't help that the first signs of another recession were already upon us. I had no idea when I'd find my next job. The fiber optic field had plenty of aspiring applicants by this time. And new emerging data products were a mystery to me, as was the market itself. I had no intention of going back into microwave; not now that I was a fiber man. In my mind, fiber superseded any phone man. Telephone companies were getting rid of them—it was cheaper to hire contractors without having to pay benefits. Many installers were taking early retirement and accepting layoffs to become contractors.

The only productive thing that happened during this trip was our house sold in my absence. The buyers wanted thirty-day occupancy. I flew home with one less problem that created another. Where would we move to? I still had no idea where the next job might come from, if ever. We couldn't move to California and then find out the next job was going to be in Atlanta, Dallas, or who knows where. I left it to the headhunters! They were the ones contracted by corporations to fill their vacancies. They would decide where we would live. Before that, we still had to move.

At least we had some cash. I had the six-month severance pay from Northern, and we'd soon have the funds from the sale of the house. It was a good feeling after eight years of bouncing around hand-to-mouth since returning to the United States. But it wouldn't last if I didn't find work soon. With a house full of furniture, two cats and a dog, we needed a place to live. It would have to be cheap. My attention was drawn to an ad for a three-bedroom house on the southwest side of Lake Lanier in the town of Cumming. It was three hundred a month. Perfect!

The owners had retired from Baltimore and were buying up affordable properties to rent out. They had just restored this one for a second time. The previous tenants had been three hard-drinking druggies who trashed the place. Their idea of fun was to use the living room wall for knife-throwing practice. I asked where they came from, thinking white southern rednecks. No, it was Michigan, right next to Ontario where I came from, proving once again the fallacy of stereotyping. The owners were happy to have a mature couple move in, animals and all. We took it for three months and filled two of the bedrooms with unpacked boxes and piled-up furniture. Surely something would happen before we had to renew the lease.

Cumming is in Forsythe County. It was one of those places the Civil Rights Movement had not yet reached. We were lucky; being white we fit right in. We could go anywhere in town and be greeted with the best of southern hospitality at coffee shops and other businesses. But not so for our movers, who were black. We'd hired them in Atlanta and they were getting nervous as the afternoon wore on. There were four of them, obviously accustomed to working together and with customers like us. At first I didn't understand, but they definitely did not want to be stuck in Cumming after dark. The Civil Rights Act may have been passed in '64, but politicians did little follow-up on implementation. Twenty-two years later nothing had changed in this town. An owner of one of the stores in town told me a tale about a black guy coming in wanting to buy a soda. He took out the soda and smashed the top off and handed it to him: "You want a soda, boy? Here you are."

Even in Atlanta many older folks stuck to the old ways. I noticed this a few months earlier when we were in Buckhead. An elderly gentleman, who in earlier times was a contractor who built many houses in the area, was talking to me in the front lawn. I commented on the weeds in my yard. He said, "Yeah, look at all those over there. Do you know what we call them? We call them cabbages because that's what the blacks eat. Yeah! They eat weeds right out of the yard." He chuckled and shook his head in disbelief. I wondered why it never occurred to him that it was likely better than starving if it was all they had. Once boiled and with a little butter and seasoning they may even have been tasty as well as nutritious. His daughter saw my pondering and whispered. "He's just old. That's the way it used to be."

When we bought the house, she commented that we were lucky to have such nice neighbors. She said, "Some are in their nineties, but they are wonderful people and have been here forever." The house had been empty for some time, and even after the sales sign came down it took us a while to move in. My first conversation with the elderly couple next door was enlightening. "Welcome," he said in way of greeting. "The house was empty for a long time and we knew why: Some black people must have bought it. They were just too embarrassed to move in. I'm glad we were wrong." I had hoped we would be accepted for something better than our color. The old gent from across the street was said to be highly respected, too. He didn't get out much and I never called on him. I'd heard enough about how it used to be. It was difficult enough to come to grips with the residue. I think they were afraid of change more than they were of another color. I lived for change.

Before Buckhead, our welcome in Gwinette County had been little better. Everyone had children in elementary or high schools. Church and sports, not only predominated, but were inseparable. The only difference between the Catholics and the Baptists was the Catholics put on their best clothes for church and went casual to their dances in the basement. The Baptists dressed casual for church and saved their best for the dance. Bloodlust was saved for sports.

Except for the family next door, we never fit in with any of them. When that family moved to Texas, the rest of the neighbors treated us as carpetbaggers not to be fully trusted: Even after we gave our best effort, their children toilet-papered the tree in our front yard. In Cummings we were suspect too. Our neighbors on one side were standoffish to the point of never speaking to us during our entire stay. After the previous tenants, who could blame them? On the other side lived a widower of Scots/Irish/Cherokee decent. He loved to pull up a couple of plastic chairs in his driveway to shoot the breeze with his daughter when she visited. I think it was his patio. He remained reserved toward us, but after a few weeks he opened up. He told me his son was flying one of the jets that had just bombed Gaddafi in Libya. Maybe that's what makes America great—hawks and doves, good cop, bad cop—the stuff that makes the world love and fear us at the same time.

Most southerners were good Christians capable of disarming anyone with their folksy craftiness. They were charming on the outside, but many carried a conditioned bias on the inside that insisted blacks were inferior to them. I found it ironic that they could be so nice, and then as if a switch was thrown, filled with suspicion and hate—another word for fear. White or not, we were outsiders and it would take a while; certainly longer than we were planning on staying in Cumming.

Cumming was a good place to hole-up in for a while. When I wasn't working the phone looking for a job, we enjoyed sailing off our dock on Lake Lanier. The three-month deadline was getting close and still there was nothing. The headhunters for the telecom industry had positions for regional sales managers in companies manufacturing products for a few Bell companies—mostly in the wrong place for me. It would be brutal in Chicago and New York, or even Atlanta and Dallas where I had few contacts. You had to be a political strategist, a smooth diplomat, a good manager and a golfer all rolled into one. And maybe a back-slapping, joke-telling salesman as well; I was none of the above. I was not looking for a title and I didn't want the pressure of meeting big quotas and managing other people. I didn't want to be a regional manager anywhere; they were always first to go. Any ambition I had for advancement had long since dissipated. I no longer had anything to prove to anyone, mostly myself.

We wanted to return to California. I wasn't getting any younger and needed something I could hang on to. There were plenty of younger guys willing to scramble for the big accounts. All I wanted was a job. It just had to be under the right circumstances. Something I could enjoy with a bit of security. Like a squirrel, I needed to start accumulating for the long winter quickly closing in.

It was a long three months, and then, as always, the unexpected happened.

After an amazing string of successes Telco Systems put their foot in it. They overstepped and had a meltdown. Up to this point their fiber success was largely due to the state-of-the-art military technology acquired from Raytheon. After winning numerous Bell contracts, they won one of the largest in the history of the industry, with PacBell. Then, they failed to deliver a working product in time. PacBell threw them out and sued for millions. Adding insult to injury they forced them to supply Nippon Electric's (NEC) 400 Mbps product to fulfill the contract. Telco Systems' chairman of the board appointed himself CEO and took drastic steps in order to save the company. He had to write off millions of dollars in their auto-dialer product line in Fremont, California. Much of upper management included my former boss, Dave, and over half the sales force was fired. The director of sales survived long enough to hire me and a few others, for the new sales team, before they fired him as well.

I had interviewed with ITT's fiber division, but the VP of sales seemed indecisive. I realized why when I discovered he too was on his way out. ITT's fiber products were not doing well against Siecor and Northern. Neither of us knew we were being interviewed by Telco at the same time, but I was hired first, for PacBell. Considering the recent law suit, I couldn't imagine a tougher assignment. The ITT guy was hired as the national VP of sales to replace Dave. His first act was to hire a friend of his to be the PacBell regional sales manager, my new boss. Neither one of them knew anything about optoelectronic products. Neither of them lasted long, either. As you can see, it was getting brutal—no more Mr. Nice Guy as the industry grew ever more competitive.

It was the same at Northern Telecom. I never thought they would close the transmission division and role it into switching, but I was wrong. They did, or at least they tried. No sooner was I hooked up with Telco Systems than Northern fired their entire transmission sales force. Suddenly, the market was flooded with telecom sales people, all scrambling for jobs. Even their VP of sales was out. He was hired as the president of Telco System's digital channel bank division in Fremont, and immediately started re-hiring his former sales force. Northern realized they paid a price for the foolish move after they started losing market share with Bell companies. Outside plant facilities were still separate and worlds apart from central office switching. Telephone company transmission engineers needed to be called on by a sales force they could talk to. Within a year, Northern had to reverse the decision and hire a new sales force. It wouldn't be their last mistake.

Telco System's new CEO/chairman also hired a president for the fiber division in Norwood. Both presidents were relatively new in their positions and had totally different ideas on what products were needed and how to run the business. With them at each other's throats, the CEO/chairman became tired of wearing two hats. He needed one of the two presidents to be the fulltime CEO. Both of them wanted the job in order to fire the other. After a prolonged battle, our guy in Fremont thought he had it. At a last-hour dinner meeting, the Norwood president convinced the CEO/chairman that it should be him. His first act as CEO was to fire our guy. The shuffling, hiring, and firings continued amid the battle of the big egos as the industry continued to expand. I was far enough down the food chain to wonder who the next VP of the month would be. In spite of it all, Telco Systems was coming back. Me too!

Pleasanton, California, was often touted as the city of the future. You could see it in the developing industrial park with the new, overbearing AT&T headquarters dominating a central position. Next to it was the soon-to-be-completed BART station that would connect people directly to Oakland and San Francisco. It would take a while, but in 2009, *Forbes* magazine would name Pleasanton as "one of Americans' top hometown spots." And after a Wall Street endorsement in 2014, *USA Today* listed it one of the fifty best cities in America to live. It was the future, but Pleasanton had preserved the quaintness of its early pioneering history. Back then it was known as the most desperate town in the west, called Alisal for the sycamore trees that abounded on the old Rancho Santa Rita. It was a stopping place for prospectors taking their gold to the banks. Shootouts in the streets were common, giving it much commonality with America today. The Alameda county fairground with the race track is still popular. How could we not want to live there?

Lesley's son Trevor, now divorced, had just received his green card and found work at the local radio station. He moved in with us for his three-month gratis period and his daughter Jessica was able to visit as well.

Jessica and Trevor

My son, Daniel, was married. He and his wife Debbie had jobs, promising careers, and had a son, Mathew. They had green cards, but it just wasn't the right time for them. It was in Pleasanton where Lesley started getting some recognition for her artwork although she had to travel to Burlingame across the San Mateo Bridge for art classes. There were art shows every year in downtown Pleasanton, but art is always the first item people cut back on during financial slumps. We could easily identify with the gold-rush folks who stopped for refuge on their way to the bank.

When stock markets crashed around the world, in '87, it became known as "Black Monday." Even Japan crashed after enjoying one of the greatest rides in history and stayed that way for decades. The United States still had legs in spite of the debt being tripled—from $712 billion, to over $2 trillion—between 1980 and '88. It was a debt that would haunt George H.W. Bush and cost him a second term. The only thing crashing in California was the ground we stood on: The Southern California earthquake in '87 measured

5.9, followed by another along the San Andreas Fault (6.9) in '89. We rode out the second one while living in Pleasanton. All our neighbors gathered around to watch reruns of Oakland's collapsed freeways and Bay Bridge, on a portable TV, in our driveway. AT&T had already moved out, leaving an empty compound of buildings in the now-struggling industrial park. With Black Monday, everything was put on hold; everything but telecommunications.

We bought a second place in Groveland and went back to the old habit of spending weekends in the mountains. Pine Mountain Lake had a beautiful man-made lake with a couple of parks and sandy beaches. If we weren't at the Iron Door Saloon, we were at the Country Club where they still had a private golf course, a good bar, and a dining room. Our first house, a few years earlier, was near the PML airport next to the equestrian center. This time we bought on the side of a mountain surrounded by towering pine trees. In the late sixties, the lumber barons of Boice Cascade developed the property as a way of leaving something behind after stripping the mountain of timber.

It started in the Hetch Hetchy Valley, where Native Americans lived for thousands of years before the arrival of Europeans. It was a valley every bit as beautiful as Yosemite, but destined to be dammed up in 1934 to create the water reservoir for San Francisco. Downstream—the Tuolumne River runs past Groveland at an elevation around 1000 feet lower. The run-off for the aqueduct to San Francisco runs right through Groveland. If John Muir had not taken Teddy Roosevelt camping in 1903, Yosemite Valley would never have been protected as a federal park. It would be buried in water for the flatlanders in the same manner as Hetch Hetchy. It may still be, depending on how much we value it, or need the water.

My regional manager had no previous Bell experience. I told him, "You take PacBell with all the money and glory, and I'll take the independents and end-users." Everyone wanted a Bell account. That's where the money was; compared to the widely scattered and lowly populated independent telephone companies. He bought it!

Central Telephone Company provided telephone services in several states. In Nevada it was commonly known as Centel of Nevada; an overstatement considering it confined itself to Las

Vegas. The rest of Nevada, aside from PacBell in Reno, was covered by very small independent companies. Centel had the same complaints in Las Vegas that PacBell had. They'd both received the same Telco Systems premature product release. After deploying the new fiber terminals and multiplexers in all their central offices, they were contemplating filing their own lawsuit. But they hadn't yet. Telco Systems had two permanent crews of installers changing out backplanes, and refurbishing everything as quickly as possible. They could not afford to have another PacBell fiasco. Neither could I.

At my first meeting with the engineering manager, he had his blackboard completely filled with every problem I'd just inherited. They didn't want to throw us out yet, but they expected us to fix the product. This was better than working with Bell where every sales call was a committee meeting with no individual decisions. I told him to leave the list up on the board until we knocked off every problem. Eventually, the blackboard was a clean slate and they continued buying over the next fifteen years of rapid expansion. It coincided nicely with all the time I had left.

I'd visited Las Vegas in the sixties, back when Howard Hughes was pulling strings from some darkened room. Casinos were drawing big-business gaming, but obviously it was flat-out gambling for anyone with money to lose. Having lost Cuba, gambling interests selected Las Vegas to build a people magnet. Now, in the eighties, *mega-casino* resorts were being built and they've been building them ever since. For the next fifteen years it was my town—at least in terms of the fiber backbone. As far as I was concerned, nothing had to stay in Vegas except Telco Systems, and me. The engineering manager had his favorite lunch spots. He and his wife always enjoyed quiet dinners in a couple of the good restaurants off the strip. I was happy that he was not a golfer. The rest of the engineers, along with their wives, liked the steak houses in the Casinos where they could play the slots for a while after dinner. We went to many shows over the years.

After my regional manager was fired, I was stuck with PacBell again. By this time there had been so many changes in Telco's management that I now had the title of *Director of Sales - Western Region* on my business card. A nice title always opened more doors and got you further up the food chain than just *Dumb-ass Salesman* on your card. PacBell needed to be stroked, but there was little likelihood of them buying any time soon. I didn't waste much time on them. That was something management in Norwood never understood. They wanted that account back and eventually assigned it to someone else. There was a lot of turnover. Their second or third attempt to fill the position was given to an aggressive lady with the promise of all the money she was going to make from commissions and bonuses. When she discovered there was no way *even she* could break into PacBell, she found a way to break into Telco Systems. She quit and sued them for all the lost commissions and time wasted. She made more money than the rest of who were still busting our butts. It may have been an equal employment opportunity, but I was damn sure I could never have gotten away with it.

  I covered everything non-Bell west of Texas and all of Canada. Most of the sales force considered it too much work with too little return, which was true. I had to search for local business everywhere, but I preferred doing that than ingratiating myself with executives by playing golf. How I survived is a mystery when you consider the number of those who didn't during that time. It was often the ones with oversized egos whose performance never measured up to their crowing, who got the axe. I maintained a low profile and never promised too much. But not where Las Vegas was concerned. Without PacBell, nobody at headquarters wanted to risk losing Centel's business. Every other success over the rest of my domain was merely a plus.

As the Internet evolved, residential and business services became more sophisticated. Software-defined networking (SDN) technologies prevailed. This was the start of newly invented acronyms describing business ventures soon to be Bell's worst nightmare. ISDN (integrated services digital network) was their preferred offering, but a host of others would soon outperform it. Incumbent local exchange carriers (ILECs), like Bell and the independents, still held a monopoly on landline services. But CAPs and CLECs (competitive access providers and competitive local exchange carriers) started up their own fiber networks and switches that competed with them. The law required incumbents to rent their competition a PoP (point of presence) in their exchanges. Now, CAPs and CLECs could compete with their own dial tone while using Bell's offices and copper lines. Bell was losing the last-mile business to the new service providers. Even more intrusive was the

Internet access from computers which could tie up switches and overload the network for hours at a time.

T-1 digital channel banks (twenty-four channels using two pairs of wires) had been around for years in the network. Newbridge, from Canada, came out with customer-premises multiplexer that proved to be strong competition for Telco Systems' product. There was plenty of business to go around. Eventually the market became saturated with so many of them. We soon introduced a line of low-speed fiber products for delivering four T-1s to small business premises that could carry up to four channel banks delivering a total of ninety-six voice circuits over fiber. With personal computers abounding, more data circuits were in demand. Many high-speed data cards were developed to share T-1 lines connected to channel banks formerly used for voice.

I had plenty of customers scattered over a very large territory. Alaska was a favorite location where Anchorage Telephone and Utility (ATU) was my largest customer, with Matanuska Telephone a distant second. During my fifteen years of traveling there, I watched the Portage Glacier virtually disappear. At first it was a famous roadside attraction with a visitor center attracting tour buses and thousands of tourists. As the glacier receded to a rocky outcrop, the icebergs melted into a pristine lake. The parking lot gave way to weeds and the building receded into its own decline. Yet, global warming was still a myth.

One of my Alaska customers from Wasilla was selling satellite earth stations in Russia. Unfortunately, a Russian company was also selling to the government and Russians didn't appreciate competition. They hired an ex-military, black-belt-type bodyguard to beat him to a pulp as they left a Moscow restaurant one night. Since his government "protection" stood by and did nothing, he refused to be taken to a hospital where he figured they'd finish the job. Instead, he demanded to be taken to his hotel. He called his wife and told her to get him out of Russia. He didn't care how, or what it cost, but he needed to be in a hospital as soon as possible. Three days later he was finally flown back and had his broken body attended to. Needless to say he gave up on selling satellite systems in Russia. We both preferred a system where competition was supposed to make you better, until it didn't.

Another customer, in Las Vegas, made up for the small amount of business I received from them, by virtue of being an interesting enigma wrapped in a mystery. It was a large contract firm working for the US government. Everything was so secret you could barely get in the building. And if you did, your contact would walk you to his office while repeating in a loud voice, "Civilian in the building, civilian in the building." I assumed I was such a pariah that everyone had to stop talking long enough to cover their desks and lock the doors. They were working on weird stuff for Area 51, where rumor had it a UFO was being studied. I asked Centel's engineering manager about this and he was absolutely sure of it. Whatever was going on, it's still going on today and it's still a secret. Is that what's meant by *What happens in Vegas, stays in Vegas*?

While living in Pleasanton we bought a 1910 heritage home in Bellingham, WA. We rented it out for five years before moving in. During those years the San Juan Islands tormented me with the idea of getting an inboard cuddy cabin for cruising around the islands between Bellingham and Victoria. I persuaded Lesley we would be located midway between two great cities, Vancouver and Seattle, with Mount Baker for a backdrop. I would convert the old garage into a studio where she could sell her paintings. We could sit in the front sunroom and watch the ships and sailboats on Bellingham Bay. There were many good restaurants to enjoy at the Marina, and all in all it was a good place to retire one day.

Chapter 14

1992-97

Bellingham, Washington

ISDN (It Still Does Nothing)

Moving to Bellingham had nothing to do with work. In the early nineties my daughter Leslie and her husband Garry were living in Seattle, where Melanie was born. Garry had been hired by Northern Telecom after they decided to rehire a new sales team. I wanted a home in the Northwest so we'd live closer in years to come. Thanks to the new emerging technologies it wasn't necessary to wait until retirement. I was able to work from home, or anywhere, and still cover the same customers over a very large territory.

The only downside was we had to hook up all over again. Think about it! There's telephone, power, gas, TV, post office, voter registration, car and driver licenses, and even more things, all needing attention. It's almost enough to turn you off moving, but not quite. It's the newness of the experience that's addictive. It's the purging of old habits and stereotypical thinking while simultaneously opening up new channels of thought that are beneficial in so many ways. Each part of the country has its own characteristics, each city is uniquely different. You only get to know them by living there.

I took a U.S. Coast Guard Auxiliary Marine Safety course and bought a cabin cruiser. I'd had boats before, but this was a whole new experience. Tides are tricky in coastal waters, and navigation skills are essential. Any place is safe enough with a good captain but I made no claim to that distinction. We did it anyway and managed to fulfill my ambition of exploring the San Juan Islands. I was more competent in a canoe where we enjoyed river trips from inland drop-points, down to the Bay. But all of it had to wait.

First, we needed to renovate the house. All the carpets and wallpaper had to be removed. We had the hardwood floors sanded and finished with the hardest surface available. It was a product that was shortly going to be banned due to its toxicity. The strength came from a formaldehyde ingredient and we had to vacate the house for three days before entering. The floors looked great, easy to clean, and probably have no scratches to this day. The wiring in the house was called knob and tube. It was done with porcelain knobs, cleats, and tubes to separate the insulated single wires and isolate them from contact with building surfaces for safety reasons. I undertook the job of rewiring the house. You needed a licensed electrician to get a permit, so I hired one to hook up a new 200 amps service entrance panel and do the external grounding. I did the wiring, fished the walls, and hooked up all the outlets, fixtures and switches.

Landscaping was a big job too. We'd rented the house to five different tenants over the years. The lawn was large and all the trees were overgrown. I trimmed the trees and reduced the size of the lawn by surrounding it with mulch. Then there was the studio for Lesley. There was a newer double garage for cars at the end of the driveway, but the old original single garage next to the alley was getting dilapidated. A huge old cedar had grown so large it took over the entrance. I removed the garage door to put in a glass sliding door and added a skylight. Also, by adding French doors on the side, it opened to a patio and became Lesley's art studio. The basement was already finished with recreation room, bedroom, and a bathroom. All I had to do was add a kitchen to call it a self-contained in-law suite for which we had no in-laws. Oscar would have loved it. It even had a billiard table. A new paint job on the exterior and it was looking good. All it needed was a wrought iron fence with gate across the driveway for the place to look like a grand old estate.

Every time I filled out a job application, I indicated I was a high school graduate. I had so many certificates from night schools, correspondence courses, college credits, and other seminars that I never thought a high school diploma important. On impulse I wrote my old high school to see if they had a matriculation program for adults by correspondence. Sure enough, they did. While I was at it, I wrote Lesley's high school and asked them to forward her academic records to the same school in order that they could include her as well. She was appalled to find out it was so easy for me to access her private information but went along with the program anyway. It took us a year to complete all the work. This time we were both honor students. Not that it mattered. Our days of worrying about such details were long passed. At last we had time to enjoy the Northwest and that's what we were there for.

Every so often we visited friends in Vancouver. On one occasion we included Reggie, who lived with my family after getting out of the Navy when my son Daniel was around five. At that time, they shared a basement bedroom in North Vancouver. After becoming a mechanic Reggie owned a garage business on the northwest side of Okanogan Lake across from Kelowna. He'd developed some close friendships with Native Americans on the reservation and was still promoting land deals in the area. Later, when he visited Ontario, Daniel went to pick him up at Union Station in Toronto. As he waited for him to show up he got interested in this rough-looking character sitting at the bar. He thought it strange to see a traveler using a saddlebag for luggage. Who travels with a saddlebag? Finally it hit him. It was his uncle Reggie.

Now he was a realtor in Langley. After his predictable divorce, he lived a rather bizarre bachelor life. The first thing I saw as I entered town was a large sign with his name covering the side of a commercial building he was selling. In spite of his image he was still a rough-talking Navy guy, which did little for his real estate persona. I found it interesting that the thought of seeing a doctor had never occurred to him. Ironically, a few years later he died in his sleep.

Lesley was the healthcare guru in our family. We had to find new doctors and a dentist. It's the most important decision you have to make. Sometimes it's the most difficult one. Often doctors are not taking new patients, especially the good ones you would want. If you can get a referral from one of their patients you may succeed, but chances are you'll end up with someone unsatisfactory. Many people take health for granted and put it out of their mind until something needs attention. Depending on the ailment, sometimes it's too late.

In 1993, when Harry Lockwood found out he had prostate cancer, he sent a letter to all his friends advising them to have their PSA checked. The first doctor I had in Bellingham turned out to be a geriatric specialist. He actually inflicted pain during a simple check-up. The second doctor was a young cyclist. When I mentioned a minor back pain, he wanted me to see a surgeon and ran down the hall to consult with one. The specialist quickly sent him back, but I'd already decided I'd pass on that. When I asked him about a PSA check he wouldn't do it. According to him, no doctors in the Northwest did it because you were more likely to die in a car wreck than from prostate cancer. He claimed that if they checked and found you were positive, the treatment would be worse than the disease, leaving you incontinent, in diapers, and impotent. Since the disease is slow growing, they argued, ignoring it was better due to the majority of men outliving it. That's a nice way of saying you'll be dead before knowing you are a victim. Many doctors still adhere to more or less that same philosophy today. No doubt they have the statistics to prove their point. Most men don't care if it's one in a thousand or a hundred thousand; they just don't want to be the one. Part of the problem is that the treatment is very expensive unless you have good insurance. Obviously it's too expensive in the eyes of insurance companies, and government funded health plans as well.

Women were universally advised to undergo regular mammogram screenings. When Lesley became concerned about a lump in her breast, her doctor wasn't. He recommended doing nothing: "Calcium build-up is common; we'll wait and keep an eye on it."

She got better advice from my daughter, Leslie. "Don't trust this to any doctors up there," she insisted. "Go to the teaching hospital at the University of Washington in Seattle." Leslie's first baby, Melanie, was born there. A good friend in California weighed in and said the same thing. Her daughter had graduated from UW. They both said, "The place is fabulous and have the best doctors."

We took their advice and went to Seattle where they took cancer seriously. The resident cancer surgeon may have had the bedside manners of a crane operator, but he was the best breast cancer surgeon in Seattle. There was a small lump in Lesley's left breast, but he was more concerned about the other side. A biopsy proved him right. It was malignant. A plastic surgeon was brought in for joint consultation on what to do. Surgery was necessary, but should it be a single mastectomy, or bilateral just to be sure? We discussed whether the left side should be cut into as well. What would reconstruction look like if it was single or bilateral surgery? No woman ever wants to make these decisions. Neither do their spouses. We agreed on the bilateral procedure. The plastic surgeon would take over after the cancer surgeon had finished. The lump in the right breast had to be removed, and the left breast was found to be completely filled with tiny cancer cells peppered all over. Seventeen lymph nodes had to be removed from the left armpit to prevent spreading. The doctors had just saved her life by recommending a bilateral mastectomy.

Hospitals typically feel it's necessary to kick you out as soon as possible after surgery. After spending a night of not even knowing if she would survive, I showed up the following morning to find her alive but looking like death warmed over. Her pain medication button wasn't functioning and she had very little sleep. The head nurse came in and immediately got her out of bed to start pacing the floor, all the while telling her how bad her left arm would be from now on. "Oh yeah, with all those lymph nodes removed, that arm will be swollen twice the size of the other one. Best thing to do is hold it straight up for much of the time to keep the swelling down. You'll have to be careful not to get a cut, insect or cat bite, on that one; it could kill you." After a short walk she almost forgot the pain while contemplating the collateral damage from having her body ravaged and irrevocably altered.

Yet, the nurse looked at me and said, "You don't look so good." I was thinking of strangling her. "Do you want a private room, to be alone and compose yourself?"

I nodded, "Yes, please," and she showed me to a small waiting room across the hall. Then it all came out: The tension for the last several weeks of not knowing if she would live, the horrible decisions to make, the worry about the operation, and then showing up to find her being bullied out of bed to march the hall while listening to the prognosis from hell. For the second time in my life I broke down. I was grateful that Margie Fink, our Palo Alto friend—the one in whose garden we were married in—had shown up the day before for moral support. But, I'd no sooner broken down than Maggie was ushered into my sanctuary by the nurse. I didn't want anyone looking at me in this state. The nurse asked again, "Are you alright? Would you like to see the doctor?"

All I wanted was for everyone to get the hell out and leave me alone for a few minutes. Without waiting for an answer, she left Maggie and ran down the hall to get the doctor while I was trying to get a grip. They quickly returned while I was still looking like a fool, only now in front of a room full of spectators. The doctor used his well-honed bedside manner to say, "What's the matter with you? Don't you realize I just saved your wife's life?" He was pissed off that I wasn't acting appropriately, with unrestrained gratitude for his skill. The only way to get out of there was to acknowledge how much I appreciated him and go for a walk, leaving the room to all of them.

I didn't hesitate to take Lesley home as soon as possible. She was recovering faster than I was. They showed me how to empty the drain cup on both sides and take care of all the dressings for the next couple of weeks. I enjoyed playing nurse and it was a battle to keep others away, especially Wendy who wanted to help. Telco System said to take as much time as I needed. Three weeks later we were at a national sales meeting in Tucson where everyone, including Lesley, went on a trail ride into the hills. Often cancer returns within fifteen years. She's now been cancer-free for over twenty. Sadly, and more poignant, our neighbor in Bellingham went into the local hospital for some surgery. Three months later he died in excruciating pain from having an instrument left in his abdomen.

A traveling salesman has to put up with much air travel and many airport delays. Too much time on one's hands can lead to dangerous contemplation. There was an incident from my misspent youth that periodically rose to the surface. In 1952, on my last summer vacation in Brights Grove, I met a First Nation lady also on vacation in a cottage close by. After a few days we had a very brief affair—a one-of—and never saw her again. Several years later, while on vacation in Sarnia, I was told she had a child she claimed was mine. Nothing came of it. I was three thousand miles away and married with my own children by then. Forty years later I still carried a sense of remorse over the possibility I was responsible.

Maybe it was just curiosity, but I took steps to track her down and found her in Alberta. When I talked to her by phone, I asked if her daughter was born in May. She not only confirmed it, but with little choice after so many years, she stuck to her story that I was the father. Her daughter was there too, married, with three of her own children. All of them were living on the reservation. This bothered me even more. She saw no reason for me to meet her daughter, but I said, "Ask, and let her decide."

The daughter was agreeable. On my next sales call to AGT (Alberta Government Telephone) in Calgary, and since it was May and close to her birthday, I took the next step and paid them a visit. I even brought some presents for her daughter and the children. This was going to be a difficult trip and I still didn't know why I was doing it.

After a long drive north, I pulled off the highway onto the reservation to find myself between two large complexes. They were the Community Centers for two different tribes, one on each side of the aisle just like Republicans and Democrats. I had no idea which camp she was in, but I knew neither would want my vote. For the next five miles the spring thaw had turned gravel road into a sea of slush. My rental car was constantly bombarded with waves of mud thrown by oncoming four-wheel pickups. Hard looking men with curious eyes, suspicious and unwelcoming, stared sideways at me while passing. They could see I was a stranger, white, and out of place. I could see I was not welcome. Eventually, I found my turn and continued down an ever-narrowing road past a couple of widely spaced houses. I found theirs at the end of the road, out of sight in a cluster of trees.

The daughter's husband had built on a piece of land where his uncle used to keep horses. With no deed, title, or transfer, they still squabbled over who had the right of use—them with the house, or the uncle with the old horses. All but the uncle and his horses were there to meet me. First was the mother, followed by daughter and husband standing before three children. A cousin presented me with a card indicating she worked for the government's family services. This was not looking good.

I broke the ice with presents for the children and we sat down for a visit. Maybe I could take them out to dinner? I gathered from their reaction it was out of the question. Possibly there were no restaurants on the reservation; at least I hadn't seen any. I got the impression they were not in the habit of dining with white men, on or off the res. I overheard a side conversation about how the daughter had been treated rudely by a lady who owned a wool store off the reservation. They had pride and bitterly resented being rebuffed by standoffish people who thought they were better than them. So far, they showed no angst toward me.

I was well aware of the problems natives faced ever since the European invasion hundreds of years earlier. In the fifties, while working in Vancouver, I'd seen the tragic results of leaving reservation life. Skid row was full of derelict alcoholics and young girls drawn into prostitution trying to survive in a white man's world. Even today there is little accounting for the lost and missing.

People I knew never admitted to being less than hospitable to Native Americans. It started with the breaking of treaties, to forced schooling, to corporate exploitation of their lands, and a host of other things including the lack of government interest in doing anything about missing, abused, and murdered females. We only see the alcoholism, crime and poverty, leaving us to believe that spending money on them is a waste of tax-payer dollars.

In recent years, the Canadian government tried to implement a $2 billion education program for native people. But the leaders rejected it and forced out the First Nation's national chief, Shawn Atleo, who had negotiated it. In 2015 the prime minister himself was voted out and replaced by another who promised $2.6 billion in education and another $500 million for infrastructure for schools. If true, it would improve the situation for generations to come. Others felt they should be allowed to live as they choose, but that's a decision better left to them after they're educated. Maybe one day they'll have their own premiers and prime ministers. And maybe that's what we fear most.

There was nothing lacking in their education or hospitality when I showed up out of the blue. Possibly they were somewhat nervous, and suspicious. I know I was. As the conversation progressed it was the daughter's husband who decided the issue of dinner. He pulled out a carving knife and trimmed up a roast of venison as skillfully as any muleskinner. I don't know which of my body parts twitched the most—scalp or testicles. When dinner was almost over, I raised a question that could have decided this issue too.

"Well, young lady, I guess this must be pretty close to your birthday?" She was already in her forties, but I had a present for her, too. I just hadn't given it to her yet. I was still wrestling with my own reservation.

"Oh no," she said. "My birthday was in March."

Whoa! I composed myself. This revelation sent me nearly slack-jawed to the point of dropping my fork with a clatter on the plate. I never saw it coming. It was like being dealt an ace to complete a straight with all the chips on the table. I swung a quick glance at her mother who was busy at the sink. She'd been following every word. I caught her just in time to see her snap back to the dishes. Both our heads jerked in such rapid succession that I doubt anyone noticed except the husband. He didn't talk much, but his dark eyes missed nothing. I didn't know how good his math was, but I'd already counted my fingers and knew there were nine months from August to May. If she was born in March, she couldn't be mine. I would never have known that if I hadn't always taken my vacation at the end of August. That's when I met her mother. I always wanted to enjoy that last two weeks of August to combine them with Labor Day before going back to school or work. And enjoy I did. No damn wonder she told me I didn't need any protection.

Keeping my cool, I asked, "Really? And what was your weight?" It sounded like something a good old-boy daddy might ask. I had other intentions.

"Seven and a half pounds," she said proudly.

Good, I thought, *nothing premature about that.* "Wow," I beamed, "you must have been a fine healthy baby?"

"Oh yes, I was," she laughed agreeably. Indeed, we were sharing a special moment.

The festivities continued unabated as the children got involved in making homemade ice-cream. To me, accustomed to pulling it out of a freezer, it looked like a lot of work. The children were having fun as they energetically did most of the work. I was wistfully eyeing the front door when the cousin brought out a camera for a group photo. Or was it to be a family photo? My mind was racing to find an exit plan. I checked to ensure that the birthday card and present were still tucked safely away in my pocket. Yep, still there! Bringing them out now could only make matters worse. All the grand thoughts of accountability and hail-fellow-well-met had tanked faster than a lead head feather. I could feel it sagging in my face and it must have been evident to all. Her cousin, from behind the camera, said, "Don't look so sad, smile!"

I forced myself. It shouldn't have been hard because I wasn't the least bit sad. I was happy! I'd been carrying this baby for forty some years. I just needed to find a way off the reservation before dropping it on them. But after such a generous reception, they deserved an explanation. Except for the mother, she'd more likely stick to her own story. Somehow, I had to break the news to them. I could just blurt it out, but who would they believe, me, or her? I could foresee a confrontation between us with me at a serious disadvantage. They'd say, "Another example of white man screwing over the natives." Between me and the freeway was five miles of native bucks looking for payback time.

I took the daughter aside, and said, "Something has come up. I can't tell you now, but I'll call you tomorrow and explain." It was the same old trick Dave used to pull when we called on MCI if they were pressing us for better pricing. He'd say, "I can't give you an answer on that right now, but I have an idea in the works. Give me a couple of days and I'll get back to you." Of course he never did. But I intended to! She needed to be convinced more than I needed someone else's daughter who came with her own three children.

With no further discussion, I got in the car and retraced my steps back off the reservation. Once on the highway, heading south, I had time to contemplate the entire fiasco. I'd arrived with an attitude of let the chips fall where they may, and put this to rest forever. For years I'd pushed it aside, refusing to admit any culpability. I was okay with that. Only lately had it grown into an interest. That just wasn't like me. It took me totally by surprise. One thing led to another until it had to be done in spite of my better judgment. It was as if I were driven by some unknown force knowing the truth that I was innocent all along. I just needed to prove it to myself. Who is capable of such twisted reasoning? Certainly not me! Other than something beyond reason, I had no idea what drove me to such an extreme. I just knew it had to be done, and I had no compunction about doing it. The revelation of her birthday lit up the room like a bolt of lightning. It revealed that I wasn't culpable at all. This wasn't the first time I'd landed on my feet after some shambles of my own making. This one topped them all! The drive back to Calgary seemed infinitely shorter than the one going.

I made the call the next morning. She seemed unconcerned about my explanation. I suggested we produce blood samples, but she wasn't interested in that either. By this time she may have known more about the subject than I did. I don't know what the others thought of my appearance from out of nowhere, only to disappear. If I left a favorable impression with any it would have to rest on the children. Perhaps they'd accept that I was the Lone Ranger. At least that's how I felt as I boarded Air Canada for the flight home. Hi ho Silver—awayyy!

When we first moved into the Bellingham house, a group of people stopped to mill around on our corner lot one night. Since there was no fence and several large trees to conceal them at that time, they polished off their beers while taking a pee. I wasn't sure what their next move was, so I called the police. The group was gone by the time they arrived. Later, we understood they were on their way back to the Lummi Reservation, a few miles west of Bellingham. These were the original people inhabiting the Puget Sound, who for centuries were hell-bent on exploring the same San Juan Islands that I was.

One day, while island-cruising with Lesley and her son Derek, we were moving along at about thirty-five knots when suddenly we were pulled to a complete and unexpected stop. The prop had caught on a fishnet strung across the entire strait between Anacortes and Lopez Island. While I was trying to free it without too much cutting, a family of fishermen showed up. They were not happy.

"Didn't you see the buoys?" one of them shouted angrily. He was a young man at the helm. The crew consisted of a young girl around twelve and a middle-aged, tough-looking, battle-scarred Neanderthal standing in the bow. He was of an age to be a Vietnam vet and very likely the father and grandfather of the other two. I would have liked to befriend the younger two, but one look at the older one squashed any attempt. Anyway, at thirty-five knots I was more likely looking straight ahead rather than to the left or right looking for buoys. I looked, and still I saw nothing. I gave them the universal body language—hunched shoulders with open hands while frowning—to make them understand I didn't know shit.

"There," shouted the one I took to be captain, while the older one's eyes pierced straight through me. He pointed toward the mainland and then over toward Lopez. I still couldn't see a thing, but then, they were known to have better eyesight than any white man. While freeing my prop to ensure a clean get away, I gave them my phone number and told them to call if I owed them anything for the damage. They never called and probably it was illegal. I wasn't going to suggest it with that guy riding shotgun. The locals bitched all the time about how Native Americans got away with fishing privileges they didn't have. I'm sure the fishermen did their share of bitching too, about people like me despoiling their fishing grounds and property with no apparent purpose.

I found Native Americans interesting. Depending on my mood I'd sometimes give them a ride. One day, two women were hitchhiking on the street near where we lived. We picked them up and gave them a ride to the reservation. One said she had lung cancer but gave it little consideration while fidgeting with a pack of cigarettes. When we arrived, family members were sitting around a bonfire in the front yard. They looked up, surprised and questioning, but not likely to invite us to join them. The two ladies, however, joined them with a cocky flair. They were enjoying their latest coup of having duped a couple of pale-skins into chauffeuring them home.

On another occasion, we'd just climbed the freeway ramp on our way to Seattle airport when we stopped for a man with a four-year-old child. They were Lakota, descendants of the Sioux Warriors who fought in the Battle of the Little Big Horn. While in North Dakota, he and some of his friends showed up to register for the army. The next thing they knew they were in San Diego training with the Navy Seals. None of them even knew how to swim. He survived the training but was still ticked off at the recruiting office for lying to him. At this time, his wife had a drinking problem and was currently on a reservation in Manitoba undergoing sweat lodge treatment. He hoped to find employment in Seattle where she could join them.

The boy was well behaved, but like any kid he had a propensity for kicking the back of the seat. His father would say, "No, my son, do not kick the seat." And then he would say it again the next time, without ever giving any indication of raising his voice or considering the next level of punishment. I reflected on my method when my kids got obnoxious—I'd swat at them from the front seat while driving. Or at least I'd make an attempt. They were in greater danger of being killed by a telephone pole than me ever connecting with one of them. I admired the man's patience and chuckled at the tenacity of his free-spirited offspring. They had relatives in downtown Seattle where we dropped them off. They'd need them, but he asked for nothing.

Lesley's soft spot was for abused women. There was a shelter in Bellingham where people could donate clothes to them. The residents were so traumatized that the sight of a man would scare the hell out of them. I was advised that I was not to go inside. When we arrived, I was allowed to briefly enter due to the size of the bundle of clothing. I'd never seen a more frightened bunch of creatures in my life. Just one look at me and they cowered in the corner, seeking safety until I left. It's hard to believe that any man could be so bent as to beat his woman into such a pitiable victim of sadistic cruelty.

There was also a halfway house for men—mostly parolees—trying to get back into society. That's where I'd drop off my discarded clothes. A neighbor of ours was a retired investment counselor who once worked at the same place Lesley had in Burlingame, California. Wanting to help the men out, he'd hired a couple of them to do some work for him. After he had full confidence in them, he let them continue while he and his wife went on vacation. Upon their return they found the safety deposit box had been emptied of all her jewels. The workers had found the combination taped under one of the drawers in his desk. He told me what one of his Jesuit school friends, a priest, had said, "What did you expect? You weren't raised with people like that. You never hung around with people like that, did you?"

He answered, "No, of course not."

"Then why would you trust them now?" The priest admonished him with perfect logic.

He had a point. But the men were doing just fine while supervised. Unfortunately the temptation was too strong while the owner was away. I doubt that the halfway house would have expected anything else. Imagine if you were just out of jail with no home, no job, and no means of getting either. That's a whole different level of desperation than even Native Americans experience. Priests, investment counselors, bankers, and politicians all have various weaknesses along with the rest of us. You see it all the time on television. Their crimes are likely far more egregious than swiping a few jewels. There's no excuse for them! Imagine what they'd do if they had nothing going for them other than a halfway house. With so much brutality and crime in our own society I find it hard to criticize Native Americans for anything.

An interesting arrest was made while we were living in Bellingham. In the Northwest, as well as other areas scattered all over the country, there are many active militia members. A more accurate description would be right-wing Nazis, or white supremacists. Whatever they choose to call themselves, they're better described as dysfunctional anarchistic racists. The arrest was for drugs, conspiracy, firearms, and explosive charges, and brought about by an FBI agent. While working undercover, he gained their trust by posing as a good source for illegal weapons. At an upcoming meeting he promised to teach them how to escape from handcuffs in case they were ever arrested. When the time came, they willingly joined in the game while he put handcuffs on everyone. Once all of them were cuffed, he produced his badge and announced they were under arrest. Now that's what I call good police work! It is specially so when a county sheriff is sometimes the most active member.

Before you get the impression I'd retired in Bellingham, I'd better get back to work. I had my corner office, as every director should, with a computer and dial-up Internet access. The "office" was in the front porch sunroom where I could transmit and receive itineraries, reports, proposals, and letters, as well as copy or send documents with my fax machine. No wonder secretaries were eliminated by the early nineties. It didn't matter who or where my customer or boss was, I always had direct communication by email. It was like being in the office next to them, only better. Not only was it at home, but it was also portable. Wherever I went, I used business centers at airports or set up an office in my hotel room. Also, my car's mobile telephone, with a transceiver the size of a cinderblock in the trunk, had given way to a cell phone. My office was always with me. Today, cell phones are a birthright, but back then it was groundbreaking territory. Travelers of every ilk were constantly showing off the latest model. It was comical to see grown men bragging about having the smallest.

With more people working this way, the telecom market was being driven by demand for more high-speed services. As mentioned before, the network was still a switched network designed for voice. It was based on the principle that people can only talk for so long. After a short call they were supposed to hang up and allow someone else to grab a line for a local call or access to long-distance calling. With home computers, more people were staying on line for hours sending emails, as well as downloading and uploading images and data. Also, with the copper pair inadequate for transmitting at high speeds, new methods were needed to increase bandwidth to the home and small businesses. The distance to reach them was a major limitation as well.

This brought about a new family of products using technologies that were evolving faster than you could keep up with them. The acronyms alone were enough to drive you mad. ISDN, DSL, ADSL, SDSL, and HDSL were the topic of every sales call. Customers were talking a language more akin to ASCII (American Standard Code for Information Interchange) than English. ISDN (integrated services digital network) had worldwide acceptance and was widely offered by Bell companies. But competition was being financed and springing up everywhere. A variety of DSL (digital subscriber line) services was evolving faster than Bell's ISDN, leaving them behind.

Large corporations like Northern Telecom were funding competitive local exchange carriers (CLECs) by selling them DMS switches entirely on credit. CLECs were increasingly offering more data services over a network designed to be shared by low-speed voice activity. Conventional switching was rapidly becoming inadequate to handle the load. Telephone companies were getting desperate. The networks needed products to separate data from voice, if they were going to prevent data users from freezing up their offices. That brought about another acronym, DSLAM (digital subscriber line access multiplexer, pronounced *dee-slam*), about which I will just say it was a product designed to strip off the data before hitting the conventional voice switch, and then sending it through routers to be transmitted over the digital network. My livelihood came largely from multiplexers and fiber products in the loop. I was competing with numerous other entrants into the market, with new and more innovative products, all fighting for the same customer-premises business. The dot-com bubble was building as data escalated and CLEC business became more unsustainable due their mounting credit from switches unpaid for.

A bubble of another sort was building at home. As much as we enjoyed the house in Bellingham, we were still faced with the problem related to my job. I'd come home after traveling all week and find Lesley in the dumps. She was alone in a big house with no family or friends close by. Often it would rain all week and then be bathed in sunshine by Friday afternoon, leaving me to wonder what her problem was. When she tried to get a painting or two into the local art gallery, they told her they only accepted Bellingham artists. She assumed she was one. Evidently you had to have been born there to develop the gloomy style favored by people living under a permanent cloud. Most market and craft-day setups were rained out anyway. She started ice-skating and met some folks, but then Bellingham shut down the arena, forcing people to drive to White Rock in Surrey, British Columbia. She went anyway but soon quit as the others dropped off.

Discontent was rising. This often happens to California people who think retiring in the Northwest is a good idea because of the low cost of housing. More often than not they are forced to return to California because they miss the sunshine. It's not natural for them to live under a cloud of perpetual drizzle. To make matters worse, our dog Georgie was now over ten years old and starting to falter. After she had a stroke, she needed to be put down. She was the best companion and security system you could have. The Bellingham house was suddenly very empty without her. As Lesley's enthusiasm for Bellingham diminished, the subject of California returned. She wanted to move back. I insisted we stay. We argued about it every weekend. She said she'd go on her own. I said go ahead. It escalated to the "D" word. Her weapon was to break into tears. Mine was to get angry and resentful. The thought of returning had no appeal for me. We were getting nowhere and needed a compromise.

I was no longer enamored with Northern California. Silicon Valley was too busy, crowded, and affected by its elitist image. Money was the driving force—the bait—and young entrepreneurs were building multimillion-dollar homes. The Bayshore Freeway was insanely busy and dangerous with congestion. Numerous commercial areas were overcrowded to the point of looking like something out of a third world country. Venture capitalists were funding ideas as much as they funded new and promising companies with actual products. And many ideas were successful. All you had to do was insert an "e" or "dot-com" in your company name and the stock would escalate through the roof. Hype had supplanted substance.

    I liked the Northwest, but I could always be persuaded to move someplace new—somewhere I'd never lived before. Bellingham had been great, but it was time to recalibrate; to get hooked up all over again. I knew LA would be too expensive. For that matter, anywhere along the southern coast would be out of reach; but what about that Orange County crisis? Late in 1994, due to faulty investments by the Tax Collector, Orange County declared bankruptcy. For a time he'd kept taxes low through income from risky bonds. When the Fed increased the interest rates, his investments crashed and dealers demanded extra payments. There's a longer explanation but the short of it was that real estate values fell for a decade. We decided to fly to San Francisco and drive down along the coast. Our targeted area was far beyond that, even beyond LA. Maybe this was an opportunity to buy in South Orange County.

Best of show- Laguna Niguel art show – 2002.

Chapter 15

1998-2001
Dana Point, California

The fall of giants

Technology dominated everything to the extent of being the core of my existence. That's another way of saying it was a thorn in my side. Most of what came out of Silicon Valley just blew me away. Even Telco Systems was no longer on top of its game. I was merely a servant to technology's mastery—somebody had to sell it. Chips determined *how* we lived. Considering the alternative of not working, you could even say they were *why* we lived. Many, especially those who stuck to the old ways and never adapted, joined the ranks of the unemployed. By adapting, I had a say in *where* we lived. We chose Niguel Shores, a gated beach community in the Monarch Beach section of Dana Point. Its location, between Newport Beach and San Diego doesn't get any better.

The same can be said for many places along that part of the coast. Laguna Beach, Capistrano Beach, and San Clemente were as good as any on the entire West Coast. But Niguel Shores had private access to a long stretch of the beach it shared with the Ritz-Carlton and St. Regis luxury hotels. It was definitely high rent, but house sales were slow and sellers were motivated. We settled in and dealt with the usual dirty little secrets that escape every seller's mind. The house had a leaking roof over the kitchen, a leaking wall in the bedroom that soaked the carpet when it rained, the smell of cat urine in the living room carpet, and a leak in the master bathroom—all missed by the inspector.

It was a beach house owned by a dermatologist and occupied by his adult children waiting for the proceeds. The two sons were in medical school, and a schoolteacher daughter was the current occupant stuck with the ageing cat and two dogs. The seller even resorted to removing many tropical plants from the patio garden, which were included in the contract. Later, when I was having some planting done, his landscaper told me that before we took occupancy he had three of his guys working for about four hours replacing exotic plants with ordinary ones. We considered taking it to arbitration, but it was easier to do the usual thing and start with the repairs and updating. We always made money on real estate; this one made more than any.

Lesley entered art shows and sold more paintings than anywhere else we had lived. She also won a couple of awards, one being best of show for a watercolor of our two Maine Coon cats. In it, Charlie stares straight at you no matter where you stand in the room—my inspiration for work—while Teddy looks wistfully toward the sky—my inspiration for play.

During this time, travel was a nightmare. San Francisco airport was next to impossible to get reservations for flights, hotels, or rental cars. San Jose airport had easier access but traffic was just as bad. I took to flying into Oakland, where I could expect to get a car without waiting in a long line up. Over the years my habit had become to arrive at the airport fifteen minutes before flight time, drop the car, and get to the gate just before last call. In San Jose it was common to see rental cars abandoned in line ups, all over the return area, as road-warriors dashed to catch flights. I worked endless hours searching for new business by visiting old customers and finding new ones. I never took *no* personally, and no rock was ever left unturned in the relentless search for yes. It was the luxury of having no employees to manage that gave me the freedom to choose. I was the scout for the wagon train, riding out front, pointing the way and opening doors. That was the joy of it. That was what turned a challenging job into pleasure and profit.

With a territory larger than Russia, I could always find business somewhere. Still, my job was only as secure as the last three-month bookings and the next three-month forecast. Beyond that I was expendable. I was on my own, but I lasted longer than most of those I reported to. They either went up, or down and out. The best boss I ever had was hardest on himself. He was a good salesman but a hard case. He approached everything, work and play, with unlimited energy. That's what got him into rehab—not once, but twice—both times unsuccessful. The last time, one of his customers from a major carrier company met him at the airport. They went to a "titty bar" for a quick beer and quickly forgot the time. His wife was enraged when he arrived home after midnight and realized everything was back to normal. You could say he enjoyed sales to the fullest, except he died in his early fifties. I didn't even start to play in this league until I was fifty.

Hundreds of hotels and motels sprang up. Available rooms became further and further away from where the action was. Houses, too, were getting further away. Tracy and Stockton were experiencing a boom, with Bay Area people migrating over to the San Joaquin Valley for more affordable housing. Prices rose there as well. When the real estate bubble burst, a few years later, prices fell at a rate that outpaced everywhere else in the country. Stockton declared bankruptcy. Even when the dot.com bubble burst it had little effect on Silicon Valley. Property there was gold. Houses bought prior to California's Proposition 13 enjoyed taxes permanently set at the 1976 rate, with limited increases as long as they continued to live there. Many people were living in houses they'd bought for less than $100K that were now valued at over a million. Even today they continue to live there for the low taxes as prices continue to rise.

As the bubble grew, Telco Systems was heading for trouble. The old product line was solid for repeat business, but competition was fierce. New business was going to start-ups that had specifically designed customer-premises products. And there were plenty of them. A new CEO at Telco thought he saw the future in routers. Many of us only had a notion of what they were, even though they'd been around for a decade in smaller Ethernet and private networks. By the late nineties, routers had worked their way into the telecom network as the Internet Protocol (IP) address. Cisco Systems was a leading manufacturer and became the richest company in the world. With each generation of new products you almost needed a new sales force. The shift to data was affecting everyone.

Before solid-state, digital, and software technologies, I thought I knew telecommunications. At least with analog switching, you could manually trace a circuit through any switch, if not the entire network. Now, you could do it all with computers and specifically designed software. Companies like Yahoo and Google were emerging with websites offering endless information on an open network. They had answers for everything—as if channeling dead people—and did it without charge. What kind of business plan was that? What sane person was going to buy their stock?

I knew communications, but little about software and the Internet. I seriously considered retirement rather than adjusting. But then I received an offer as Director of Western Region Sales from a Silicon Valley start-up called Mainsail Networks. They had a new generation of multi-service access solutions for optical networks. At least it was hardware—something you could see, feel and touch—on the outside. Inside, who knew? I wasn't needed for that. It was only my network—my customer base—that made me popular.

Lesley, filling in at a trade show.

In addition to my West Coast territory, I now had Nextlink Communications Company nationwide. Nextlink was a competitive local exchange carrier, started in '97 and based in Bellevue, WA. This meant I had to travel to places like Miami, Nashville, Chicago, and Dallas, as well as all the western cities. The main attraction of working for Mainsail was the sign-up bonus and stock options. Start-ups were great opportunities for people on the ground floor. It's a very big leap from start-up to market acceptance, no matter how exciting the product is. All too often they exhaust the venture capitalists' money by demands for third and fourth rounds of financing. When that happened to Mainsail, it was bought by

Terayon, whose stock had shot up with their video modem product. But then Terayon got in trouble over a bad microchip selection and their stock quickly dropped, making the takeover not so attractive. My stock options dropped more each month until I sold and quit for a better offer.

By the year 2000, data was taking over the network. Telco Systems' entry into router products was difficult and they were struggling to survive. That same year, they were acquired by BATM Advanced Communications, an Israeli firm that had their own line of routers. It was a good acquisition for them. They had the new technology, and Telco System had the customer base of US telephone companies. They offered me my job back, but I'd already accepted another offer from Integral Access in Chelmsford Massachusetts. They had the latest voice-over-Internet-protocol (VoIP) technology. It was no longer a question of voice sharing its network with data; voice was now hitching rides over the data network as if hobos on a freight train. It was degrading, but I had no pride. I abandoned Mainsail and jumped on board when they offered me a job with better stock options and bonus program. Hobo or not, I wanted to play one more hand before getting out of the game. There wasn't much time left. People got rich on this stuff, why not me?

I'll tell you why! Let me count the ways. The market was being saturated to the point of stagnation. Customers were calling "time-out." The rapid growth of so many alternate providers was ebbing. And although Integral Access' VoIP technology was good, the product needed considerable fine-tuning. It was not at the modem plug-and-play stage yet. Field trials and early deployment required the assistance of engineers. The market demanded a product that anyone could receive by mail and easily install. It was the best of times and the....No! We've already been there. But let me give you one more: It was time to retire.

After several rounds of financing, it became obvious that Integral Access, too, was running out of time. And so was I. I needed sales *now*, not years from now. Integral Access was a second potential windfall of stock options not to be realized. The entire DSL (digital subscriber line) market was waiting for the next gigabit wonder product to win the last-mile business. We were on the cusp of another generation of new products about to make VoIP look like Western Union. And we were about to fall over a cliff.

During the build-up to the new millennium, everyone was panicking over the Y2K glitch. Every computer with storage (related to the practice of using two digits instead of four for identifying a year) made years after 1999 distinguishable from the twentieth century. The 21st started all over again with 00, 01, 02 etc. From the birth of computers two or three decades earlier, two zeros had never been used since 1900. They never appeared again for a hundred years. It was a simple thing, but it was a major software problem. Even humans had to reset their thinking. I recall this because we were on Catalina Island for New Year's Eve. The next morning, 01/01/2000, Lesley bought a painting from an art shop. When the owner was writing the bill of sale, she stalled, confused. Stammering, she said, "Gee, I've never done this. How am I supposed to write the year? Zero zero means nothing. Am I supposed to put in those zeros?" We thought about it and none of us were sure. We all agreed to just go for it, no matter how strange it appeared. I'm sure people all around the globe had to adapt just as quickly in a single day.

Prior to this, many people thought Y2K had the potential of wiping out everything from bank accounts to property ownership and portfolios, once the clock tipped over to the new millennium. As the countdown grew closer, concern grew to the level of panic. I found it strange that people could get so worked up in response to a bunch of fear mongering. Surely greater problems faced all of us. Late in 1999, I wrote an article called *The Y2K Hysteria* that was published in the Orange County Register. Had I been clairvoyant, I could have warned about the dot-com bubble just around the corner.! I could have warned about Al-Qaeda terrorists coming to America, the second Iraq war, or the real estate and financial meltdowns. This was stuff worth worrying about—the perfect storm of train wrecks.

The Y2K glitch didn't amount to anything, aside from its own cottage industry of opportunists who profited from it. But everything else soon fell apart. I have revived the article here for one more reading. It still contains an ominous message.

The Y2K Hysteria

Yes, we need to worry about potential disruptions, but not to excess.

Whenever confronted with the Y2K problem, I am reminded of my friend in Montreal. One weekend, back in the seventies, she wanted to drive to Rimouski to visit her family. Her husband, unconvinced of her driving skills, tried to discourage her by saying the tires were bad and it would be too dangerous. She insisted and went anyway, all the while worrying about the tires. About halfway there, a dashboard light came on and remained on for the rest of the trip. This was easily put out of her mind because of her husband's persistent warnings about the tires.

When she arrived at her destination the car was smoking. It turned out the motor burned up because it was out of oil. As she told me the story, I naturally sympathized with her husband who had to buy a new motor. To my surprise and amusement she cut me short. "Fiddle on that," she said, "I'm just mad because I spent the entire trip worrying about the wrong thing." Now, I'm wondering, how we will feel early in January 2000 if the wheels don't come off?

If we are worrying about the wrong thing, what then should we be worrying about? It seems like the world is now split into two camps: Those who profit from the great millennium bug, and the victims, those who obsess to the point of panic. Obviously we should worry about the victims, but more to the point, the victims should be worrying about those who profit by the panic. They will be found giving seminars, consulting, doing media appearances, and selling everything from books, software/hardware fixes, including complete new computer systems, and everything right up to and including bomb shelters. It doesn't stop there. Money is to be made from this in practically every sector of the economy. Y2K has become a standalone industry generating millions of dollars in profit for those willing to exploit an opportunity.

"What's wrong with that?" you may ask. "After all, isn't that the American way?"

Well, it certainly falls within the parameters of capitalism, but like my friend's husband, it takes a partial truth and exaggerates it to instill fear in order to manipulate the victim.

Media hype helps feed the frenzy. I'm amazed at the number of people moving to the Northwest who cite Y2K as a reason. I even know people in the Northwest moving to the islands to escape something they're not sure of—perhaps the starving barbarians from the South? I can understand a little stockpiling toward the end of the year and expect everyone to give some thought to it. Even I plan on laying in a couple of extra six-packs, but the hoarding has already begun on a large scale. Also, religious fervor is at a new high. And the Internet is expanding exponentially with instructions on everything from what bottled water to stock to how to survive global war.

Governments are saying, "Everything is under control, and, besides, in the event of trouble the troops are prepared."

Am I missing something here?

It's not the tiny software glitch that needs to be fixed. The same nerdy bunch that created it will do that. It is society's naïve vulnerability to everything coming at us from the media—TV, movies, video games, and especially the Internet and the computer itself. In the same way that television has had a negative impact on every civilized society on earth, the computer can do a thousand times more damage. With an unregulated Internet multiplying like a runaway virus rampant with anonymous predators—from snake oil salesmen to pedophiles— this is worth worrying about. Every mile we go down this road we compound our problems with more casualties from violence; more addictions to sex, drugs, and acquisitions; more alienation from society; and more family estrangement from lack of communication.

For some, the computer can provide endless hours of entertainment, and that doesn't make them worse than those hooked on the more benign TV. But chances are there are millions more who are isolated and highly focused on the interactive potential for destructive purpose that computers, video games, and the Internet can provide. In the same way that my friend's red light went on, our society may be flashing warning signals not to trust this Trojan horse of technology. Why are we so easily led to believing Y2K is the problem and so oblivious to accepting the real menace that slowly but surely continues to get worse the further we go?

The first step is to recognize the problem and stop worrying about some trumped-up Armageddon that's likely to be an inconvenience at worst. We need to recognize the consequence of continuing on before we can start to fix it. It will take one heck of a mechanic, but when enough people feel strongly about it, we'll have one in the same democratic process that allowed the situation to get out of hand in the first place.

Computers are here to stay, just like guns and automobiles. We need to learn how to use them, and more importantly how not to use them, in order to avoid the same type of frustration and disappointment that my friend experienced.

The world has long since forgotten what the Y2K excitement was all about. Many may have even forgotten the dot-com bubble. However, in the light of Internet activity today, the article may have understated those things we needed to be worrying about.

In September 2001, there was a sales meeting at Integral Access' headquarters in Chelmsford, MA. On those occasions, salespeople survived by their ability to spin great optimistic forecasts, no matter how unrealistic. Anyone who could not produce the numbers had no business being there, but you could always bullshit another quarter's worth of fiction. My customers were pulling back as they saw signs of the final clash of the giants. It was voice versus data—telephone companies wanted to get into computer services, and computer companies were already overtaking the networks. The battle was fought with takeovers, bankruptcies, spin-offs, and technology. The bubble grew and the stock market soared, even as corporate money disappeared and evaporated. It made no sense. My sales were drying up from customers whose stock market value was rising. Everyone was fudging numbers.

The smart move was to go to the sales meeting, declare my territory dryer than a witch's whatever, and get fired. It would have cost them. But they'd already been generous with a sign-on bonus, unrecoverable advance commissions, stock options, and even bonuses for finding others to fill empty positions. Such offers were common during this affluent period of telecom history. Soon they would have to start letting some go. It was the top of the bell curve prior to the fall. The boom was on its last legs. Nobody at the sales meeting would admit their well was dry, that nobody was buying, except me. Maybe theirs wasn't, but mine was. I didn't go to the meeting. Instead, I quit.

I felt the only thing to do was go away quietly, to disappear to start a new life the same way as all the Bells, ILECs, CAP's and CLECs had to. Had I gone to the sales meeting, I would have taken

Lesley and stayed over the weekend to visit friends in Maine, as we tried to do every year. And if we had, we could very well have been on the American Airlines Flight 11 from Boston to Los Angeles. As you know, it was hijacked and crashed into the North Tower of the World Trade Center. I've never regretted quitting when I did. Integral Access soon retired, too. Having run out of cash after a third or fourth round of financing, it was acquired by BATM and rolled in with Telco Systems. Life went on for those who had the accounts to continue. Others looked elsewhere.

The CLECs' initial public offerings (IPO's) contributed greatly to the bubble that burst by 2002. With easy financing from companies like Nortel and others competing for their business, these IPOs were highly leveraged. Actual earnings did not warrant their Wall Street successes. Consequently, and with few exceptions, every communications company and tech stock crashed. American ingenuity and know-how seemed to implode, except Cisco. The network was now saturated with routers.

Ma Bell's break-up two decades earlier had led to competition from Sprint and MCI. In exchange, AT&T got access to the computer business but failed miserably with Computer Systems and other acquisitions. All her babies had been sent to seven different foster homes called Regional Bell Operating Companies (RBOCs) which became known as the Baby Bells. Then she herself was acquired by SBC Communications—one of her own babies—previously called Southwestern Bell. Having gobbled up so many of its siblings, it was only appropriate that SBC rename itself AT&T Communication, just to put a good face on it. Even Western Electric was spun off as Lucent, only to be acquired by Alcatel, a French company. That's just part of the carnage that was started when poor old Ma Bell had her breakdown. MCI had infiltrated her backyard and that was just the beginning of problems.

For example, in 1983, Bernard "Bernie" Ebbers from Alberta had grown from high school basketball coach to owner of several motels in the south. Soon, he was the CEO of a company providing alternate telephone services called LDDS (Long Distance Discount Services) in Hattiesburg, Mississippi. After a series of acquisitions, LDDS became WorldCom and merged with MCI. As head of MCI, Bernie became so wealthy he even tried acquiring Sprint. But he'd been investing in too many other unrelated personal ventures that benefitted neither stockholders nor Wall Street, only himself. Time was not on his side. With the industry in decline, he ran out of creative accounting procedures used to disguise his losses and insatiable greed. His MCI/WorldCom dream created the largest accounting fraud in history, until Madoff's Ponzi scheme. In 2002, WorldCom was forced into bankruptcy, and in 2005 Bernie Ebbers was convicted of fraud and sent to jail for twenty-five years. The pieces were picked up by Verizon which had already grabbed all the remaining Bell Atlantic Baby Bells. Verizon survived and fought to stay afloat in a sea of integrated services.

    The poster boy for all corporate insatiability was Kenneth Lay, the CEO of Enron Corporation, an energy company. I only mention it here because they were aggressively entering the telecom and data markets. They were offering voice and data service over power lines that also managed power usage and home security systems. Nobody ever gave up territory in this business, but I declined an opportunity to give a product presentation to Enron engineers in Portland. I offered the entire account to one of the Midwest guys. I'd already been down the road of dealing with growing companies spreading, acquiring, and ultimately crashing due to some egomaniacal CEO. Besides, I wasn't planning on hanging around long enough to see it come to fruition, which it never did. Kenneth Lay saw it coming first. He liquidated over $300 million in falling Enron stock in spite of his compensation package of over $42 million, all the while encouraging employees to buy. The Enron scandal was so appalling it even caused the dissolution of the nation's largest accounting firm, Arthur Anderson. In 2006, Kenneth Lay died of a heart attack while facing a possible thirty-year prison sentence. After his death, the same federal court judge that convicted him vacated the judgment to free his survivors from any civil litigation. Everyone else lost money.

    I would be remiss if I didn't mention Northern Telecom (Nortel). They benefited immensely from deregulation, only to have a similar ending in spite of their celebrated Digital World image. By the mid-nineties, they dominated the United States and much of the world with DMS-100 switches for public and private networks. With the market demanding multiprotocol networking over the Internet, they bought Bay Networks and changed their name to Nortel Networks. The stock continued to climb in spite of poor profits in a market that was becoming saturated. It was during this time that I tried to get Nortel to acquire Mainsail Networks. Later, while working for Integral Networks, I tried to get Cisco to acquire them. On both occasions, I set up meeting with the appropriate marketing people in charge of acquisitions. Nortel and Cisco had been buying smaller companies struggling in the industry everywhere. They were doing so well, they only had to throw stock at a smaller company and take them over. But it was too late to get them to strike a deal. The giants were hiding problems visible only to those at the top.

From 1998-2000, about $3 billion in Nortel's revenue was improperly booked. In 2000 the CEO reportedly cashed as much as $135 million in stock options. In 2001 Nortel had nearly $16 billion in write-downs. When the bubble burst, Nortel stock fell from nearly $150 to less than $1. It was a crash that left sixty thousand employees out of work. The company evaporated, taking down everyone except the highest management. In 2003 the top forty-three managers were rewarded with a total of $70 million in bonuses, of which, due to erroneous accounting, a dozen of them had to return $7.8 million. Don't take my word for any of this, ask Google; it'll tell you for nothing. I should have asked them what stocks to buy since mine all crashed and theirs went up.

Collectively, it sounds like an obituary for the telecom industry. But if you recall my earlier assertion, life is like a deck of cards. New opportunities always proliferate at the same time as others decline. Even Steve Jobs was forced out of Apple at the same time as new technologies were appearing. He had won, and then lost, in a high-stakes game where other technology companies continued to grow and blossom. But they, too, were subject to self-destruction or driven out by another generation of products. Steve Jobs wasn't a loser at Apple; he merely folded and dropped out for a while. He got back in the game with *i-products* like iMac, iTunes, iPod, iPhone and iPad. He connected everyone in the entire world to everyone else. It wasn't long before individuals and groups were connecting, searching, texting, tweeting, and sometimes even talking far and wide. Jobs played a hand that would take digital technology and turn all of us into a generation of *I-Selfs*, with a capital I. The millennial generation would have everything it needed. One day, people may wonder what happened to books, newspapers, and even conversation; but they'll be able to access the accumulated knowledge of mankind or run a major business from the palm of their hand. The industry didn't die, it just changed.

When data took over, telecommunications didn't die, it just changed. Phone Man didn't die either. I'd spent the entire fourth quarter planning for this moment. Not for recognizing what it was, or when it would happen, but to stay in the game as long as I could and then get out. With the clock running down, I picked up the ball and headed for the sidelines before I got clobbered. Others had the same game plan. Some of us survived intact, but others were trampled in the scrimmage. It was no longer about one man or team, or any one game; after rising to unprecedented heights, the entire league imploded taking down everyone with it. It's only one man's view, but it's a close one and I don't mean from the bench. I was in the middle of it.

Life is all about work. You grow through the career you choose and advance by the amount of effort you put into it. Work is the chisel you need to carve a life out of a hard place. You work to ensure you get the most out of life that you possibly can. And you work in order to get benefits such as healthcare, sick pay, vacations, pensions, retirement plans; otherwise why bother? Given a choice, you might prefer going from school to retirement and pick up the benefits without lifting a finger. But what would that teach you? Where's the satisfaction of pulling in all of the chips if they've just been handed to you on a silver platter? How would you know the joy of winning if you'd never felt the pain of losing? How would you gain the skill to win without ever having played the game? Everyone has a talent for something. You just have to find it. If you can do that without working, more power to you.

    The secret is to find something you love and then do it. Work at it and work hard, because if you love it, it isn't work at all. That was how I felt through fifty years in the telecommunication industry. But maybe I had it wrong. The problem with work is that most jobs suck. Chances are the people you work for do too. I was never suited to factory work. I never tried office work, shift work, construction, or any kind of union work. None would have satisfied my curiosity and lust for freedom and change. It's much better if you own your own business. I tried that, too, only to completely fail. That's why I switched to sales where I enjoyed the freedom away from factory confinement and routine. Sales work was something else I wasn't suited for. I was in it for the travel. Sales work was just the wind beneath my wings.

Part IV

2001 – 2013

Lesley on the beach.

Chapter 16

2001-03
Dana Point, California

Hopi holiday

At the beginning of the twenty-first century, women were as productive as men; they just didn't get paid as much. In spite of all the promises of new technology, jobs were being lost, eliminated, or shipped overseas. Across the country people complained they had no work. Others complained they had too much. They needed two or three jobs just to get by; wives and mothers included. Many men, tossed out of their well-paid blue-collar work, stayed home or took menial jobs while their wives became breadwinners. Roles were shifting. Everything changed.

I was retired and we were living at the beach. I had a kayak for paddling around Dana Point Harbor and surfing gentle waves at Capistrano Beach. Niguel Shores had a Men's Golf Club where we played golf at various courses including Camp Pendleton because many of the members were retired military. Life was good, maybe too good. What is it about golf that people obsess over? Is it the social aspect or are they seriously trying to improve their game? Either way, I can understand both. Some strive to play professional golf. Others hate *their* game as much as they love *the* game. Many are just narcissists; they love the game because they see it as a manifestation of their skill and talent. I wish I could say that. I guess I just did, but it didn't apply to me. They work to play golf at every opportunity and then retire to play full time. It wasn't long before I'd had enough of both, golf and beach. Let's face it; I wasn't suited for retirement either.

New York City was very much on my mind on the morning of September 11. I was going out the door for a game of golf when the TV showed the first plane crash into the World Trade Centre building. This was a real game changer; a mindless act that changed everyone's life. Would anything ever be the same again? Nobody knew, but everyone worried and with good reason. Life in the Shores was a stark contrast to the forces soon to be released. Somebody had to pay, and this time the troops would have to be ready. Civilian rounds of golf at Camp Pendleton were replaced by troop rotations. At the beginning of the twentieth century, the "war to end all wars" was fought. The twenty-first century introduced the war to end the end of war—creating a perpetual state of war.

Dana Point retiree – 2001.

I thought about the young Hopi who briefly worked for me in San Carlos in the early sixties. Why had he suddenly quit his job and moved back to the reservation? If he thought life in white man's country was screwed up back then, he should have stuck around and got a load of what I saw. I had to find out what motivated people like him. We drove east on Highway 40 across the desert. The traffic and road rage withered behind us along with all the other trappings of the last century. Somewhere east of Barstow, I shut off the cell phone and visualized it bouncing along the freeway until tumbling to the edge of the desert with no more significance than an empty beer can.

The desert vacuumed my brain of everything important, leaving little more than visions of tom-toms and smoke signals.

Shunning the car's air-conditioning, I opened the windows and basked in the rush of whistling tepid air. Now I was riding the pony express. Nobody needed anything faster. I was tired of emails, meetings, schedules, forecasts, budgets, and all the rest that went along with holding your ground in an insanely competitive world. Even golf was old. The twentieth century had ground to a halt after a tired and overextended stay. I was escaping back in time to see my one and only Native American friend. I always liked them. Rarely was it mutual.

Across the Colorado River lay Arizona, an ancient land with a million ghosts of prehistoric people going back thousands of years. With so much to learn, we needed a tour guide. This is what we learned, more or less: *The Navajo were the last of the tribes to settle there. They came from the Northwest around AD 1400, but were far from the last to arrive. The Spanish came in 1540 and established an Empire in 1692 that lasted until 1821, and then the Mexican period lasted a mere 25 years until 1846. After that, the Anglos arrived in numbers not even the Navajos and Apaches could stop them. Before the Spanish settlers arrived, the Hopi flourished across northern Arizona and parts of Utah, Colorado and New Mexico. Land was plentiful, and they traveled freely while practicing communal living based on dry farming and trade with other cultures as far away as the west coast. They became excellent builders, preferring to live in terraced apartment-style compounds made from stone and adobe. The Spanish called them pueblos (towns), usually found on the high mesas. Oraibi, at Third Mesa, has been continuously occupied for over a thousand years, making it the oldest continuously occupied settlement in the United States.*

To reach the Hopi reservation, no matter what direction you came from, you had to go through the Navajo reservation. Before entering Navajo land, we stopped at the side of the road while our Hopi tour guide performed a tobacco offering to the spirits. She requested we join the circle and listen to the words of peace and harmony. She recited, *"Leave all negativity behind and enter this land with respect, forgiveness, and positive thoughts. For in forgiveness is strength, and to not forgive is to create your own hell. We should open ourselves up to the maker; listen in silence, find beauty in others, and in the land."*

I thought, easier said than done. The raging wind whipped at our clothes and lashed our hair into the likeness of wild banshees.

Tobacco flew from our hands across the dry and desolate reservation. Like an unseen power, it seemed to shout, *"You are trespassing, not only into ancient land but also ancient time."* It demanded respect.

The Hopi never went to war with the US government. Consequently, with no treaty, they lost much land and ended up located in the middle of the Navajo reservation. They are the most peaceful of all Native Americans. Quiet and highly spiritual, they maintain kivas for religious purposes. Their kachina secret society believes in gods, spirits, and departed ancestors. Many Hopi still live in villages—concentrated square-shaped pueblos—on top of mesas where they can see for miles and look over their crops. At church and ceremonies, unlike the Navajo, they dress plainly with no jewelry to avoid offending the spirits. The Hopi and Navajo are two completely different cultures. In spite of their differences, they coexist peacefully under extremely difficult conditions. They do, however, share a belief in spiritual beings, respect, and harmony with each other and with Mother Earth. Caught up in times of rapid change, they have adapted to the white man's ways and rely on the courts to settle their differences. The rest of the world would be well served to emulate them.

When we reached Oraibi I was surprised by the antiquity of Third Mesa. It was in ruins, with weather-beaten shacks clinging to thousand-year-old building blocks slowly decaying from sun, wind and time. A series of scattered wooden outhouses with doors facing the land below stood at various angles at the edge of the village; questionable conveniences to contemplate cherished patches of corn at the foot of the mesa far below. We were told that much of Oraibi was sacred and not to be walked on or photographed. We proceeded to the jewelry store located in a building that looked more like a 1905 land office. Inside, the Hopi girls were well educated, polite, and charming with a serene sort of beauty. I soon discovered that much more had been invested in people than in the land. Sacred land had no need for grandiose structures and expenditures.

As we returned to the van we met a young man selling kachina dolls. He was an artist, and, like most Hopis, lacked the hard edge for closing. Behind him ran a little brown-eyed three-year-old who left me regretting the no-photography rule. Her jet-black hair had a life of its own, leaping in all directions before falling gracefully to a point down her back. It framed a small round face that rose out of a little red dress shading her bare feet. She looked wild, angelic, shy, and mischievous, all at one time.

    The first village we entered at First Mesa was Hano. Next to it was Sichomovi, and then Walpi at the end of the road. To me they appeared as one. All were ancient, dusty, wind-blown and desperately poor as they clung to a narrow outcrop of rock a thousand feet in the sky. Although water was piped into the community, Walpi intentionally had no services of any kind. Only foot traffic was possible through narrow lanes separating the densely packed pueblos. The non-existent yards dropped off sharply but were of little importance compared to the dark, mysterious kivas lying beneath the surface of the rocky brim. They were inviolable stony chambers revered as churches and only visible by the tops of ladders extending through their roofs. However inconspicuous, they were devoutly protected. The kivas beckoned to those who would descend into solitude to communicate with spirits and other worlds.

They lived on mesas for a good reason. While contemplating this, I stood overlooking a vast empty desert, trying to visualize the Spanish arriving. They'd come on horseback with shiny breastplates and helmets reflecting the sun. All I saw was a modern hospital with an abundance of solar panels. Then, a few miles to the left, coming from the east, I saw a tiny orange object rapidly closing in on the mesa. It grew in size as it climbed the serpentine road to the top where it unleashed a disciplined army of small invaders into the narrow lanes of Sichomovi. Two disciplined regiments, one male and the other female, marched off individually and in small groups. They were armed with books, knapsacks, and newly created works of art. As quickly as they entered the pueblos they re-emerged with elevated energy. They brandished bats and all manner of balls for throwing, kicking and bouncing. The dusty streets became a combat zone with staccatos of shouts, squeals, and laughter. My concern for their survival diminished to the level of my concern over the Spanish.

    It was time to leave. On the way out we drove through Hano and I locked eyes with another small girl in a circle of her friends. She stopped playing long enough to pantomime sadness at our departure. With a small closed fist she brushed an imaginary tear from her cheek. *Sign language*, I thought, *a two-second communication but worth a thousand words.* The silent voice, from the soul of a child, with the power to etch a lasting memory and disarm more skillfully than force could ever accomplish. Like a veil, shifting ever so slightly, it revealed the secret allure that binds them together. That was what pulled people like my Hopi friend back to their land.

Today, most Hopis live off the mesas near Second Mesa where more modern conditions exist. Some say the Hopi pioneered solar energy just for powering their TV sets. If true, they showed greater wisdom than the federal government in the matter. Jimmy Carter tried to implement subsidies and created a 100-million-dollar solar bank. He even installed solar panels on the White House roof, but Reagan's first act was to tear them off. Oil and coal predominated for another generation, maybe two.

The number of vehicles in front of the Hopi administration office suggested that the community itself was by far the largest industry. Coal mining existed, but gambling had repeatedly been voted down. There was a cultural center with a museum, a thirty-three-room hotel, and a restaurant. The parking lot had many artisans and craft people displaying their wares. They patiently awaited the dubious pleasure of receiving visitors. This is where I found my friend.

He was a retired sheriff from the Hopi police force and lived in a small house near the Community Center. His son crafted kachina dolls for a living and his daughter was away at university. He, like his noble ancestors, thrived without the burden of affluence. It was no surprise when we didn't recognize each other after so many years. In fact he didn't remember me even after I introduced myself. His memory became clearer when I reminded him of a book I'd lent him on Hopi anthropology. I didn't ask him to return it. In his culture I supposed it was an honor to give freely and I would have lost stature. After forty years I would have been a dick in any culture. Suddenly, his face lit up and he immediately gave me a hug. Then he surprised me by producing a camera. I thought it was taboo, but very likely that only applied to the sacred areas. Lesley took our picture using his camera, and another using mine.

Since he'd been a sheriff, I pressed him about his Wild West gun-toting law enforcement days. He laughed and said he only had to pull out his gun out once. I was disappointed. I expected more, having grown up on Hollywood images of shootouts and war parties. Where were their Sioux Falls massacres and the Gitchie Manitou murders that were typical of the seventies? I wanted to know what life on the reservation was really like. To appease me he revealed a more dramatic story about losing all seventy of his cattle while he and his family went on vacation. He had several acres of dry empty land out in the desert, and he instructed a friend to keep an eye on the cattle. The friend neglected to visit and never noticed that the well pump had ceased to function, yet power failures were common. When he returned, he found his herd sprawled in ghastly death throws surrounding the dry water trough. It doesn't get any more horrific than that.

I couldn't resist asking, "Is that when you drew your gun?"

"No," he quietly replied, "No, he's still a good friend. I drew my gun to scare someone who was being belligerent when I stopped him for driving recklessly." It still felt short, but at least it was closer to home.

As we turned west on Highway 40 to return, I wondered where our perception of Native Americans became so distorted. Was it how history was taught? Was it TV, movies, or was it all about a land grab? Were we actually capable of genocide just to gain access to minerals, grazing land, and homesteads?

I received no visions nor saw any kachinas, other than the ever-present dolls, but then, how could I? In the land that abounds with visions, spirits, and prophecies, it takes quiet contemplation to realize that the wisdom of the ancients endures forever. It takes practice to apply what civilization rarely remembers—patience, compassion, generosity, and acceptance—yet it's all there, buried deep in all of us. Too often the direct opposite pervades by sitting on the surface. How we think and what we practice should not be left to others, especially the media. The Hopi are very much aware that it's up to them—the media is not their message—action speaks to who they are, and some things are sacred.

Modern wisdom, even with all the science and technology, suddenly seemed temporary and shallow by comparison. Then I recalled the Hopi prophecy that said, *"The spirit of the ancient ones will return in the children of the white man, and they will become our new friends. Red, yellow, black, and white will join to form the Rainbow Warrior, we will be one people and the healing of Mother Earth will begin."* Have we ever been one people? Was there ever a time without war? If there is any hope for our planet, someday we will have to become that Rainbow Warrior they're waiting for.

Until then, I wasn't holding my breath. With that thought in mind, we left the land of the ancients to their solar panels and wind and remained nomads for years to come.

Chelsea, our cat, died from heart failure while suffering from kidney and urinary problems. Lesley needed a quick replacement and wanted a Maine Coon cat. We found a breeder in Maine with two or three almost ready for adoption. It was time for a vacation, so we immediately left in hot pursuit. When we saw them, they were six weeks old and so irresistible that we had to have two. By the end of our vacation they were old enough to fly home with us. We carried them through security and kept them caged under the seat on the plane. When we arrived home it took them only minutes to adjust. Within days they knew every corner of the house better than we did. As we became more familiar, it didn't take long to know that one was Teddy, and the other Charlie. Cats can adapt without losing their personality or who they are. But as you know, cats will be cats. The hardware may change but they come prewired with all the software in place. No training is required, but be prepared to be trained by them.

Teddy, Chelsea's ghost, and Charlie.

Niguel Shores was one of those places where locals said, "People move in and never move out." That was before they met us. It was the perfect place for retirement, maybe too perfect. Somehow, perfect was not for us. We operated on five-year plans. After three years I'd get antsy. At five years it was time to move, assuming we hadn't already done so. There was too much stuff out there, too many options, and too little time.

We were ready for another move.

Chapter 17

2003-04
Savannah, Georgia

Way down south in Dixie

Savannah is the kind of place they write songs about. How many cities have songs written about them? Think of New York, Chicago, San Francisco, or Paris, and you'll immediately think of at least one more—Savannah—and she may have more songs than any of them. Johnny Mercer was a song writer who wrote over a thousand songs. I don't know why he wrote so many, but I do know where much of his inspiration came from. He was born in Savannah.

    We immersed ourselves into the midst of that steamy hotbed of southern sophisticated backwardness for a full year. Whenever I hear one of Mercer's songs I think of Savannah. Just one word or a couple of notes from certain songs, and Savannah rushes in like warm bourbon over ice. It's like 2003 all over again, and we're downstairs at the Pink House restaurant's bar enjoying an after-dinner Irish coffee. The sultry voice of Gail Thurmond is at the piano crooning "Savannah Moon," "Stormy Weather," and a host of other songs. It's still an escape now, as it was then, no matter where we live.

    Savannah is magical! Little city squares with cobblestone streets abound with architecture from centuries past. Trolley cars, horse carriages, and tour buses navigate through foot traffic respectful of the old southern tradition of simply strolling. Forsythe Park, with its grand fountain designed after the one in the Place de la Concorde in Paris, attracts everyone. It's a lifestyle tolerant of all the misfits and oddballs. Only in Savannah would a man totally immerse himself in Spanish moss to become a grotesque statue to shock and entertain tourists by unexpectedly waving an arm. And who could not be seduced by the history, lush foliage, and antique shops? Restaurants welcome you with everything from international cuisine to soul food and little tea shops. All of it is harbored and at peace among beautiful old weathered homes sheltered by towering trees.

Nowhere was Savannah better portrayed than in John Berendt's book and subsequent movie, *Midnight in the Garden of Good and Evil*. We wanted to live among those characters in that beautiful city with all its intrigue and love of tradition. It's a place where magic washes over reality, making it seem like fiction; a city filled with characters both real and fanciful. Even murder adds charm to a city so dedicated to maintaining its history.

And then reality set in. A thunderstorm with showers was casually forecasted on the radio. I'm not sure why they called it that. As I recall, what followed was rain in volumes I'd never experienced anywhere but Florida. We were not concerned about the thunder; it was lightening that got our attention. As a child I had learned to measure how close lightening was by counting the time from bolt to sound. There wasn't any! Both were all over us blinding and deafening simultaneously. In the middle of the night we watched from an upstairs window and saw the most amazing display of electrical energy ever witnessed. Just when we thought it could get no closer, a thunderous explosion blew up a transformer in the alley right behind us. It set fire to a tree and showered the house with shooting stars and rocket-like embers. The power failure set off our unfathomable alarm system with a hidden horn loud enough to drown out any storm. This was our introduction to Savannah.

In the days to follow we added other charming characteristics. Gnats became number one. The locals were so indifferent to them that they affectionately named their baseball team after them. My first encounter happened while tending the garden. It resulted in red welts all over my body that continued to grow, itch, bleed, and leak fluids for the next three weeks. Like black flies in Canada, they recognized new blood and went berserk. And then we discovered hurricanes.

Savannah normally escapes the worst hurricanes. But just for us this one dropped unprecedented levels of rain accompanied by winds that blew tidal water fourteen miles inland to the city. Power lines failed and storm-sewer sump-pumps quit. The entire neighborhood flooded. Streets filled with water and ran up driveways to encircle houses, sometimes rushing uninvited into living rooms. We watched as it rose toward the last high-water mark on our basement furnace. The St. Patrick's Day parade was a washout, or would have been in any lesser city. The Savannah Irish with their marching bands and thousands of revelers slogged on undeterred through the deluge. It would take more than a hurricane to stop a parade in Savannah. And then came spring with another surprise known as humidity. Savannah's speed was already governed by it: Slow. Coming from the West Coast, it stopped us dead.

Our street, a boulevard actually, was often referred to as one of the prettiest in Savannah. It had huge oak trees that created two tunnels along the entire length of it. The tree in our front yard was so large it penetrated the driveway, creating an obstacle to navigate around. It's the same all over Savannah. Trees tear up sidewalks and streets, with roots and oversized trunks, causing huge upheavals of concrete. You have to be constantly vigilant when riding a bike or walking. Rather than complain, Savannah folks have a saying. *"In Savannah, you can get away with murder, but they'll hang you for cutting down a tree."*

Many thought our house was the prettiest on the block. We were referred to as "the party who bought the *Barfield House*." We already knew we were the third party to buy it since it was built for the Barfields, who died thirty years earlier. Surely one of our predecessors must have made an impression over the span of an entire generation? No, not in Savannah! We, too, would have to wait for acceptance and could be just as easily forgotten as the others.

A strategy was needed. We broke the ice with a cocktail party. There's another saying in S*avannah: "In Atlanta, when you meet a crazy person you lock them up. In Savannah, you invite them home to dinner."* Of course nothing could be further from the truth. They will, however, go to any length to receive an invitation to *your* party. Nonetheless we wanted to meet the neighbors. In the past I'd always relied on a bar with a good happy hour to meet people, often with questionable results. Even in Savannah I couldn't resist inviting a couple of locals from the bar at Johnny Harris Restaurant on Victory Drive. One of them was a middle-aged buxom blonde who owned a home-based manicure business. She was married to a shrimp boat captain, which in my mind made her all the more appealing. Unfortunately, the captain was a no-show at the party. This left her winging it alone while spilling out of both ends of a very short pink cocktail dress.

Lesley wondered, "Where did she come from?"

I explained: "I thought you might need a pedicure one day or something." I didn't know pedicure from manicure, but I liked what I saw.

My other contribution from Johnny's bar was Jim Bob—a dark, sinister-looking, CIA-gone-rogue-type looking individual who owned a place on Skidaway Island. Lesley found him to be downright scary, but I needed a place with easy access to launch my kayak.

Again, I explained the importance of the connection: "He said, 'Come on out. I'll get you in the water.'"

She replied, "Yeah, along with all the other bodies."

Who was she to talk? One of her starving artist friends didn't show up until everyone else was leaving. She wore a multicolored hippy dress recycled from the seventies, accessorized by homemade long-strung bead necklaces. I don't think she came for the party. She was more interested in the leftover hors d'oeuvres which she took home with her. Not that any of it mattered. Aside from the previous owners, we never received a return invitation from any of them. Not even Jim Bob.

With a sponsor you can join one of the many clubs in and around Savannah. Starting with a membership fee of five or ten thousand dollars, you can pay as little as $100 for a very humid game of golf, or sit around the pool sipping mint juleps while watching kids squeal in the water. The better class of people always joined these golf and tennis clubs. There are dozens of them. In fact they are the backbone of Savannah's society. The old guard sticks to them through generation after generation. Children grow up in them while their fathers swing deals and mothers plan parties. Newcomers with upward mobility flock to them. Politicians get elected by them. We didn't play golf or tennis, have kids, or any interest in society and politics. But we did join the First City Club downtown which had a dining room with gourmet food and a decent bar. Even there, most of the members were business people making connections, or aspiring politicians trying to get elected. We'd drink too much, eat overrated food, and drive home without meeting anyone we needed to see again. We could do that in any bar in town.

Bars are not the best place to improve one's social life. However, that's exactly what happened in the bar at the *17Hundred90 Inn and Restaurant*. We ran into a Jewish crowd who occupied two or three tables every Thursday night. They called it their club. Upon invitation, we joined them and soon became regulars. They didn't drink all that much. They just enjoyed each other's company and always had a good laugh. Soon we found ourselves going to art classes with them. I painted my first and only oil painting which still hangs in my daughter Leslie's office in Raleigh. When Bubba Horowitz had his seventieth birthday party at Johnny Harris' convention hall, we were invited along with a couple hundred of his lifelong friends. Had we stayed in Savannah, it would be because of this wonderful group of people.

When Lesley started having problems with high blood pressure, she needed a doctor. One was recommended by someone we knew, but he was not taking new patients. We tried another and then another. Then, largely due to the humidity, she started having other problems, like swollen glands, thyroid disorder, and an inner ear infection. She was rendered deaf in one ear for four months. Each doctor uttered a worse prognosis than the previous one before referring her to the next. She learned never to tell a doctor what illnesses her parents may have had, to avoid being tagged with that as well. None of them wanted new patients, especially patients on Medicare. She finally resorted to calling her California doctor for consultations.

My own search for a doctor was just to have one. After a couple of refusals I ended up with a young fellow just out of medical school. He looked about sixteen. Perfect, I thought, by the time I need him he'll be right on top of his game. My problem was boredom, a very serious disorder that causes me to do strange things. Like move to Savannah in the first place.

For a while I entertained myself by riding my bike to explore the city. Often I'd end up at the courthouse to watch court cases being tried. During a trial it's always best to sit on the same side as the victim's family. They might wonder who you are, but that's better than appearing sympathetic to some felon or rapist. Trials can be boring with all the waiting, discussion, and procedures. But think about what's at stake. The victims must sit there and reveal everything, often very personal and embarrassing things, in order to ensure that justice will prevail. The perpetrator's lawyer will try every trick they can to avoid a conviction. This is old stuff that we've seen forever in movies or on TV, only wrapped up in an hour or two. In a courtroom you are right there in the middle of it for weeks or months, and seemingly forever. What makes it palatable is that both you and the perpetrator know that if proven guilty this is his last look at freedom. While I was there, I found myself wishing they'd wrap it up in half an hour. Instead I'd have to return again and again for days before completion. Too often I'd miss the verdict and have to search the newspapers for the result. More often I'd search from courtroom to courtroom, only to find endless procedural matters being whispered and discussed over some traffic or other benign offence. Even in Savannah there wasn't enough rape and murder to keep me happy.

One of Savannah's drawing cards was that Leslie, my daughter, lived on Kiawah Island outside Charleston. She and Garry had two children, Melanie and Gordon. We were able to see them more often. We even took their Shih Tzu dog, Polly, for a month while they were on vacation in Asia. Polly drove us nuts! Between our two Maine Coon cats and a strange environment, Polly was not happy. She had a novel way of expressing it—by using any room in the house for a bathroom. I tried to take her for walks, but I could never get her past the door of my car. I'd have to carry her a few blocks away in the hope that she would walk home, and *bingo*. No such luck! She would just stand there looking at me. If I tried to pull her, she'd sit down and skid along the grass on her rear end.

Garry, Melanie, Leslie, and Gordon Forbes.

The one good thing about having Polly was that I found "the puppy club." Every night at 9:00 p.m. a number of guys would gather in the neighborhood on the mall in Baldwin Park at Atlantic and 45th. They walked their dogs there and shot the breeze for a couple of hours while the dogs sniffed each other out on leashes. Some guys brought their martinis in a "traveler"—another Savannah custom. One guy carried a handgun because they'd been held up one night. Polly gave me a legitimate reason to participate, but she took great offence at any uninvited sniffing. Even here I would have to pick her up in order to protect her from getting killed by some dog ten times her size after she attacked it. Polly didn't like the puppy club any more than she liked living with us. When we finally threw in the towel and took Polly to her vet's kennel back in Charleston, it created a rift between us and the Forbes family that was as great as anything between us and Savannah.

Garry and Leslie on our new patio.

I needed to get out more. I was looking for something stimulating, something I could be involved in. I tried volunteering for Habitat for Humanity and was assigned to a house under construction by a close-knit, well-heeled group from one of the exclusive developments on the outskirts of Savannah. They were proud of their service toward providing underprivileged and disabled people with affordable housing. It was just the kind of thing I was looking for. They worked in pairs. I had no idea where to start and nobody was interested in working with me. Finally I was inflicted upon one disappointed chap who looked like he'd just been demoted. We were applying vinyl siding since that would have been the simplest task. But even that proved too much for me when halfway up one side someone pointed out that the color had shifted to a slightly darker shade along the way. You had to stand back to see it. Somehow the different shade got included in the shipment. Naturally it had to be entirely my fault. All conversation was over as my ill-fated partner angrily started removing the dark panels until reaching where the shift had occurred. I stuck out the day but once was enough. The nice thing about volunteer work is they can't fire you, and you can quit any time you want. These guys were too cliquey for me.

Next, I noticed a small two-line ad in the paper. It read, *Electricians wanted*, and added a number. I'd never been an electrician although I'd thought about it a few times. Once was in California, a couple of decades earlier, when I was thinking about moving to the Sierras. I went into real estate instead. That was another mistake. Before that I'd wired a campground with outlets for trailers and RVs. That didn't work out too well either. But I did rewire a house in Bellingham, updating knob-and-tube wiring to 110/220 VAC service. Maybe that would count. I made the call.

"This's Tom," he casually answered. It was a cell phone. I could tell he was on a job site by the voices shouting to be heard over a background sounding more like a war zone.

"It's about the ad," I said. "Can you tell me more about the job?"

"We've a contract do'n electrical work for a car dealership. Rat now we're do'n the Caddy dealer. You n' electrician?"

I was prepared. "Not licensed, no, but I just retired from the telecommunications industry."

I needed more! Selling fiber optic transmission systems hardly qualified me. "I've been around it all my life...and I've rewired houses."

That was a stretch! I could have talked about being a regional sales director but that would have been a deal-breaker.

"Would age be a problem?" I asked, to throw him off track.

"Not if you can handle the work. My ole daddy worked 'til he was seventy-five. It ain't easy, no dime sane?" It took me a couple of seconds before I got it—*know what I'm saying?* It was a lazy and easy way of talking that most southerners are prone to. I found it infectious and knew I'd adapt quickly.

"No problem. I've just finished renovating an old Federal here in Savannah." Another stretch, I thought, reflecting on the two young men I hired to do the repairs to the roof, fix up some dry rot around the windows, and rebuild a couple of sashes in the sunroom. Most of the work was on a brick patio with a fountain in the center. They did that too. However, I did install a ceiling fan with a light in Lesley's studio. Surely that would qualify me?

"How much are you paying?" I asked, just to get past the interview. I wasn't really interested in the money

"If you can do it, it pays fifteen bucks an hour. Y'innerested?"

"Just tell me what time and give me some directions." I hadn't worked by the hour since BCTel and wasn't interested in doing the math. If he'd said ten bucks I would have given the same response. I just wanted something to do.

I was up at six in the morning and excited. Lesley eyed me with suspicion, wondering what latent primitive male instinct was driving me this time. Not wanting to restrain me, she insisted I eat a big breakfast. I arrived before eight as the sun was creeping over the trees. Half an hour later a Toyota crew cab rolled up with four pairs of eyes checking out my STS. Opening the door I dropped one work-booted foot before exiting in my Levi's and T-shirt. I popped the trunk and strapped on my tool belt before pulling out a bright orange Home Depot pail full of tools. This ought to impress them.

"I see you remembered your tools," someone snickered from the truck's rear seat.

The bastards are laughing at me, I thought. I ignored them and approached the older blond-haired one who just emerged from riding shotgun. He was about forty, short and stocky with a round gut that looked as solid as the rest of him. I said, "You must be Tom?"

"Hi Al, glad you made it." The other three joined us. "This here's Cole," he said, pointing to the six-foot-four, 220-pound driver. Obviously this was Tom's second-in-command. Turning to the other two, he briefly added, "Jason and Judd."

They looked surly and suspicious, or maybe just curious. I knew southern boys would be respectful of my age—they'd be thinking about their ole daddies. That wouldn't last long! Performing would be something else. I had a better chance with this crew than the snobs at the last work site. With handshakes over, I followed them around the building. The project was financed by a company that built to the automobile company's specification, and then leased to various dealerships. After the electrical contractor defaulted, the general contractor called Tom's boss, who owned a company in Atlanta. They normally worked on residential and commercial properties in that area, but they'd done similar dealership buildings and were asked to finish this one.

The large parking lot was still being bulldozed as we stepped over the chaos of a work in process. Out back, their construction shack was a thirty-foot aluminum trailer overflowing with and surrounded by material. It sat on landfill that had recently turned to mud from the rain. At the back of the trailer was a small pond that once covered the entire site for countless years, it was now a shrunken, murky refuge for two young alligators. They were no more than three feet in length and no doubt abandoned. Now they were accustomed to handouts tossed by the crew. This time it was raw hamburger pulled out of a wrapper and rolled into gory-looking red baseballs for ease of throwing.

"Damn freezer in the RV crapped out," Judd explained as he tossed the meat, bringing the young alligators to life.

I said, "Good training! See man, see food." Then I wished I hadn't. I noticed Jason look at me with renewed interest. Cole and Judd were barely in their twenties, but Jason was several years older. He'd been around and would be wondering if I was a smart-ass.

The ceiling in the service area of the Auto-Mart was around thirty feet high. They had already placed the conduit and pulled the wiring in that part of the building. My job was to install the high-intensity light fixtures. Looking up through the metal framing, I could barely detect little rat nests of wire sticking out of outlet boxes all over and woven in along with gas, water, and sprinkler systems.

"Y'ever hook-up one'a these?" Tom asked as he cut open a large box from a stack of forty. He removed a 600-watt, 26-inch aluminum high-bay intensity lamp. It must have weighed forty or fifty pounds.

"No! But if you show me how to do the first one, I'll do the rest." It came out with more bravado than I felt. "There's only one thing...." I paused, concerned over what his answer would be.

"Whazzat?"

"How the hell do I get up there?" I asked, pointing to the ceiling. If he says that three-piece ladder lying over there in the corner with a stack of reels, I'm outta here.

He turned and said, "Y'ever run one'a them things?" I followed his finger to an oversized cast-iron coffin painted bright yellow with a metal guardrail around the top. I'd seen them before. They were mostly around job sites, warehouses, or storage yards along the side of freeways. This was the closest I'd ever been.

"I've seen them around for a long time, but I've never used one."

"It's a scissor lift. Tak'ya rat up there. Come on, I'll show you."

With no effort he threw the light fixture into the lift. It was already loaded with a number of boxes carrying clamps, connectors, plastic wire wraps, and a roll of heavy 12-gauge, 4-conductor, rubber-coated cable to be run between the fixture and the outlet box. With barely room to stand, I clung to the guardrail as he manipulated levers to spin us around and lift the platform. It swayed as we elevated into the mass of ironwork and pipes until it was stretched to the limit and as close to the ceiling as possible. With deft movements he went through the installation procedure while casually talking as though just shooting the breeze. He exuded confidence. Nothing showy or impatient, but enough to confirm he was a pro. My apprenticeship took less than an hour. It consisted of Tom hooking up the fixture and explaining the lift. The more he talked the better I understood him. The accent was easy enough to comprehend, but the man himself was more complicated. His mind was as quick as his hands. I was soon left to install the remaining fixtures on my own.

A week later he threw the switch and they all lit up. Everyone laughed and gave me a high five. I think they were taking bets. I played it cool. "Wha d'ya'll expect? Damn roof blow off?"

Two more "electricians" showed up a few days later. I could sense the crew's reluctance to warm up to them in the same way I was shunned at the last job. At lunchtime we went our way to Mexican, pizza, or Italian restaurants while they ate something bought on the way to work. The older one was called Booker. He was in his forties and the younger one, Deford, around twenty. They were black, and I gathered they were uncle and nephew, possibly cousins, but certainly not electricians. I could see Booker had some training. He sheltered Deford by whispering instructions that none of us could hear. Tom, or one of the crew, would show them where to hang the conduits and junction boxes and then leave them to pull the wire in. I followed along, installing fixtures and hooking them up. They badly needed this job and found it the same way I did with the ad in the paper. I was comfortable enough with them, but far too curious for their comfort.

I admired their brand new Explorer and asked Booker how he liked it. It wasn't his, but they needed a vehicle to get to work. With no fixed address they had trouble renting one until they went to the Savannah airport. Residency was neither required nor expected at the airport, but it was expensive. The two of them would have to work at least two hours every day just to pay for transportation. That was as much information as I ever got out of them. I could see they had a hard life. They didn't have many tools, but I was happy to lend them what they needed. At the same time I made sure I got them back at the end of the day.

For lunch they'd sit in the Explorer eating chips and whatever they'd picked up while filling the tank. It was no use pumping them for more information. They preferred talking in low voices between themselves. Booker did most of the talking. When they started taking off early, Tom never said anything. They'd told him it was for court appearances, but he never mentioned it to me. And then they were gone altogether. Booker apparently learned his trade while doing time in prison. With their absence, I assumed they'd received their sentences and were now returning for another semester in electrical contracting. It hardly seemed fair. They would have done anything to keep that job while I was just doing it for fun. I still wonder what their crime was. Hopefully they would receive more electrical training and never to return to jail.

Whatever Tom and his crew's home situation was, they wouldn't be living much better than Booker and Deford while on this job. They were temporarily living in a trailer park outside Savannah in the boss's RV. Over lunch they would entertain me with stories of their bachelor existence. Chaotic, is the only way to describe it. In between the drinking, cooking, cleaning up, and watching TV, they occasionally got some sleep. Dirty tricks and pranks were rampant. I couldn't imagine an RV large enough to contain all four of them at one time. At work they were a team of professionals with a clear line of authority and pride in their performance. At lunch their iced tea was sugared to the point of clogging a pulmonary artery, and they consumed enough refried beans to blow up Hoover Dam. Pizzas were the thick-crusted type overloaded with cheese and pepperoni. Everything was fortified with salt.

I asked Jason, "Why so much salt?" He was in his late twenties and contained his long hair pulled back into a pigtail with an elastic band.

"My daddy always said it was the best thing about eating. You can put salt on anything and make it taste better. Says so in the Bible, too! My daddy always puts it in his beer and if you try it you'll see what I mean. Hell yeah! Even makes beer taste better."

He'd been a radio operator on a Navy SEAL gunship designed to make clandestine drops in foreign destinations. While stationed in San Diego he'd married a Mexican girl and now they lived in a mobile home near Atlanta. He told me that she'd recently returned to visit her family in San Diego, taking their two little girls with her. It was a trick! After she left, he found out she had no intention of returning. His remedy was to fly out and bring his daughters back on a Greyhound bus.

I asked, "Do you think she'll give you any trouble?"

He firmly said, "There won't be no trouble. I told her I'm com'n to get my kids and bring'em home. She can do what she wants." The steely look in his eyes reflected his Navy SEAL training. Or perhaps it was from Gettysburg, and beyond.

I said, "Some of those Mexican girls have pretty big families. Maybe she won't be alone."

The conversation was over when he replied, "There won't be no trouble."

I supposed that if he used his training he'd be in and out town before his wife even knew he was there. There was no doubt he'd accomplish his mission; I just wondered how he'd handle the occupation. Raising two kids in a trailer park while working in Savannah might be too much even for a Navy SEAL.

Judd was younger. What he lacked in outside experience was made up for in energy. At twenty, he was rail-thin and six foot tall with closely cropped hair. He was wiry and almost spastic in his quickness. The others told me he had a black belt in judo. I took their word for it. I called him, "Gitterdone." He approached every task with the same expression: "Well okay, let's gitt'er done." One day in a pizza parlor he pointed to an electrified backlit picture on the wall. It was a woods scene with a bright blue river constantly tumbling over a white bubbling waterfall into a flower shrouded pool. The water moved as if real. All it needed was a Budweiser sign flashing on and off. I thought, *Thomas Kinkade on steroids.*

He said, "That's what I'm buying my bride for a wedding present when we move into the new mobile next month."

"You might want to run that past your bride before spending the money," I said. "She may not like it."

He looked at me as if I was from Mars, "What for? She's the one what picked it. Beautiful, ain't it?"

"Yep, good choice," I agreed. The squint in his eyes suggested he doubted my sincerity. I may have been living in Savannah, but he knew a damn Yankee when he saw one.

Cole was not much older but beyond age in his fullness. After high school he started working for Tom to save up for college. Three years later he knew more about electrical contracting than most engineers ever would. He and Tom thought as one; anything Tom wanted Cole got done with no words wasted. Together they were a well-oiled machine. When we went to lunch, Cole drove effortlessly as if just willing the truck to where we were going. Unlike Judd, who steered in short, quick movements, impatient to arrive. He worked the same way.

Tom was occasionally generous with his expense account and paid for lunch. Sometimes I sprang too. They talked about some of the bars down on River Street in Savannah, and where to get the best oysters. I went bar hopping with them one night, drinking beer and slamming down oysters. Jason and I were playing pool on the only table when a guy left the bar and asked if he could join the game. He sounded like a northerner, maybe New York. I would have liked to hear what his story was, but Jason wasn't interested. With a sharp "no" he decided the matter without even looking up from his shot.

I thought, *so much for southern hospitality*. I think the stranger had the same instinct. He backed up a few steps beyond the reach of a pool cue before returning to the bar.

I would entertain Lesley with stories about the crew. In spite of their homespun beliefs, they were intelligent and possessed remarkable skills as electricians. It was generous of them to accept me into their tight-knit circle. I couldn't begin to keep up with them in energy or knowledge. At the same time they rarely mentioned politics or religion except in conversation together. It was clear to me where they stood on both fronts. But they weren't clear about me. I was just an enigma they never fully understood. They kept me on a short tether and it wouldn't take much for them to turn me loose.

When I invited them home for a barbeque, they cleaned up pretty well. It was still cut-off jeans and sneakers, but they'd showered and put on their best behavior to meet Lesley. The neighbors may have had some misgivings if they saw them unloading in our front yard at dinner time. They'd more likely assume we were having our kitchen remodeled. But I knew we were in for a better time with the crew than with any of them. Lesley was looking forward to it, too. At the first sight of Jason coming up the walk with his ponytail and cut-offs, she commented wistfully, "He has the most incredible legs."

He rose further in her favor when he looked inside the living room and said, "Wow! I always wondered what it was like inside these houses."

The weather was hot and humid—a perfect evening for a cooler full of beer on the patio. We stood around the grill, drinking beer and anticipating the aroma of steaks being seared over hot coals. Then the rain came, slowly at first in scattered drops, and then sprinkling its way on up to buckets.

"Uh oh," I said, "I guess we'll have to wrap it up." Everyone looked at me, slack-jawed, as if I'd just spoken in tongues.

Jason spoke first, totally deflated. "What? Y'all not have'n the barbeque?"

I choked on my beer while stifling a laugh. "Sure we will. We'll just have to eat in the dining room." Then we all cracked up and started picking up plates and cutlery to rush inside.

"Well, I can live with that," Jud said. "Let's gitter done."

Lesley's family had lots of antiques, dishes and silverware left over from nearly forgotten ancestors. Her parents weren't rich, but they had preserved everything they could, and she followed the tradition by hanging on to everything she'd grown up with. The dining room's softly dimmed chandelier hovered over the rarely used silver serving trays and tea sets. Oil paintings surrounded the elongated table now hastily set with paper plates and beer cans. Still, it was an elegant setting for the ragtag noise and laughter that followed.

Tom revealed why he'd never reached a higher station in life. It was due to one of his three children with special needs requiring extensive medical care. If he made more than $30,000 a year, he would be on his own and never able to afford it. If less, the state picked up the medical expenses and she received the best of everything. The arrangement with his employer would never make him rich, but he knew a good deal when he saw one.

Jason had just returned from California with his two school-age daughters. A family member was looking after them until the dealership was finished. I could see he was worried about when he took over and reality set in. Judd was close to marrying his childhood sweetheart. There was not much point in telling either of them anything. They'd already cast the mold for years to come, just as I had fifty years earlier.

        Cole was uncommitted. He clearly loved what he was doing, but options were still open for him. He'd have to break away from Tom and go back to school for a degree. I couldn't see it happening. It would be difficult to finance four years of college without any income. Little did they know how much I had in common with all four of them! These are all basic issues ordinary people face all the time. Overall, the entire evening was enjoyable, and Lesley had as much fun as I did. But we were outsiders; in fact, far more so than with our neighbors.

When the job ended, I went back to being as edgy as Lesley. With her it was bugs, heat, humidity, and southern culture in general. I was just bored, but my son Daniel had a cure for both of us. He was getting married again after his divorce a few years earlier. It was a good time to visit the entire family because I never had much opportunity to watch the grandchildren growing up.

        After returning from the wedding, Thanksgiving was near, and we had plans. Ten years earlier, while living in Bellingham, we'd bought a timeshare in Whistler, British Columbia. After moving away, it proved disappointing. Anytime we wanted an exchange, we'd give up a beautiful two-bedroom apartment in a world-class resort to receive a small studio somewhere in the boondocks in return.

Jeanne Lindsay and Daniel Rankin, Burlington, ON – 2003.

Alexandra and Mathew Rankin on left with Becker, Melanie and Gordon Forbes on right with Polly.

    I'd always wanted to go to Key West. When we moved to Savannah, the first thing I did was reserve a week at Thanksgiving. This was our timeshare's last chance. We needed a change of scene and Key West was the answer. Lesley worried about the accommodations. To me that was secondary. I wanted the revelry, the bar-hopping and even Hemmingway's cats. I didn't care. More than anything I wanted to see what people went there for. Besides, it was a 4-star resort, how bad could it be?

    She'd been burned too many times before to not know the answer to that. On the drive there she kept repeating, "It better not be a dump."

    I'd counter with, "Hey, you've seen the pictures? It's a big hotel, right there overlooking the marina with all those cigarette boats for drug running."

    "It better be just as good as Whistler."

    "Well, it may not be a two-bedroom unit, but we only need one anyway."

    "It better be nicer than the last one. At least it had better be cleaner."

    "You worry too much. It'll be fine." Whenever I said *that* about something, she'd say, "Yeah! Fine, fine, we'll all go to

Houston!" It was the line Jane Kaczmarek spat out at Robert De Niro in the movie *Falling in Love*. Just when she thought it couldn't get any worse, it did.

Lesley was right. It was a disaster! Not only was the room barely large enough to accommodate a bed, but the kitchenette was squeezed into what used to be a single closet. And forget about a view! Our unit had a window onto the outside open hallway directly in front of the elevator. I knew what was coming: "This is just not acceptable," she said.

"I've already checked with the office. It's the only one available."

"What's that horrible smell? It smells like urine. Somebody had a dog in here. Can't you smell it?"

"It's nothing, maybe a little mildew in the carpet. I'll get the manager to spray it with something."

"Oh, my God, *mildew*! My allergies are acting up." Things degenerated rapidly. The manager sent maintenance up with a dehumidifier that rattled and whined for an hour as the argument intensified. Her declaration of dog urine rose in direct proportion to our tempers.

"It's not about the damn room," I shouted. "It's about Key West!"

She shouted in return, "Fine, stay if you like, stay forever for all I care. Take me to the airport. I'm going home."

I couldn't remember how De Niro handled it, but I shouted back anyway and stomped out with the luggage. I didn't check out. I was coming back for a world-class party. I drove to the airport in stubborn silence. Vacationers spilled over the sidewalks into the traffic, causing my anger to intensify with jealousy. I envied and hated the bastards at the same time. It was a New Orleans Mardi Gras without the floats and beads. Everything I'd hoped it would be.

Lesley's fuse was shorter than mine—spontaneous, short-lived, and followed by remorse. Mine was long-simmering until rising to the level of borderline personality disorder before sinking to moody petulance with ongoing resentment.

She broke the silence and looked at me for the first time since leaving the hotel. "You missed the turn. Where are you going?"

"It's too late to catch a flight. You need a room for tonight and I just noticed a Hampton Inn."

"Well, okay! But what are you going to do?"

"I dunno. Maybe we should have dinner. Get a bottle of wine. Talk about things?"

"Yeah, I could use a drink." She was already over the hissy fit and suddenly agreeable.

"Me too," I grumbled.

The next day we drove to Anna Maria Island and booked into a motel. It was a week under a banner of truce. I tried to pretend that Key West never happened. But after Savannah, it still gnawed away at me, intensifying the resentment. Something was wrong. We'd been through many tiffs before and always emerged united. This time it was dividing us. Maybe it wasn't Key West. Maybe it was my recent electrician fixation, her health issues, or our marriage itself? Or was it all about Savannah?

Whatever it was, Anna Maria Island was intended to still the water. Harry and Karen Lockwood had recently stayed with us on their way south from Canada. I could see he was quite taken with my kayak, so I'd said, "Take it, it's yours. You'll get more use out of it on Anna Maria than I will here." He insisted on paying for it, so we settled for half of what it cost on the condition I remained half-owner, which I ignored. Had I known how soon I'd be back in California, I would have kept it. Anyway, now it was at their Anna Maria beach house

By the time we arrived, Harry had become accustomed to paddling around the Gulf beaches. One of his favorite destinations was a sandbar a few hundred feet in front of his place, where he occasionally saw small sharks swimming around. He was drawn to them in the same way he was drawn to alligators and manatees swimming beside his boat or canoe further inland. The first day we were there, he said, "You take the kayak, I'll swim." With that, he tossed a brutal-looking commando knife into the kayak, followed by his bathing suit. Buck naked and indifferent to the people on the beach, he added, "Stay close. If sharks attack, use the knife."

He started swimming toward the sandbar, leaving me little option but to follow him. I knew Harry had always been an incurable practical joker, but I also knew he fancied himself as some sort of a poor man's Rambo. Which was it this time? I had no idea. As I followed him I resisted the temptation to shout "SHARKS!"

On the last day, he scheduled a deep-sea fishing trip. When we arrived at the dock, the captain failed to appear due to a severe hang over. I gathered that Savannah's Tybee Island wasn't the only drinking island with a fishing problem. After a long lunch, we returned in time to take the ladies out to dinner. I continued to party out of sheer resentment. It was a long night; my last opportunity to wash Key West out of my system. It was time to go home.

Northbound on I-75 was a logjam. We moved over to the 301 where the locals drove pickups with flood lamps and shooter-seats over the cabs. Floridians know how to kick ass. The best I could do was buy a rubber plant at a nursery as a peace offering. Along the way, I waxed on fluently about the problem with Savannah and what we should think about doing. When I casually mentioned California, she stopped me cold.

"California?" she said in the midst of my rambling. It was just one word—one word buried in a string heedless of consequence—spewing from the depth of my nearly recovered psyche. It was the same old wanderlust that had plagued me my entire life, and not always pleasing to her.

"Huh? Oh, yeah! Well, sure, now that you mention it, why not?" I boasted full of confidence. "We can do anything we want, can't we?" It was true. Alone we were misfits. Together we were unstoppable.

"But we just got here. It's not even a year yet," she reasoned more than protested. "We'd have to sell the house. You know how slowly they move in Savannah."

"I'm not saying tomorrow. It would have to be next year, if at all. I'm just saying we should think about it. Okay? Jesus!"

She sank back into the seat, frowned, and said, "Fine, fine, we'll all go to Houston."

It was a done deal!

At least our squabble was over. I'd planted a new seed with little confidence of it ever sprouting. Now I knew it was a go; at least as far as she was concerned. It was inconceivable that we'd contemplate another move across the country this soon. We'd been down this road too many times. But once united in similar follies we were an overwhelming force. This time it wasn't a question of what we were going to do; it was a question of how we could pull it off.

The only thing more stressful than selling a house is buying one before you sell the one you have. That was how we got there, but not the way back. The housing market in California had not tanked at all. Selling there now would not be a problem. In spite of 9/11 and the tech stock crash, prices continued to climb, slowly at first, then with ever increasing demand in a market short of supply. Where were all these people coming from? Where did they get the money? Didn't they know we were fighting two wars in the Middle East and a bunch of terrorists at home? In Savannah, houses took forever to sell. Every month would throw us further behind. Our selling price would likely drop in direct proportion to the escalation of California prices. We'd never get out of here.

As I drove, Johnny Mercer's lyrics resonated in my head. It might have been "Georgia on My Mind," but more likely, "Something's Got to Give," or "Fools Rush In." I don't know, but suddenly I remembered something our realtor had said when she was showing us properties: "I've been busy all morning showing a pocket listing."

"Pocket listing," I'd asked, "what's a pocket listing?"

"Oh, that's just a client who doesn't want to put their house on the market for fear of what the neighbors will say," she explained. "But if they want to sell it, they allow me to show it."

When we arrived back in Savannah, I gave her a call: "I remember you once mentioning pocket listings—houses you show clients when it's a good fit."

"Yes, why are you asking?"

I think she knew. "I'll explain later but I thought maybe you'd like to put our place in your pocket?"

Not surprised in the least, she asked, "How much do you want for it?" After some dickering, where I explained all the improvements we'd made, she said, "I'm with an out-of-town client right now. I think she would like to see your place. Can I bring her around?"

This was even quicker than when we sold our house in Groveland to Merrill Lynch, thanks to Northern Telecom. The only hitch was, as in Buckhead, the buyer insisted on thirty-day possession. Not even a year yet and we were selling our house with no idea where the next one was. We only knew it was going to be in South Orange County. But we'd have to be quick. The fire was already lit under that market. And it involved another double cross-country trip just like all the others: The first trip was for house hunting, and then to leave Lesley's car there. The second was to get us and the cats there in my car. The buyers must have seen us coming. The feeding frenzy for house buying had already started.

Close to the beach was out of the question. Laguna Beach, Monarch Beach, and Dana Point were all too expensive. It was even a land rush in Capistrano, Aliso Viejo, and Mission Viejo. If you saw a house in the morning, it would be sold by the afternoon. We checked the 55+ communities where there seemed to be more inventory. Other locations were shunned due to earthquake, fire, and floods. Californians coveted beachfront property, cliff-hangers, and anything with a view of the ocean. They had a passion for rebuilding properties up ravines with dry shrubs and trees every ten or twenty years between fires. We'd been in an earthquake that swung the chandelier the width of the dining room table amid books falling off the shelf. That was enough! We'd never experienced a forest fire, but we'd seen homes devoured by fire hurling down a mountain or up some canyon, driven by winds that even Savannah had never seen. By the end of the week we found two houses in a gated community in Mission Viejo. It reminded us of Tuscany, with tall cypress and palm trees jutting out of properties visible in all directions from one vista to another. Both houses were sold before we got there. That afternoon another one fell out of escrow after being tied up for months. We jumped on it before they thought about raising the price.

Mission Viejo, CA.

Now that we knew where we were going we needed to downsize. Both of us are incurable collectors. The evidence spilled out of the garage and along the driveway right up to the six-foot gate at the side of the house. Our garage sale ad stated *Saturday, 8 a.m.* They started arriving at seven-thirty. First it was the professionals, or at least the ones who knew what they were looking for. I assumed they wanted anything they could resell at a flea market the same day. They kept clasping the top of the fence and peering over to ask when I was opening the gates. I held them back until the advertised hour to give the neighbors an equal opportunity. I didn't mention that the good stuff was already sold to the new owner. The pros made a quick sweep and were out of there in minutes before moving on to better pickings.

The rest of the day was typical Savannah. No one was in a hurry. They casually walked in from around the neighborhood, or rode up on bikes to browse and socialize. One by one, all the books, dishes, linens, pictures, tools, furniture, and various questionable treasures were bid, bartered, and sold. What was left at the end of the day was sent off to a Goodwill drop-off point. Nothing was stolen as in Bellingham where my marine radio and sonar disappeared. I'd seen the guy looking at them. The next time I turned around they'd gone—him too. Savannah may tolerate a few murders, and be proud of their dueling ancestors, but they have little patience for lesser crimes.

Bubba and friends expressed regrets on hearing of our departure. They couldn't comprehend why we were leaving so soon. How could we explain it to people so deeply entrenched? They loved Savannah! I suppose we did too. I wouldn't want to have missed the experience for anything. Had we stayed, it would only turn bitter. Maybe she was just too much for us. Rather than becoming resentful, it was better to take her fond memories, charm, and mystery with us to California. We still have them today. That's what Savannah folks do. They never let go.

Chapter 18

2004-13

Mission Viejo, California

Enough with the clubs

There must be something in California that keeps bringing us back. If you count the times, you'll find this is the fifth. Without the water from mountain run-off, most of it would be desert.

The first thing we saw after crossing the desert, on Hwy.10 westbound, was a sign for an Indian Casino. Yes! Palm Springs at last! The Cahuilla Indians lived there for hundreds of years and called it "Se-Khi" (boiling water). When the Spanish came they called it *La Palma de la Mano de Dios* (the palm of God's hand). Later, the first Europeans shortened it to Palm Springs. Whatever it's called, water boils out of the ground in summer temperatures as high as 123 degrees Fahrenheit.

Early in the twentieth century it developed a reputation as a resort town. Around mid-century it was very popular with movie stars and other notable individuals. They built second homes but invariably vacated the place, leaving it to the desert for much of the year. By 1980 it was largely year-round living with much of it gated communities. Take away their air conditioning, and in summer there would be nobody left but *desert rats* and *snowbirds* living on *La Palma de la Mano de Dio*s and drinking *Se Khi*. We were a short drive away from our destination, but a long way from stopping.

All that's needed to make things grow is water and sunshine. There's no shortage of sunshine, and between mountain run-off and the Colorado River, water was plentiful. Sprinkle enough of it along the West Coast where the temperature is moderated by the Pacific Ocean and everything grows, cities included. That's what makes it the best state in the union. That's what brings us back.

Our gated community was waiting, and we were ready for a long stay. It had close to two thousand homes, two community centers with pools, lawn bowling, and shuffle board pavilions. It was nice, but further from the beach than our previous home in Niguel Shores. Once moved in, the renovations began. Every year there would be something else. The kitchen, bathroom, hall closets, windows, and patio were all worked on until the place was to our liking. It was an investment. We always relied on upgrades to increase the value.

Another way to increase the value is to get lucky. For the next four years, real estate value rose at an unprecedented rate. Many who bought during this time would be disappointed when the housing bubble burst. That partially explains our long stable period of almost ten years without moving. After the crash in '08, it took another five years for houses to regain their previous value. The other reason is we were quite happy there. What's not to like? It was near Lake Mission Viejo and surrounding beautifully landscaped rolling hills. Inside, there were wide streets and sidewalks, and it was less than ten miles as the seagull flies to Laguna Beach. Many people had moved in at age fifty-five and were still there thirty years later. In our case, that would take us to well over a hundred years old. Maybe we'd get lucky with that, too.

Rules are necessary in any community. They had rules on top of rules in a fifty-page rules book. Many thrived on the politics of it. They campaigned to get elected and once successful, have control of how and where the association fees were spent. We're talking millions here. You can see the motivation as well as the responsibility involved. There are volunteers with good intentions found at all levels. We were not good volunteer material. I do understand the need, but also found it offensive to have someone walking around my house looking for violations—garage door left open, parking violation, birdfeeders attracting rats, water fountains and birdbaths attracting mosquitoes, patio extensions exceeding the limits—to name a few. We called them (privately) clipboard man (or woman). Once cited, you would receive a notice to correct the situation or pay fines until you did.

Lesley got cited for speeding once. I went to the hearing with her to make sure she didn't fire off and end up paying the hundred-dollar fine. I knew the secret with these people was to pretend remorse (grovel) before them in order to avoid a fine. A grand body of people assembled to confront her, as well as numerous other offenders, all in turn. The general manager was the only friendly face among them. He wasn't elected. He was hired, making him the only professional among them. It helped that he'd previously bought one of Lesley's water color paintings at the annual craft show and hung it in his office. When her turn came up we entered the tribunal room and sat facing a U-shape table. The president sat centered in the middle of the U, with various secretaries of this and that on either side of him. Lesser officials sat on both sides, scowling with intimidating expressions that suggested maybe Metamucil would help. There were twelve in all. The entire administration had assembled to punish her for goosing it up a hill slightly over the limit.

I thought she did very well. She channeled her sweet innocent little-old-lady who had always served her well with traffic cops. They capitulated but expected an apology. After a warning and self-congratulatory words in regard to the great service they were compelled to perform in order to keep everyone safe, she still needed to tell them she was sorry. It was too much for her. She turned on them and said, "I'd just like to know if there are any among you who has not at some time exceeded twenty-five miles an hour on these streets?" She had them! There wasn't one who didn't squirm, grin, or shuffle in their seat. The general manager actually guffawed. I'd never heard Lesley paraphrase the Bible before and hoped she wouldn't make a habit of it.

Biblical or not, I could see the hundred bucks coming back up on the agenda. There's one thing I learned in sales: When you have the purchase order; it's time to shut up. Before they could collect themselves, I grabbed her arm and said, "Thank you gentlemen," and ushered her to the door.

While living there, I joined the men's golf club. The course had a variety of birds, including a large number of Canadian geese that I admired. I can understand why some golfers detest geese on their fairways, but what turned me off was clubbing baby rabbits to death with a driver. It was done by some brave soul in a foursome somewhere in front of us—one I'd never want to play with. I never liked golf that much anyway. Soon, I quit playing altogether.

It was the shuffleboard club that held my interest longer. This is a game you can play at any age. There was one lady in her nineties who always managed to beat everyone without even raising her heartbeat. It's also a game that can reveal people's best and worst tendencies in terms of over-the-top exhilaration or self-flagellation. You could see it with the squeals of childlike euphoria when they vanquished their opponent, and in borderline manic depression after making a bad shot to end up "in the kitchen" with minus ten points. We had two home teams that regularly competed, as well as away games that took place with other gated communities in the area. I'd never played before but soon caught on and became the instructor teaching new members. But as in golf, shuffleboard only lasted a while.

I often went to the lapidary room which was equipped with everything you needed to cut, grind, and polish stones. We went to the desert to collect rocks to work on, and every year we'd go to the Orange County Gem Fair and stock up on pearls and stones for making jewelry. I stayed with it until all the girls in the family got something from my basic craftsmanship—mostly appreciated, sometimes not. I'm not social enough to belong to clubs. The only one I stuck with was the vegetable garden club. Here, I talked to the plants and they never talked back.

I had a twenty-square-foot patch of ground where I planted fruit trees and vegetables, just like everyone else. We could plant whatever we wanted as long as no rules were broken. Many were obsessed with trapping poachers such as raccoons, rabbits, and voles, which I never found to be a problem. How could you kill a living creature over a carrot? I grew more vegetables than I could eat, anyway. It was mostly voles who found their way inside my fence, and how much could they eat? With all the vegetables I had it was necessary to resort to army-style cooking. I used a large boiler pot for making zucchini soup and then froze it in smaller containers for instant meals all year round. I never made less than three loaves of zucchini bread at a time, and I always went large on spaghetti sauce and salsa. Lesley's specialty was making lemon marmalade, as well as pesto sauce from the basil.

I could write a chapter on the subject of how to deal with rabbits. Sure, there were too many of them, but we were okay with that. The community's way of keeping the population down was to hire exterminators to trap them. Catch and release, they called it, but never fully answered the question of where they released them. I think you know! Trapping wasn't productive enough, so they started shooting them as well. It was more efficient with the same result.

When you have rabbits you're likely to have complaints about them eating flowers and destroying lawns, but you will also have coyotes. For a while, it was common to see one or two coyotes walking along the street or resting in your backyard. They are the natural predator that keeps the rabbit population down. Once the rabbits were gone, the coyotes starve until they, too, became scarce. You can never get rid of either one for long. But as the rabbits dwindled in number, coyotes attacked unsuspecting pets. People complained about losing their cats until they learned to keep them inside. Small dogs were vulnerable even while walking on a leash with their owners. A coyote would eat everything, including the collar if it was leather. If you wanted a memento it was best to buy plastic. With or without dogs, most people walked with a cane or golf club in hand in case coyotes were in the neighborhood. Rabbits were not treated so kindly in spite of their gentleness. One sighting and the subject of extermination would erupt all over again.

Given a choice between rabbits or coyotes, there was no question about what side Lesley would come down on, unless cats were in mix. Cats, it seems, are at liberty to kill at will. To quote another Churchillian classic: *Cats look down upon a man, and a dog looks up to man, but a pig will look a man in the eye and see his equal.* Don't take it personally. I'm sure Churchill would have produced more evidence than I ever could. If I was to guess at a rabbit's thoughts, I'd say, *Rabbits look at a man and see a golf club.* Or maybe a trap, or a dart gun—but they'd never hang around a coyote long enough to see anything.

Lesley wasn't into clubs any more than I was. But she did join the Orange County Art Association She had a website and always displayed her work at the Balboa Island Art Walk. Artists are a special breed. They usually have enough in common that they develop many lasting friendships. That's why they go to art classes where they dress similarly and think liberally. Otherwise they'd go mad locked up in their studios slapping paint on canvasses until they ran out of money, walls, attic space, and closets to store their unappreciated creations. Supplies are expensive. Matting and framing are prohibitively so, unless you do your own. Even then it's not cheap. Exhibiting your work is time consuming as well as expensive.

Most people who cruise art shows know nothing about art. It's an outing for them. Maybe a cheap date with free wine and cheese followed by dinner at some overpriced restaurant while the

Lesley at Balboa art show.

artists repack their paintings to take home. Lesley's paintings are like babies she's created. She remembers who bought every one that she ever sold. Her friends are the same way. She also enjoyed ice-skating at the Aliso Viejo arena, and her love of travel and cats has never diminished. While others relied on the community center, clubs, bus trips to the Reagan Library, Las Vegas, and other local casinos, we occupied most of our time elsewhere.

Clubs and familiar faces are important to most retired people. I liked them too, but not for a steady diet. I also liked change. I found cruise ships boring and likened a cruise to being trapped in a Las Vegas casino with no means of escape. Our bus trip around France and the Russian river cruise were much more interesting. It's the unexplored territory that makes life interesting. Our most successful vacations were renting a car and take off on our own itinerary across places like Portugal, Spain, Italy, Ireland, United Kingdom and Australia. Fortunately we shared the same interests.

In 2011 I had a gall bladder attack and went in for what was supposed to be a four-hour stay in the hospital and home that night. Four days later I was home. The surgeon performed a laparoscopic gallbladder removal but found it completely encased in gangrene. Had he known, he would have had me on antibiotics for a week beforehand, and cut instead.

The operation took much longer than expected because of the size of the stone and all the clean-up required. One stone alone was the size of an egg. Other doctors in the room said, "Cut, cut!" But he said, "Nope, I told him I was doing it this way and that's what I'm doing." After going home I was draining my chest through a tap in my side for a week.

While in the hospital I had a "roomy" from Dana Point who had a similar thing happen to him at the same time. His was an appendix attack. The gangrene was life-threatening in both cases. We had the same surgeon and there's no doubt he saved our lives. We swapped jokes and told stories while becoming good friends. His wife loved to throw parties and have all their eclectic friends gather at their house overlooking the ocean. They were not club joiners either unless it was at Agostino's Italian Restaurant in Capistrano Beach. They knew everyone on Friday nights and often acted as if they were the reception committee. This was a club we could both join.

The following year I joined another club. I called it the PCC, for the prostate cancer I'd just inherited. While waiting for the biopsy results we took a trip to France. Upon returning, I expected more change then even I would want.

Nice, France.

Every move I ever made was in search of a dream, some elusive, and some thrown right at me. For me there is no end game or destination that qualifies as success. Each success you achieve is only one more step along an endless road of education toward being the best you can be. Most people are content no matter where they are. If that's your goal, call it a successful life and make up your mind to be happy. But will it be fulfilling? I don't think so! Try and tell that to a Canadian goose, the caribou, or even Monarch butterflies. Nature abhors a constant.

I was recently in a BMW dealership when I noticed a sign on the men's room wall over the urinal where I couldn't miss it—seeing it, that is. It read, "Happiness is not about the destination, it's about getting there." It sums up my philosophy. I'm talking about life, not a BMW. As long as there's gas in the tank, why not use it? As long as there's life, it compels you to look over the next hill.

Our next hill was in Canada, starting in 2013. The last thirty-five years had been practically void of family life. We had plenty of good family visits, but they were few and far between. We both had people in Canada who we rarely saw. For that matter, we saw too little of Canada, too. The subject often came up in conversation with friends. "Canada," they would say incredulously, "What would you move there for?" *Family* was the only answer that would satisfy them as to why we were thinking of moving after ten years. It was the only answer they would accept because family to them was a constant and usually close by. But we had our own kids, and grandchildren having our great grandchildren that we rarely saw .

Nobody we knew would move there. California people would never consider it. In their minds, Canada was French, over-taxed and cold with bad health care. They had a point, but they were only partly correct. The health care is not bad; it's just a tad slow. That's only because everyone in the country receives it in equal measure. It's also paid for in equal measure through taxes, with some being more equal than others depending on how much they consume.

No country in the world could have provided better service, training and activities than what my son Leonard enjoys every day. Starting in 1975, Ontario decentralized the care of mentally and physically challenged people to community-based services.

*As you can see,
he's come a long way.*

Thousands of adults with developmental disability were moved from institutional environments to new homes in communities close to their families. It not only resulted in huge savings by eliminating expensive outdated facilities, it stimulated the economy in communities all over the province. The challenge of caring for them would destroy any parent, but the care provided by government funded non-profit organization like Mainstream's is phenomenal.

My birthday falls in February—every year, same day—and I'm a guy who hates redundancy. The countdown in 2014 was met with two heartbreaking events: one expected, and the other taking everyone by surprise. No one was surprised when Harry Lockwood, my lifelong friend, died two days before my birthday. He'd been surprising everyone for years. As his prostate cancer advanced he kept fighting and lived longer than anyone expected. The other event, one day before, caught all of us unaware. My ex-wife, Doris Townsend died.

After many years of estrangement, we were actually seeing signs of unification. At first she'd seemed uncomfortable with my sudden appearance after thirty-six years, but gradually she became more pleasant. On several occasions I had reason to visit her in St Catherine's where we shared stories about Leonard. She offered to show me her house, backyard, and art studio. Lesley even talked about the possibility of them painting together. At a family shower, just a week earlier, the two of them sat together and had an enjoyable conversation with no indication of past acrimony. After the devastating loss of her husband she was getting back on her feet, slimmed down and looking good. Her death was due to a heart condition that no one suspected. One day she was there, and the next she was not.

Additionally, in a period of two years, I lost one brother (Bill) and two first cousins. People were dropping off all around me. They rarely mourn the death of loved ones any more. Instead, it's called a celebration of life. It's an opportunity to share memories, pictures and conversation about the departed one. If they've been long suffering it should be considered a blessing and well worth celebrating. At other times it's more difficult to put a happy face on it. One way to do that is to think of the Phoenix, and I don't mean Arizona. I mean the bird of Greek mythology that takes on new life by arising from the ashes of its predecessor, symbolizing rebirth—the victory of life over death—and immortality.

It's a wonderful metaphor of a long-lived bird forever being regenerated and reborn. I needed to look no further than my own two little birds, my great-granddaughters Zoe and Nora, to see new life rising. With more pending, I see all of them as my door to immortality. But this is not the time to burden them with that. We still have plenty of time before testing the Phoenix theory.

In 2017 we returned to California. No matter how many times I burn the bridges, California always finds enough ashes to bring us back. I knew I loved the place, I just didn't know how much until we returned.

The End

Nora and Zoe.

Epilogue

Writing this has been a time-consuming and rewarding experience. I'd recommend everyone to write their own memoir. My initial motivation was to leave some record of my existence just in case any of my grandchildren and their children became interested in those ancient times of the twentieth century.

Once started, it quickly became a selfish motive. I had what I considered to be an interesting life and wanted to share it with others. I also wanted to prove I could write. I never realized there were so many ways to say the same thing, or that there were so many rules. Every genre requires a different style, and while I'm not sure if I got it right, I have strived to maintain my own voice in a world of literary experts.

We lived in Ontario for three and a half years. Yes, it's cold in winter, taxes are high in any season, and it is a bilingual country forever. It was the cold that changed our minds. We moved back to California for the sixth time. This time it was Laguna Woods Village.

Laguna Woods Golf Course.

Brandon Wilson and Mathew Rankin with me and Daniel.

Jaime, Leslie, Lesley, and Jeanne.

Alex Wilson, Leslie and Zoe Wilson.

*Leonard with his friend Cathy.
Go Lenny!*

Wendy

Jessica and Trevor

Derek and David

Acknowledgements

Of those who helped with this book, I am most grateful to my wife of thirty-eight years, Lesley Joyce Rankin, who always encouraged me to write. She suffered the most by reading many flawed early attempts, and never complained about my absences while lost in the computer doing so. Also, I want to thank Richard Bisson, multi-language translator by profession and poet by nature, for his lessons on how to write. I am especially grateful to Miranda McPhee for her editing and publishing support. Her patience and expertise has made this possible. Warm thanks must also go to the Laguna Woods Publishing Club and all the members for their encouragement.

Made in the USA
San Bernardino, CA
23 March 2018